FAITH, FILM AND PHILOSOPHY

BIG IDEAS ON THE BIG SCREEN

EDITED BY
R. DOUGLAS GEIVETT
AND JAMES S. SPIEGEL

IVP Academic
An imprint of InterVarsity Press
Downers Grove, Illinois

InterVarsity Press
P.O. Box 1400, Downers Grove, IL 60515-1426
World Wide Web: www.ivpress.com
E-mail: email@ivpress.com

InterVarsity Press® is the book-publishing division of InterVarsity Christian Fellowship/USA®, a student movement active on campus at hundreds of universities, colleges and schools of nursing in the United States of America, and a member movement of the International Fellowship of Evangelical Students. For information about local and regional activities, write Public Relations Dept., InterVarsity Christian Fellowship/USA, 6400 Schroeder Rd., P.O. Box 7895, Madison, WI 53707-7895, or visit the IVCF website at <www.intervarsity.org>.

All Scripture quotations, unless otherwise indicated, are taken from The Holy Bible, English Standard Version copyright © 2001 by Crossway Bibles, a publishing ministry of Good News Publishers. Used by permission. All rights reserved.

Design: Cindy Kiple

Images: sign: Image Source Pink/Getty Images
        marquee: Todd Harrison/iStockphoto

ISBN 978-0-8308-2589-9

Printed in the United States of America ∞

Library of Congress Cataloging-in-Publication Data

Faith, film, and philosophy: big ideas on the big screen / edited by
R. Douglas Geivett and James S. Spiegel.
   p. cm.
Includes bibliographical references and index.
ISBN-13: 978-0-8308-2589-9 (pbk.: alk. paper)
1. Motion pictures—Moral and ethical aspects. 2. Motion
pictures—Religious aspects. I. Geivett, R. Douglas. II. Spiegel,
James S., 1963-
PN 1995.5.F35 2007
791.43'75—dc22

                                                                      2007026753

P	21	20	19	18	17	16	15	14	13	12	11	10	9	8	7	6	5	4	3	2	1
Y	25	24	23	22	21	20	19	18	17	16	15	14	13	12	11	10	09	08	07

Contents

117124

Acknowledgments

This volume is the product of much work on the part of many people. We wish to express our deep appreciation to each one. First, the team at InterVarsity Press. We are especially grateful to Andy Le Peau and Gary Deddo for their enthusiasm and vision for this project from the beginning. We thank Jennifer Seidel for her meticulous work double-checking script documentation and assisting with style. Thanks to Joe Stamm and Sally Sampson Craft, we have enjoyed creative support for the release of this book. And thanks to Gail Neal and Ross Inman of Biola University for their assistance with the index. Jay Hawthorne, an independent contractor, is responsible for the wonderful design of the website for this book: www.faith-film-philosophy.com.

We could not ask for better contributors. Each one was on the A-team we wished to assemble when we first conceived of this project. With trepidation, we pitched the idea to each one and invited each to propose films and topics that he or she would most enjoy writing about. Not only was there no overlap, there was remarkable diversity and balance in the preferences expressed. Because of them, this book offers something for everyone. We thank them all for their hard work and patience. It has been most rewarding to work with such a talented group, whose contributions surpassed even our loftiest hopes for this book. They descended from the comfortable altitude of the ivory tower and gave us essays to enrich the film-viewing experience for all of our readers.

We are also thankful to the colleagues, friends and family members with whom we have discussed film and philosophy over the years. Their observations and insights helped to shape this volume in many ways. The philosophical analysis of popular culture, perhaps more than any other area of philosophy, is properly a community affair. We are blessed to be part of academic communities that significantly enhance our capacity for this work. We thank our colleagues at Taylor University and Biola University for their continuing support, both professional and personal.

Finally, we thank our wives, Amy Spiegel and Dianne Geivett, for their constant encouragement during this project. In addition to their usual patience and good humor, they have provided especially helpful comments and suggestions. We dedicate this volume to them, our favorite film-viewing companions.

Introduction

JAMES S. SPIEGEL

* *

Plato once said, "Those who tell the stories rule society." In America today, it is quite clear who the principal storytellers are: filmmakers. Hollywood's influence on our culture can hardly be overestimated. From comic-book superhero adventures and sappy romantic comedies to epic dramas and independent art-house films, the movie industry's products, for better or worse, influence the way people perceive the world and their place in it. Our values are also affected by the films we watch, whether those values pertain to lifestyle choices, aesthetic concerns, moral priorities or political aims.

Films are, at the most basic level, stories. Whether mythical, like *The Wizard of Oz* and *Forrest Gump,* or historical, like *Cleopatra* and *Saving Private Ryan,* films present narratives aimed at informing, persuading, challenging or inspiring us. So, of course, they are really more than mere stories. Every film offers a worldview, a set of beliefs and values for understanding how the world is and how it should be. Such beliefs and values are philosophical in nature, which brings us to another main subject of this book: philosophy.

To quote another ancient Greek thinker, Aristotle said, "Philosophy begins in wonder." This observation is confirmed everywhere in human experience. At some time or another we all find ourselves wondering about such things as life's ultimate meaning, the morality of abortion or euthanasia, the best form of government, the nature of consciousness, the difference between good and bad art, and what it means to have knowledge. As we begin to entertain answers to these questions and to debate them with others, philosophy begins.

Many films demonstrate that philosophy is irresistible and that big questions are not just for scholars. Films often deal directly with significant philosophical issues, including moral issues like abortion *(The Cider House Rules)*, euthanasia *(Million Dollar Baby)* and capital punishment *(Dead Man Walking)*. Some deal with free will and determinism *(Gattaca, Minority Report* and *Donnie Darko)* and personal identity *(Memento* and *Eternal Sunshine of the Spotless Mind)*. And in two recent films, *Waking Life* and *I ♥ Huckabees,* worldview analysis is itself the central project. We are, by nature, curious creatures. It is no surprise, then, that filmmakers should be so interested in philosophical issues. But the question arises, how can we assess the worldviews and truth claims implicit in the films we watch? And that question leads to another: what can films teach us about our beliefs, our values and the way that we go about developing our worldviews?

This book aims to address these questions. With a roster of fourteen authors, the philosophical subject matter is wide ranging, but the authors are united by their common Christian perspective and their concern with another crucial question: how should our faith perspective shape the way we interpret and assess film? Each offers a unique approach to this endeavor, bringing his or her own style and voice to the issues discussed. In many cases the philosophical positions advanced by the authors do not represent a consensus among Christian philosophers. But each nonetheless arrives at his or her position through a careful integration of philosophical method and Christian conviction.

Philosophical Method and Christian Belief

A few words about philosophical method are in order. First, philosophy is especially interested in the analysis of *foundational* issues, such as the meaning of life, the existence of God, the problem of evil, the nature of human freedom, the immortality of the soul and the nature of knowledge. The philosopher considers different views on such issues and critically assesses them for their truth value, asking questions such as, is belief in God, freedom or immortality logically consistent and does it square with the facts of experience? Some views may be substantially correct but contain misleading or false elements. The philosopher aims to preserve the insights of particular positions while rejecting the mistakes within them.

Second, philosophy involves identifying *presuppositions,* the unrecognized or unspoken assumptions that we make about different issues. Many times our convictions about even the most important subjects are rooted in personal prejudices rather than in objectively good reasons. For example, many students enter college with strong political convictions, often completely in line with a major political platform. Some of these may be well-supported beliefs, whereas others are merely dogmatic biases. The philosopher aims to expose these biases, however painful that process may be at times.

This leads us to a third aspect of philosophical method: the use of *arguments* and evidence to justify beliefs. There is a difference between knowledge and mere opinion. Socrates, the father of Western philosophy, proposed that the difference lies in the fact that to know something is to be capable of providing some sort of account or justification for believing as one does. While philosophers today debate whether such justification is a necessary condition for knowledge, it is a matter of common sense that the more evidence one can provide in defense of a view, the more rational one's convictions will be.

A fourth feature of philosophical method pertains more to its broader aims than to its means. Philosophy is interested in *worldview development*—the development of a comprehensive set of beliefs about the most fundamental issues that we face as human beings. What are human beings, and what is our place in the universe? Were we created by God? If so, what is God's nature? Are humans basically good, or are we morally corrupt by nature? Do we have immortal souls? Are we free and morally responsible? If so, then what moral standards should guide our conduct? All of us have certain beliefs regarding each of these questions, and these beliefs cohere with one another more or less well. Ideally, one's worldview should be such that the various elements are consistent with, and even mutually explain, one another. Furthermore, and most importantly, one's beliefs should be true: they should reflect the way the world really is.

As noted above, each contributor to this volume is an avowed Christian. With the concept of worldview in hand, we are now in a better position to spell out just what this means. Each author affirms the following: Human beings have been created for the general purpose of glorifying their Creator, and all human activities, in one way or another, should reflect this. God is almighty, all-knowing, perfectly good and loving, and he is working out his plans in human history. Human beings are indeed free and morally responsible, but we are also morally corrupt, having inherited a natural tendency to selfishness and pride, bequeathed to us by our forbears, Adam and Eve. But, graciously, God has intervened on our behalf in the person of Jesus Christ, whose life, death and resurrection carry the promise of our redemption and ultimately the transformation of humanity itself.

While some of the chapters in this book feature philosophical discussions of some of these core Christian doctrines in the context of film analysis, many other issues are addressed from the vantage point of Christian conviction. The subjects and styles of the essays are intentionally wide ranging, and one reason for this is to display the breadth of Christian philosophical inquiry. The specific aims of the chapters vary accordingly, but they nonetheless fall roughly into three general categories. Contributions by Kelly James Clark, Caroline J. Simon, Sara L. H. Shady and Douglas K. Blount aim to enhance or inform a Christian worldview using insights gleaned through film analysis. The chapters written by R. Douglas Geivett, David P. Hunt, Gregory E. Ganssle, Brendan Sweetman and myself (James S. Spiegel) intend to highlight or illustrate philosophical themes using the films in conjunction with Christian ideas as conceptual tools. James F. Sennett, Greg Jesson, Dallas Willard, Ronald K. Tacelli and Winfried Corduan offer critical analyses of philosophical contents of films, some of these revealing problems with the worldviews implicit in the films.

The chapters are diverse in a further respect. Doug Geivett and I wanted to have a varied sampling of films in terms of genre, period, theme and country of origin. Consequently, the films discussed here include classic and contemporary films of domestic and foreign origin, and the range of genres includes drama, science fiction, horror and documentary. But one thing all of the films have in common is a certain richness of content and theme that invites philosophical discussion. While any film can be analyzed philosophically, some films are more interesting than others in this respect. Those discussed in this volume especially warrant such analysis, though any number of other films might have been chosen. We encourage readers to bring the same critical Christian consciousness modeled by our authors to bear on other films they view. However much readers might disagree with some specific claims of the authors, they can at least profit from the model of Christian philosophical inquiry on display here.

Overview

The chapters are arranged thematically, beginning with the issue of the human condition or, as it sometimes called, philosophical anthropology. Sennett's leadoff essay on *Citizen Kane* makes the provocative claim that Hollywood has betrayed the thesis of its greatest masterpiece. Orson Welles's classic tale of the self-destructive nature of wealth and power provides a penetrating and startlingly biblical portrait of human depravity. The sad truth about human nature is that it has tragically fallen from its original created state of moral purity, and Charles Foster Kane is emblematic of that Fall. However, the American film industry today not only rejects this stance, but also promotes a vision of humanity diametrically opposed to Welles's own. This, suggests Sennett, constitutes the "*Citizen Kane* mutiny."

On a more constructive note, Clark dives into the dense narrative of Tim Burton's *Big Fish,* garnering insights about human life, love and relationships that dovetail with a Christian perspective. The film's medium is also its message, to laypersons and philosophers alike: some truths are best—or only—communicated in story form, especially the deeply personal truths about our identities as individuals and within families and communities. Each of us lives, moves and has our being within a narrative structure; our lives cannot be adequately understood except in this light. Christians would do well to appreciate this fact about our lives and, more than this, to recognize what Burton seems to miss, namely, that we are all part of a divinely orchestrated grand narrative which ensures that there is meaning and significance to all of our individual stories.

Jesson discusses the vision of romantic love in the films *Pretty Woman, Legends of the Fall* and *The Bridges of Madison County*. While these might at first blush appear to be inconsequential love (or perhaps lust) stories, Jesson shows how these stories actually attempt to find hope in some seemingly hopeless situations and, in this regard, are significant statements about the human condition. They powerfully convey the universal yearning for love. Furthermore, in spite of themselves, the filmmakers show how romantic love, even in its most fantastic forms, is a pathetic, even tragic substitute for *agape,* the unconditional love of God. Such love—radical, beautiful and rare—is the essence of Christian hope.

The next four chapters take up the nature of knowledge and the human mind. In the first of these, Geivett discusses a cluster of epistemological issues raised by *The Truman Show,* explaining why knowledge is valuable and the tight connection between knowledge and human flourishing. Through its depiction of a man whose entire life is a theatrical façade, *The Truman Show* illustrates the basic epistemological features of the human condition, including the roles of curiosity, evidence, cognitive dissonance, community and intellectual virtue in the quest for understanding. Geivett shows how such matters play out in the context of religious belief and in the challenge to believe responsibly on other matters of great significance.

As in *The Truman Show,* the central character of *The Matrix* lives in an artificial world and is forced to choose between life in that world and the harsh, unknown reality that lies beyond it. But here the parallels end. As Hunt shows, *The Matrix* raises fascinating issues related to metaphysics, epistemology and value theory. For instance, in what sense, if any, is the world of *The Matrix* real? How can we know that the scenario posed in the film is not true? And, in the end, does it really matter what is real? The film has been touted for its philosophical relevance and also for its apparent Christian themes. But Hunt reveals how the film's implicit theology is actually gnostic: it emphasizes secret knowledge as the key to human liberation and assumes a negative view of the body and the physical world—themes that are anything but Christian. Hunt thus provides an important corrective to a common interpretation of the *Matrix* films, a misconception under which even many Christian viewers labor.

Ganssle's chapter discusses the philosophical theme of personal identity running through three Charlie Kaufman films—*Being John Malkovich, Adaptation* and *Eternal Sunshine of the Spotless Mind.* What *is* personal identity? Just what is it exactly that makes me *me?* Am I merely a physical body or something else as well? Any plausible philosophy of mind must answer these questions in a satisfactory way. Ganssle uses these films to review and explain major theories of consciousness. He also shows how the Kaufman films illustrate a view of mind that is most at home with the historic Christian (or, more broadly, theistic) view: mind-body dualism. One of the distinct advantages of this theory of mind is its ability to explain the persistence of personal identity even through the assaults on consciousness depicted in these films.

In the last chapter in this section, I discuss a philosophical subject raised in two films that otherwise have little in common: *It's a Wonderful Life* and *Run Lola Run.* Both films feature counterfactuals; that is, they consider events that might have happened but did not (what *if* George Bailey had never lived in Bedford Falls?) or that might yet happen but have not (how *would* things go for Lola, depending on certain choices she could make?). These are counterfactual conditionals, and I use the films to explain this concept. Along the way,

I discuss other issues raised by the films, including human freedom and divine providence. Also, I note how the narrative structures of the films reveal their assumptions about each of these issues.

The theme of the third section of the book is the moral life. Many films offer a vision of what human life and community should look like, while others make significant assumptions about morality. Dallas Willard discusses three films—*Pleasantville, American Beauty* and *The Cider House Rules*—which embody a moral outlook that is increasingly prevalent in contemporary American culture: a deep-seated cynicism toward moral rules or any kind of moral authority. In fact, as Willard points out, such films see the very notion of moral rules as quaint and inimical to human growth. Instead, they recommend liberation from such rules and any constraining moral authority in favor of personal autonomy. The path to moral liberation lies in following one's feelings and desires, especially those of a sensual sort. Such a vision for humanity fundamentally opposes the Judeo-Christian convictions that there is such a thing as moral authority and that abiding by moral standards is actually necessary in order for humans to flourish.

In the documentary *Bowling for Columbine*, Michael Moore shares his own vision of the good life for human beings, albeit in primarily negative terms. The Columbine High School shootings in April 1999 were symptomatic of a growing trend of violence in American culture. We are prompted to ask, what is wrong with us? Moore's answer is that this violence is a product of a culture of fear, perpetuated by the media through its endless reports on violent crime. This culture of fear is aggravated by the endorsement of violence, via the U.S. military, by national political leaders. Shady responds to Moore's assessment in light of the Christian social philosophy of John Macmurray, who recommends as an antidote the building of communities characterized by trust and justice. Such community is informed by a concept of Christian love and the recognition by each individual citizen that one's self is tied up with community.

Mystic River is another film that treats issues of violence and our response to it. Simon discusses a number of moral issues raised in the film, including the moral legitimacy of revenge. When, if ever, is revenge appropriate? Is forgiveness a proper moral response to harm? If so, is repentance on the part of the wrongdoer a prerequisite for forgiveness? Simon shows how unconditional forgiveness, though absurd from the standpoint of many worldviews, is perfectly rational within a Christian theological framework. And because of this radical doctrine of forgiveness, the Christian response actually holds out the most promise for ending cycles of violence, whether involving single murders, random school shootings or even international conflicts.

When we think about violence in connection with film, our thoughts may naturally turn to the horror genre. But is there anything of philosophical interest, much less of a moral nature, lurking in that dark corner of the film world? Tacelli shows us that, ironically, horror films—*especially* the really bad ones—illustrate a deep moral truth. Films such as *Lemora*, *Silence of the Lambs* and *King of the Ants* fail as horror films precisely because they do not acknowledge the reality of a human good. Without objective goodness, there can be no real evil. And, of course, without the threat of evil, there can be no genuine horror. Christian ethicists, among others, have often argued that the notion of the Good is an indispensable category for ethics. Tacelli demonstrates that it is indispensable even for a popular art form ostensibly unconcerned with moral goodness.

The book's final section features three essays that treat films with religious themes. Sweetman discusses several philosophical issues raised in the science fiction films *Contact* and *2001: A Space Odyssey*. Both films offer plenty of fodder for discussion of human nature and free will, and they prompt questions regarding the age-old debate between naturalism and the religious perspective. Sweetman shows how the issue of the rationality of religious belief is dramatized in *Contact*, particularly through the conflict between the main characters, who embody devotion either to scientific methodology or to religious faith. Stanley Kubrick's *2001* is a bit more subtle in approach, but its assumption that intelligence and consciousness can be produced in a purely physical system suggests a naturalist perspective. Sweetman also discusses how in both films the prospect of life on other planets raises further questions about religious faith. If life on our planet provides evidence for God's existence, then wouldn't the presence of life elsewhere only strengthen the case?

Corduan discusses so-called Hong Kong films, the most popular among them starring Bruce Lee or Jackie Chan. Western fans of these films typically are ignorant of just how thoroughly and consistently Chinese philosophy and culture are woven into them. One example is the Confucian virtue of filial piety, or respect for one's family, especially parents, which is a theme or background assumption in most Hong Kong films. Another pervasive theme is the Chinese ideal of balance, the harmonizing of the opposing forces of yin and yang. This aim is paramount in both Daoist and Confucian traditions, and the struggle to achieve this equilibrium is another common theme in Hong Kong films. Such uniformity of values and religious expression within the films of a particular culture is unique. Corduan's analysis is therefore instructive regarding both the Chinese mind and, by contrast, the Western mind.

In the book's closing chapter, Blount analyzes themes in U2's music documentary *Rattle and Hum*. In particular, he notes the themes of despair and hope, what he calls "the blues of human wretchedness on the one hand and the gospel of promised redemption in Christ Jesus and his kingdom on the other." U2's honesty about the darker side of human nature is comparable to Friedrich Nietzsche's, but there, as Blount notes, they part company. What Nietzsche calls a mere human invention in the wake of the death of God, U2 declares as the only hope for humanity. In the final analysis, the verdicts of Nietzsche and U2 might exhaust our alternatives: utter despair in the face of our own wretchedness and mortality or rejoicing in our forgiveness and eternal hope in Christ—requiem or gospel, death or life.

Together the essays in this book treat most of the central doctrines of Christianity: the nature of God, divine providence, the human soul, original sin, grace, atonement, *agape,* moral absolutes and *koinonia* (Christian community). Many perennial philosophical issues are discussed as well, including human nature, free will and determinism, the theory of knowledge, faith and reason, the mind-body problem, and the nature of the Good. Whether the authors' perspectives and attempts at integrating these doctrines are satisfactory must be left to the reader to decide.

The specific aims of the chapters have been distinguished above. Let it be noted that the principal and overarching aim of this book is to demonstrate how insights in each of the three subject areas—philosophy, theology and film—may mutually inform one another. It has been a long-standing conviction (though hardly a consensus) among Christian scholars that theology and philosophy may (and should) be integrated. A more recent conviction within mainstream academic circles (which is also far from being universally affirmed) is that popular artworks like film are a potentially fertile source of scholarly insight. The authors of these essays share both of these convictions. What makes this book distinctive is its integration of these endeavors.

You will find that none of the chapters presupposes acquaintance with any of the others. We encourage you to jump around and read the essays in any order you wish, dictated perhaps by which films you happen to have seen or perhaps by those you would like to see. If you take this latter approach, please beware that many chapters contain spoilers. The authors take no responsibility for ruined surprises! We do take responsibility for our efforts to instill you with the wonder of philosophical inquiry and the love of Christian theology. And we hope this study will better prepare you to apply a Christian philosophical method to every aspect of life—including the world of film.

PART ONE

THE HUMAN CONDITION

1

The *Citizen Kane* Mutiny

What Hollywood Knows and Will Never Admit About
Life, Love and Human Relationships

JAMES F. SENNETT

● ●

All the characters I've played are various forms of Faust.

Orson Welles

In 1998 the American Film Institute kicked off its "100 Years" series by naming *Citizen Kane* the greatest film of all time—an assessment with which virtually every poll of industry professionals ever taken agrees.[1] The reason for such amazing unanimity is clear. *Citizen Kane* was a transitional film in virtually every aspect of the industry, and it is often regarded as the birth of contemporary cinema. In his acclaimed text on film craft Louis Giannetti chooses *Citizen Kane* for the subject of his chapter on synthesis, in which all the various "language systems" of contemporary cinema discussed in the book (photography, mise en scène, movement, editing, sound and so on) are studied in terms of their relationship to one another and their contribution to the whole.[2] The film introduced, improved or mainstreamed many techniques and practices that have become hallmarks of contemporary filmmaking: deep focus, low-key lighting, steep angle shots, discontinuous and overlapping narrative streams, just to name a few.

It is ironic that this film—so universally acclaimed and admired—presents a view of life, love and human relationships that is ignored at best, and ridiculed at worst, by much of modern cinema. While *Citizen Kane* has been praised and emulated in every aspect of its technical nature, it has been discounted and derided in every aspect of its moral nature. While it has been overwhelmingly applauded as a work of art, it has been overwhelmingly rejected as a work of literature. Hollywood has engaged in a systemic mutiny against the message of *Citizen Kane*—a message that rings familiar and true in the ears of anyone acquainted with the gospel.

My thesis is that *Citizen Kane* presents a biblical and realistic picture of human nature—one that is denied and denigrated by the Hollywood mainstream. This thesis will be developed by examining the character of Charles Foster Kane and focusing on the issue that is clearly his driving, though usually unconscious, motivation—the desire to be loved. This desire, coupled with a pathological fear of giving love in return, is Kane's tragic flaw and is exercised to his own detriment and that of almost every person he cares for. His predicament is consistent with biblical anthropology and largely out of step with contemporary cinema's picture of humanity. Cinematic culture more often glorifies the very aspects of Kane's life that most directly contributed to his downfall.

"Maybe Rosebud Was Something He Couldn't Get or Something He Lost"

One of the most celebrated aspects of the script of *Citizen Kane* is its use of multilayered narrative. The story of Charles Foster Kane is told six different times, once by a newsreel and five times by people who knew him well—his guardian Mr. Thatcher, his business manager Mr. Bernstein, his best friend Jedediah Leland, his ex-wife Susan Alexander and his butler Raymond—all of whom are interviewed by Hollywood reporter Jerry Thompson. These layers reveal different and often conflicting pictures of the illusive figure that is the film's subject.

However, the stories offered by those who knew him best and cared for him most (Leland and Alexander) provide us with a picture of Kane that makes sense of many of the enigmas generated in the outlying narratives. These two central accounts are surrounded by pictures of Kane that are obviously one-sided or otherwise inadequate. The newsreel leaves the discerning viewer with the same sentiment expressed by the studio mogul Ralston: "It isn't enough to tell us what a man did; you've got to tell us who he was." The narratives by Thatcher and Bernstein aren't much help, representing opposite poles of opinion—Thatcher's disdain and Bernstein's idol worship. And Raymond's cynicism, while a fitting coda to the enigmatic story, tells us almost nothing about Kane that we don't already know.

Nevertheless, each of these stories provides hints about the character of Charles Foster Kane. The newsreel shows in a glance the peaks and valleys that defined Kane's search for validation. The Thatcher narrative contains one of the most self-reflective lines Kane delivers in the film: "You know, Mr. Bernstein, if I hadn't been very rich, I might have been a really great man." Bernstein takes a break from his incessant adoration of Kane to observe, "It wasn't money he wanted. Thatcher never did figure him out. Sometimes even I couldn't." These two insightful glimpses prepare the audience masterfully for the detailed revelation of Kane's character to come. And near the film's end, the contemptuous Raymond delivers the startling and revealing tale of Kane's childish temper tantrum after his wife's departure from Xanadu (although the clueless servant can offer no better commentary on the bizarre event than "he did crazy things sometimes").

But Leland and Alexander were closest to Kane, and from them we get the deepest insights into who he was. They are both disillusioned disciples: though they are caught up initially in the promise of Kane's charisma, they come to a gradual yet resolute refusal to pay the price for fulfillment of that promise. Leland observes early on, "I was his oldest friend, and as far as I was concerned he behaved like a swine." In the argument leading to their breakup, Alexander offers this indictment: "You never gave me anything in your whole life. You just tried to buy me into giving you something." Yet when Thompson ends their interview with the observation, "All the same, I feel sorry for Mr. Kane," Alexander replies, "Don't you think I do?"

Those who know nothing else about *Citizen Kane* know the first word spoken in it—Kane's dying word, the word that defines the mystery that drives the film, the word that holds center stage in its climactic scene—*Rosebud.* "Rosebud was a sled" has become the film industry's most famous spoiler. But Rosebud is more than a sled. Rosebud is a metaphor for lost love, lost security, lost happiness. In the final scene from Kane's boyhood home in Colorado, as his sled is slowly buried in the Rocky Mountain snows, all validation of Kane as a person is buried with it—his mother, his home, his childhood, his innocence. In what may be the movie's most ironic line, Thompson expresses skepticism over Rosebud's significance. "It wouldn't have explained anything. I don't think any word can explain a man's life." But for the careful student of this powerful screenplay, *Rosebud* explains everything. It explains Charles Foster Kane.

Both Leland and Alexander confess complete ignorance concerning the identity of Rosebud. This is not surprising. Kane is not a man to reveal his vulnerabilities to anyone, not even those closest to him. However, both his friend and his wife know far more of Rosebud than they suspect. In their stories they tell us much about the great man who is, in the end, just a lonely little boy crying for his sled and the happy memories it represented.

To Thompson's query as to whether or not Kane had ever loved his first wife, Leland responds, "He married for love. Love. That's why he did everything. That's why he went into politics. It seems we weren't enough. He wanted all the voters to love him, too. That's all he really wanted out of life was love. That's Charlie's story—how he lost it. You see, he just didn't have any to give. Oh, he loved Charlie Kane, of course, very dearly. And his mother, I guess he always loved her."

This comment reveals much. Kane is a man starved for love, so starved that the unconditional love offered by those who cared most for him is inadequate. He needs love poured over him in massive doses. In their argument following Kane's trouncing at the polls—the argument that led directly to the severing of their friendship—Leland chastises the great man: "You talk about the people as though you owned them. As though they belonged to you. Goodness. As long as I remember you've talked about giving the people their rights, as though you can make them a present of liberty, as a reward for services rendered."

Kane's need for love, fueled by its premature truncation when his mother sent him east, is insatiable. And as a result, Kane cannot recognize the love he already has. Instead, he must forge ahead in relentless pursuit of the love he always senses is just beyond reach. In perhaps his most insightful observation on this subject, Leland concludes their argument, "You don't care about anything except you. You just persuade people that you love them so much that they ought to love you back. Only you want love on your own terms. It's something to be played your way, according to your rules." Here the irony leading to Kane's destruction is fully revealed. His deep sense of lost love leads to a terrifying insecurity, which in turn leads to the requirement that the love he so desperately craves be delivered in nonthreatening, controllable ways. This, of course, is a psychological impossibility. Genuine love, in order to be given and received, requires vulnerability, openness, taking risks. Kane needs the former but cannot risk the latter in order to gain it.

In another argument, the one that leads to the dissolution of their marriage,

Susan Alexander struggles to articulate why the opulence and luxury of a life married to Kane—which he took to be undeniable proof of his love—is so woefully inadequate. In her first attempt to express this inadequacy, which she makes as they ride to a Kane-ordered picnic in the Florida Everglades, she says simply, "You never gave me anything I really care about." This cryptic comment is explained later in their tent, when she says, "Oh, sure, you give me things, but that don't mean anything to you. [. . .] It's just money. It doesn't mean anything. You never give me anything that belongs to you, that you care about."

Even Alexander—depicted throughout the film as shallow, uneducated and frivolous—sees through Kane's pathetic attempts to purchase the love he fears he can never procure through legitimate channels. Even she knows that the one requirement for genuine love—the unfettered giving of oneself—is beyond Kane's capabilities. When he pleads rather pathetically, "Whatever I do, I do because I love you," she retorts, "You don't love me. You want me to love you. Sure. 'I'm Charles Foster Kane. Whatever you want, just name it and it's yours. But you gotta love me.'" When he slaps her for this comment, she responds emotionlessly, "Don't tell me you're sorry," to which Kane replies in kind, "I'm not sorry." The next day she packs and leaves him forever.

Kane's character, as revealed by Leland and Alexander, is deep and complex. One central theme emerges, however, around which all other dimensions seem to revolve. Kane is, above and before all, a man who desires to be loved, but who has no idea how to go about winning or keeping the love of the people he cares for the most. As a result, he is a man of contradictions and a man who relies on manipulation and domination. This passion for love, together with his inability to procure it to his satisfaction, is the tragic flaw that defines and destroys Charles Foster Kane.

"Not That Charlie Was Ever Brutal, He Just Did Brutal Things"

Theories of biblical anthropology vary widely, depending often on the starting point selected. If one begins with the doctrine of the Fall, biblical anthropology takes a decidedly pessimistic turn, focusing on the predicament of spiritual despondency in which human beings find themselves and on the utter hopelessness of their ever contributing meaningfully to any kind of deliverance from it. On the other hand, if one begins with the doctrine of humankind being made in the image of God, the biblical model of humanity is more optimistic, emphasizing the indelible mark of the divine that defines and individuates humanity—a mark that, though dimmed by human sinfulness, is never fully extinguished and that provides a sort of homing signal that can, if heeded, draw us back to our origin and purpose.

A proper biblical anthropology lies within the tension created by these two contrasting emphases. Human nature is, in an important sense, contradictory: we are drawn seductively toward the dark promises of personal hubris and physical gratification, and yet we are beckoned gently but forcefully by a clarion call to value and purpose that transcends the feeble promises of ego and corporeality. We are in the world but not of the world. We are the image of God, but it is an image stamped indelibly into physical substance.

Such a paradoxical anthropology is skillfully displayed in *Citizen Kane*. In the delightful sentiment that constitutes the title of this section, Leland captures perfectly the love/hate relationship with its title character that the film forces on the viewer.[3] We want to be best friends with Kane, but we feel in our bones the porcine essence of his actions. We do not know whether to be Thatcher or Bernstein. We cheer when Alexander walks out, yet our hearts break for Kane as he treads zombie-like between the infinitely reflecting mirrors. His graciousness is as genuine as it is irresistible when he charms Alexander out of the pain of her toothache. But the unyielding domination that forces her into the pain of her ludicrous opera career strips us of any admiration we might earlier have felt. We are tossed relentlessly between approbation for the qualities that reflect the image of God and could have made Kane "a really great man" and disgust at those carnal attributes that remind us continually of the degenerate nature of one separated from his Creator.

Theories concerning the image of God abound, of course, and I have neither inclination nor room to present, defend or dispute any of them here.[4] I will assume only that our being created in the image of God implies that many of the significant characteristics of God have their reflection in us. Dorothy Sayers, for example, notes that the dominant characteristic of God in Genesis 1 is that he is the Creator; so when we read in Genesis 1:26-28 that we are created in God's image, it is only natural to assume that our capacity for imaginative creativity is a reflection of that image.[5] I wish to focus on the dominant characteristic of God that is reported in 1 John 4:8 and intimated on virtually every page of the New Testament: God is love.

As beings created in God's image we are dependent for fulfillment and validation on the establishment and maintenance of genuine love relationships in our lives. One need not be an expert in clinical psychology to know that many emotional and behavioral problems are traceable to the absence, destruction or perversion of the deep and authentic human connection that is the purest referent of the overworked English word *love*. What is often missed, however, is how such a fact of human existence is attuned to biblical anthropology. Given the centrality of love in the biblical conception of God and a doctrine of humanity grounded in the image of God, one would expect that breakdowns in vital love relationships would lead inexorably to breakdowns in human psychological stability.

This, of course, is precisely what we find in *Citizen Kane*. Our only encounter with the child Kane provides us with the most important thing we can know about the man Kane. The love relationships in his home were precarious and weak. His father impresses us as perhaps well-meaning, but he is hopelessly naive at best and cruelly abusive at worst. He tries to care about his son, but hasn't the least idea how to go about it. His mother, who obviously loves him very much, is crippled by a quasi-Victorian detachment and sense of helplessness in her desire to protect Charles from his father. In the very few minutes we have to get to know her, we find it no wonder that she jumps at the opportunity, afforded by the unexpected gold fortune from the Colorado Lode, to get Charles away from his father and onto the road to opportunity and affluence. She does this because she loves her son, and she sees her actions as the only way to save him. Despite her distant stare and the disconnectedness of her every mannerism, we hear the deep conflict of love and concern as she utters her most poignant line, "I've got his trunk all packed. I've had it packed for a week now."

His mother's motivations of love notwithstanding, young Charles has no choice but to see her actions as a rejection of him and the end of everything he cherishes. Throughout the scene in which his mother is signing away his future in an effort to save him from a life of abuse and deprivation, the boy frolics carefree outside the window, yelling and running and sledding and having the time of his life. If he is abused or deprived, he knows nothing of it. He chatters nonstop, making the best of his solitude and turning a snowbound wasteland into a winter wonderland. He is lighthearted, untroubled, innocent. But all of that changes in a matter of seconds with his mother's announcement that he is leaving with Thatcher. And in the last glimpse we have of the child, his face is fixed in a snarl of defiance. Leland has his friend pegged correctly: he is not a brutal man. He is a lonely child. He is a creature of God, an image-bearer called into being to love and be loved. But his capacity for both is crippled in a single ironic act of love made frantic by desperation.

"There's Only One Person in the World to Decide What I'll Do, and That's Me"

But were Kane's need for love the whole story, the infuriating bundle of contradictions that constitutes his persona would still lack explanation. If we need something, we go out and find it. But Kane cannot find the love he needs because he is pathologically unable to make himself vulnerable and available to those whose love he desires—a necessary condition for receiving such love. There may be many psychological explanations for this failing, but whatever plausible reason is given will dovetail with the standard Christian doctrine of the Fall. Kane cannot (or does not wish to) find it in himself to respond appropriately to those around him—and therefore recognize and receive the love he desires—because he is fallen, in rebellion against his Creator.

Perhaps the most telling dimension of the doctrine of the Fall for understanding Kane is that the Fall was motivated by human desire to be like God. Theologically, there is an immeasurable gulf between the words of God in Genesis 1:26, "Let us make man in our image," and the words of Satan in Genesis 3:5, "You will be like God."[6] The Fall can be understood as the unwillingness of humans to "settle" for the former, striking out instead in pursuit of the latter. Seen from this perspective, the image and the Fall are in direct opposition to one another. Kane's desire for love results from his being made in the image of God. His fear of making himself vulnerable and available results from his desire to be like God. Such an analysis squares perfectly with the Bible's surprising contrast of love not with hatred but with fear (1 John 4:18-19).

With the Fall comes a distortion and perversion of the most fundamental of human concepts. While Scripture identifies love as the defining characteristic of God, those not intimately acquainted with the Creator would most readily name power and control as the essential mark of the divine. Charles Foster Kane is no exception. That Kane is fallen man desiring to be God can be seen in the tools he uses to carve out his special place in the world: his wealth and position, his charm and his relational detachment. All of these instruments are aimed at one primary goal: the acquisition, maintenance and growth of power and control on all levels—personal, social and political.

Kane is a man of great wealth and position, and he uses this to insure his dominant power in every dimension of his life. Kane's use of his money and his status as a newspaper publisher to exercise power is witnessed early in the Thatcher narrative, when he is depicted as orchestrating the Spanish-American War with all the lackadaisical whimsy of a fraternity prank. To follow the development of his life through the overlapping narratives of the movie is to witness the steady increase in Kane's use of his wealth and position for the forceful acquisition of power. He finances a blitzkrieg political campaign that comes within a hair's breadth of succeeding. When Alexander's talent is insufficient to secure her operatic fame, Kane uses his money and the influence of his newspapers to manufacture the façade of a successful career for her. And when the real world comes tumbling down around him during the Depression, he runs off to Florida and builds a world of his own, one that will acquiesce to his every whim and desire. Leland comments on the exotic and elaborate Xanadu, the pleasure palace Kane builds for himself: "He was disappointed in the world. So he built one of his own, an absolute monarchy." The man who would be God, in his final act of desperation, creates his own universe over which he can rule.

But money and status are not the only weapons at Kane's disposal in his pursuit of power. Charles Foster Kane, wealthy newspaper tycoon, is also "good old Charlie Kane," a man of endearing personal charisma and magnetism. He is a consummate gentleman who exercises the social graces to perfection. He is the life of any party—witty, articulate, suave and jovial. In Bernstein's narrative he is even portrayed as deferential, concerned that his own interests not carry undue weight—as when he instructs the *Inquirer*'s society page editor not to treat his wedding announcement differently from any other.

It is both appropriate and ironic that the most charming picture of Kane in the entire film comes from Leland's narrative, as he tells about the night Kane first meets Susan Alexander. She is suffering from a toothache and Kane's primary concern is to get her mind off of it. He is more playful, more genuinely warm and cordial in these scenes than anywhere else in the film, as he wiggles his ears for her, makes shadow puppets and insists that she sing for him. He displays a rare moment of vulnerability when she quips, "I don't know too many people," to which he replies, "I know too many people—I guess we're both lonely." And in one of the most heart-rending lines in the film he asks her, "You really like me, though, even though you don't know who I am?" But most of the time Kane's charm and affability are directed clearly and intentionally toward manipulation and control—as in his forceful but utterly smooth and refined takeover of the *Inquirer* offices, his wooing of the voters, and the way he directs and molds conversations and confrontations throughout the movie.

A third tool Kane uses for achieving and maintaining power over his world is a detachment and aloofness designed to send the message to all around him that he is not interested in negotiation, compromise or any of the other standard activities of peer-level human interaction. He knows what's best for all concerned, and he will have his way. When Alexander's voice coach begs to be released from his duties, bemoaning the fact that Alexander simply lacks the requisite talent, Kane ignores him completely and instead turns to Alexander with the words, "It's all right, darling. Signor Matiste is going to listen to reason." There are times when Kane even appears to acquiesce a bit, only to wind up sending the message that he is more in control than those around him had imagined. When Leland offers the stinging criticism that Kane is looking for love but insists on having it on his own terms, Kane pours himself a drink and offers "a toast, Jedediah, to love on my terms. Those are the only terms anybody ever knows—his own."

The most blatant and defiant displays of his detachment come in his relationship with Alexander. When she implores him to let her stop singing and complains that she does not understand why he insists on her going on, he thunders, "My reasons satisfy me, Susan. You seem unable to understand them. I will not tell them to you again. You will continue with your singing." And the beginning of the end of their relationship is heralded by the following interchange across the cavernous, echoing chambers of Xanadu:

> KANE. I thought we might have a picnic tomorrow, Susan. Invite everybody to spend the night in the Everglades.
>
> SUSAN. Invite everybody? Order everybody, you mean, and make them sleep in tents. Who wants to sleep in tents when they got a nice room of their own with their own bath where they know where everything is?
>
> KANE. I thought we might have a picnic tomorrow, Susan.

When Kane speaks his will in such final, nonnegotiable terms, he sends the unmistakable message that the issue has been settled and resistance is futile.

Here we see the interplay of all the tools at his disposal. When his charm cannot overwhelm those around him, he is quite ready to use his wealth and position to overpower them. And he can afford to exercise such domination because his aloofness and distance protect him from the pain and wounding that would ordinarily follow from such relational trauma.

But his deep need for and relentless pursuit of power and control cannot separate Kane completely from the true meaning of the image in which he is created. Throughout the film Kane couches his exercise of power in the guise of love and the good of those around him. And we have the definite feeling that these expressions are not insincere. He insists to Thatcher, "I am the publisher of the *Inquirer.* As such, it is my duty—and I'll let you in on a little secret, it is also my pleasure—to see to it that decent, hard-working people of this city are not robbed blind by a group of money-mad pirates because, God help them, they haven't anyone to look after their interests!" In his campaign speech at Madison Square Garden he intones boldly, "I'd make my campaign promises now, if I weren't too busy arranging to keep them!" And as we have already seen, he tries desperately to placate Alexander's final barrage of accusations with his special plea, "Whatever I do, I do because I love you." Throughout the film we are afforded glimpses into the heart of this desperate, confused, conflicted man. And it is a heart of flesh, though encased irretrievably and sorrowfully in impenetrable stone.

If there is a final break where we know that the Image cannot win out over the Fall in Kane, it is when he fires Leland after finishing the devastating review of Alexander's opera performance that his friend had begun. Leland emerges from his drunken stupor and his office just as Kane is putting the finishing touches on the article.

KANE. Hello, Jedediah.

LELAND. Hello, Charlie. I didn't know we were speaking.

KANE. Sure we're speaking, Jedediah. You're fired.

Leland has been the one person who can get through to Kane, with whom Kane cannot bring himself to be distant. But Leland has forced Kane to look at the real world—and himself in relation to it—once too often. Leland insists on being Nathan to Kane's adulterous, murderous King David, on uttering his prophetic "Thou art the man!" But Kane does not have the spiritual conviction that will allow him to confess, as did his regal Hebrew predecessor, "I have sinned against the LORD" (see 2 Samuel 12:1-14). He cannot heed the message, so he has to kill the messenger—and with him, any hope of redemption.

"I Am, Have Been, and Will Be Only One Thing—an American"

The picture of Charles Foster Kane drawn over the last two sections is one perfectly consistent with and explainable by a biblical anthropology grounded in the tension between our status as divine image bearers and our status as fallen rebels. Of course I am not suggesting that this consistency is intentional. The last thing screenwriters Orson Welles and Herman Mankiewicz would have cared about was constructing a character who illustrated biblical doctrines. Nonetheless, it is a testimony to the power of the biblical picture of humanity that such a perceptive and sensitive view of what might drive a man like Kane squares so well with it. And I believe it is further testimony to the authenticity of biblical anthropology that the truths revealed in the character of Charles Foster Kane are so summarily dismissed, ignored and railed against in contemporary cinema.

It is prudent at this point to restate the thesis of this chapter: namely, *Citizen Kane* presents a biblical and realistic picture of human nature—one that is denied and denigrated by many films being made today. The former part of this thesis has been demonstrated in the previous two sections. There remains now only the defense of the latter. This will be done by returning to the three weapons of power at Kane's disposal, which were examined in the previous section: his wealth and position, his charm and charisma, and his aloofness and relational detachment. We have seen how the use of these tools constitutes Kane's tragic flaw and leads to the systematic thwarting of the very love he is so desperate to gain. In this section we will examine how they constitute some of the most celebrated and enviable traits of the most popular heroes of modern cinema.

Before doing so, however, it is important to note that many films recognize the following two truths implicit in *Citizen Kane:* (1) that wealth, position, charisma and control cannot bring happiness or substitute for authentic love relationships, and (2) that to be human is to live in the tension created by our image-bearing status and our fallen nature. The films of Frank Capra two generations ago and those of Nora Ephron in the present generation are among the better known examples of films that, while admittedly formulaic and platitudinous, nonetheless concentrate on the more relational aspects of human existence and demonstrate such to be diametrically opposed to the pursuits of wealth, power and control. In such films the characters must always choose between the formidable temptations of their fallen nature and what their image-bearing souls know to be the path to fulfillment and happiness.

But such films are most often overshadowed—both in the critic's corner and at the box office—by those in which wealth, position, charm, detachment and power are celebrated as the truly respectable and enviable attributes of contemporary Western humanity. At the time that I originally wrote this essay (June 2005) the two most popular films in America were *Batman Begins,* the latest in the incredibly long line of incredibly successful comic-book hero movies, and *Mr. & Mrs. Smith,* the latest in the incredibly long line of incredibly successful movies glamorizing and glorifying a life of international crime and intrigue. Not a single film in the top ten box-office draws at the time came close to reflecting the biblical anthropology of *Citizen Kane*—with the possible exception of Ron Howard's *Cinderella Man* (which was hovering at the very bottom of the list and making its case for the 2005 "sleeper of the year" award).

All three of Kane's weapons of power are fully used and applauded in the longest running film series of all time—the James Bond movies. From the glory days of Sean Connery to the jury's-still-out Daniel Craig era, for over forty years Bond has represented the ultimate in male sophistication, magnetism and machismo. He always has the coolest cars, the sexiest women, the most advanced toys, and the calm and suave demeanor that never flaunts or showcases any of it. He is the ultimate twentieth-century Western hero. And everything that failed miserably for Charles Foster Kane works flawlessly for "Bond, James Bond."

Four of the most famous words in the history of Hollywood capture the worldliness of James Bond—the maximal sophistication that creates humanistic redemption out of the fallenness of carnal egotism—"Martini. Shaken, not stirred." All of Kane's weapons are present in this picture of Bond, painted by this seemingly innocuous wet-bar order: wealth and position (the martini is the drink of the social elite), charm and charisma (the confident tone of the words and the patented half-smile with which they are delivered codifies the entire Bond persona), distance and aloofness (his martini must be prepared in a way that sets him apart, letting everyone know he's not just another one of the sophisticated crowd). The subtle differences in taste and texture between a martini shaken and one stirred are apparent only to the elitist of the elite.

Perhaps the most obvious rebellion against the message of *Citizen Kane* is seen in the amazing success of the comic-book film genre. Here is an admittedly incomplete list of heroes from the pages of DC Comics, Marvel and their second-tier competitors that have made it to the big screen in recent years, many with multiple movies to their credit: Batman, Blade, Catwoman, Elektra, the Fantastic Four, Hellboy, the Incredible Hulk, Lara Croft (Tomb Raider), the League of Extraordinary Gentlemen, Spider-Man, Superman and the X-Men.[7]

While the personalities of these many heroes differ wildly (it is hard to imagine two more disparate characters than Spider-Man and Superman), the instruments of power used by Charles Foster Kane permeate their ranks. Super powers and secret identities—the staples of any comic-book hero's repertoire—serve by default to set the tabloid champions apart as aloof and distant figures.[8] And, of course, such separation is necessary for the aura of mystique that surrounds such figures and gives them a necessary advantage over friend and foe alike. Not all superheroes are wealthy, but they are all people of status, simply by virtue of their being superheroes. And, of course, their entire station and purpose in life are governed by this special position. As for charm and charisma, who ever heard of a dull or boring superhero? While some are unbearably obnoxious, conceited or out of touch, it is the industry standard for each to possess the uncanny ability to say or do exactly the right thing at exactly the right time to win over exactly the right people to exactly the right position. They always have exactly the right friends and exactly the right enemies.

The final sets of films I wish to examine bear a striking resemblance to the comic-book movies in the development of their heroes, though both series are based on original ideas and not on any preexisting comic-book series. (Both have, not surprisingly, given birth to their own line of comic books, however.) I speak of the *Matrix* series and the *Star Wars* series. These wildly popular movies again reflect all of the weapons in the *Citizen Kane* arsenal of control and power.

While the protagonists of both series are decided underdogs without the advantages their dominating foes possess, they nonetheless manage to have access to whatever resources they need to accomplish the task before them—including what must be inordinately expensive technological equipment. The actual wealth and position are not present (in fact, the source of the funds needed to procure this equipment is not quite clear in either series), but the unmistakable perks of such, which ultimately enable them to triumph, abound. Furthermore, explanations of how victory comes their way are provided by each series' equivalent to the super powers the comic-book heroes possess—the Force at the disposal of the Jedi and the quasisupernatural powers available to anyone who understands how to manipulate the matrix. Charisma and charm abound in the heroes of both series—characters do not come more disarming than Neo nor more delightful than Yoda. And again we are reminded at every turn of what seems to be a dogma of Hollywood heroics: that detachment and remoteness are the price to be paid by one who wishes for the advantages necessary to save the universe. From Obi-Wan's hideaway cave on Tatooine to Morpheus's private refuge behind his trench coat and customized nose-pinching sunglasses, the message is repeated and clear—those who would make a difference must remain distant from those on whose behalf they are making it.

Conclusion: "It Will Probably Turn Out to Be a Very Simple Thing"

Examples of Hollywood's glorification of the Kanesian hero can be listed ad infinitum (or ad nauseam, whichever comes first). I have not even touched on the glorification of the criminal life represented paradigmatically in Steven Soderbergh's wildly popular remake of *Ocean's 11* (and its predictably disappointing sequels, *Ocean's 12* and *Ocean's 13*) or the disturbingly successful tough-cop series, such as the *Dirty Harry* and *Lethal Weapon* movies, that blur beyond all recognition the line between good guy and bad guy. But I must move on to some closing remarks concerning this picture of the Hollywood hero that was unfolded over the previous section. I have three such remarks in conclusion.

First, I believe that the admittedly brief examination presented here offers good evidence for the second half of my thesis: that the typical Hollywood message of heroism and success is in direct contradiction to that of *Citizen Kane*. The American film industry is much more interested in the myth that Charles Foster Kane bought into than it is in the cold hard truth that formed his unfortunate legacy. The double-edged lie—that power and control are the proper end of human existence and that wealth, position, manipulative charm and relational aloofness are the proper means to that end—is alive and well in our nation's entertainment capital. Again, I do not pretend that this verdict applies to contemporary cinema across the board. But inspection of the top box-office draws at any given time over the past generation or two reveals an unmistakable balance in favor of movies that glorify what Orson Welles and biblical anthropology denounce—the myth of the modern American hero.

Second, we must be careful what we conclude from this. I do not mean to imply that those who produce contemporary films are engaged in some industry-wide scheme to perpetrate a fraud on the American moviegoing public or to promote any explicitly and intentionally anti-Christian agenda. I am no conspiracy theorist. I do not believe that Hollywood has an "agenda." American filmmakers are much more interested in providing entertainment and making money than they are in sending messages of any kind. Multimillion-dollar corporations want to know what will sell, not what will preach. As long as the *Citizen Kane* mutiny continues to produce blockbusters, the production companies and film distributors will continue to generate films that reflect it. The myth of Charles Foster Kane lives in the hearts of the American people, and it is this perpetual fable that motivates the mutiny. The pipedream that we could all be Kane, and be happy and fulfilled as such, keeps driving us back to the matinees and feature showings to immerse ourselves just a little longer in the warm, soothing bath of fallen self-deception.

Third, I want to be clear that my argument is not a call for rebellion against the film industry, for boycotting of movies or studios that promote a nonbiblical anthropology or for social action of any kind. I love movies. I watch them more than I should and love to talk about them long after most people around me have tired of the subject. They are one of the great defining elements of contemporary culture, and I believe that they can be enjoyed and appreciated as works of art, works of literature, works of technological achievement without such appreciation translating into endorsement of the worldview elements of the films. (If I read and enjoy Homer, does that mean that I approve of or believe in the polytheism and hubris that permeate and drive his plots?) This chapter is an exercise in social criticism informed by philosophical and theological reflection, and as such it is a call to awareness of one dimension of one major element of the culture we share. Lacking the requisite omniscience, I will forego the task of prescribing application of this awareness to the lives of my variegated audience.

Story-Shaped Lives in *Big Fish*

KELLY JAMES CLARK

When my youngest son was born I sent an electronic announcement to the faculty and staff at my college:

> Kelly Clark is pleased to announce the birth of Evan Clark. Evan was 22 lbs., 14 oz. He walked out of the womb and greeted his parents in French. Our impeccably handsome boy can read Latin. He's an accomplished pianist and has a flair for the culinary.

The literal facts of Evan's birth would have been decidedly bald (pun intended):

> Evan Clark, son of Kelly and Susan Clark, was born on June 22. Evan weighed 8 lbs.

Which statement communicates better the unique value of Evan in the eyes of his parents—of the weight of his life, not of his body? While not entirely factually true, the announcement was a mythic expression of the excitement with which we greeted his birth and of our hopes for his future.

Big Fish, directed by Tim Burton, is a magical tale that demonstrates the transforming power of stories. Drawing on Daniel Wallace's novel and John August's superb script, Burton shows the power of story to shape a life. The Big Fish (Edward Bloom) is a person whose life and life story are about to slip away. He is dying. But his stories, like most fishing tales, are exaggerations. What do his stories communicate about the value of the Big Fish, of the weight not of the fish but of his life?

Big Fish, though not explicitly Christian, is philosophically and morally rich in ways that are congruent with Christian belief. It shows the power of grace and redemption in human lives. And it occasions the opportunity to reflect on narrative, which is essential to self-understanding. For those Christians not yet convinced of the power, virtue and even necessity of narrative, I defer to the fact that Holy Writ is God's narrative self-communication. Stanley Hauerwas writes of the power of biblical narrative, "The narrative of Scripture not only 'renders a character' but renders a community capable of ordering its existence appropriate to such stories. Jews and Christians believe that this narrative does nothing less than render the character of God and in so doing renders us to be the kind of people appropriate to that character."[1] *Big Fish* occasions reflections, both generic and Christian, on narrative.

As we reflect on narrative, we may ask: How do stories "render a character"? How do stories shape and even transform lives?

Quick Review

The young Ed Bloom was the big fish in his small town of Ashton, Alabama. The old Ed Bloom is on his deathbed, estranged from his son, Will, who resents his physically and emotionally distant father. Will believes his father has hidden himself behind the fantastic yarns that he impulsively spins. The film recounts Edward's life through the medium of his mythic tales. Adolescent Edward scores the winning touchdowns and saves the neighbor's dog. Finding Ashton too small a pond for the big fish he longs to be, Edward sets out for a wider world, where he meets a witch, a giant, a naked nymph and circus freaks. A detour through the town of Spectre, populated by happy failures, nearly traps Edward in complacency. Then he's off on his odd quest for fame and fortune.

Will, a newspaper reporter, returns to his father's bedside to sort reality from fantasy: "I'd just like to know the true versions of things. Events. Stories. You." To the literalist Will, these stories are an annoyance and a ruse behind which his father hides. He believes his father tells his tales to keep his son and the real world at a distance. Ironically, yet tellingly, Will is the film's narrator—telling his father's story.

Demythologizing

The central myth, related by Edward, concerns an uncatchable fish: "There are some fish that cannot be caught. It's not that they're faster or stronger than other fish. They're just touched by something extra. . . . One such fish was The Beast." As Edward tells the story at Will's wedding, Will departs in disgust, missing the meaning behind the myth (the compliment to Will's mother and wife): "Now, you may well ask, since this lady fish wasn't the ghost of a thief, why did it strike so quick on gold when nothing else would attract it? That was the lesson I learned that day, the day my son was born. Sometimes, the only way to catch an uncatchable woman is to offer her a wedding ring." Will's inability to sympathetically understand his father's stories renders him incapable of understanding his father's life and loves.

The myth of the uncatchable fish also serves as a metaphor for human significance. The adolescent Edward tells us, " 'Kept in a small bowl, the goldfish will remain small. With more space, the fish can grow double, triple, or quadruple its size.' It occurred to me then, that perhaps the reason for my growth was that I was intended for larger things. After all, a giant man can't have an ordinary-sized life." So begins Edward's gigantification. Edward departs Ashton's small bowl, setting off for a bigger pond.[2]

We learn that his quest for significance hits rough patches—a dark forest of aggressive trees, spiders and bees. Outside of Spectre, Edward glances across a river and sees an alluring woman; as he fights a snake, she swims away. The woman represents Edward's destiny, the adventure that life could be. But his destiny was nearly snuffed out not so much by a poisonous snake as by a stick. Spectre is the town of deferred dreams that Edward departs immediately before conventional "happiness" overcomes him and deprives him of his dream.[3] He is warned that all people will eventually lose their dreams, that everyone will settle for their mediocre place in the cosmos. The very old Edward laments, "As difficult as it was to reach Spectre, I was fated to get there eventually. After all, no man can avoid reaching the end of his life." After all, what is his destiny? He becomes a traveling salesman.

We learn through these stories of the great-souled man that lived them and now tells them. The older Edward is a fading, flawed hero, if ever a hero at all. Wishing the world and his place in it to be a certain way, he tells fantasies of how things ought to be (or ought to have been). He is old and dying, mostly alone, estranged from his son, leaving behind a grand house and soon-to-be-forgotten stories. The Big Fish is drying out in bed, shriveling before his own eyes.

The film ends with Edward slipping into the great stream as he's transformed, literally, into the big fish.

Edward is a slippery character whose life nearly slips through Will's fingers. Will nearly fails to catch his father's generosity, courage, dogged determination and, ultimately, his love for his wife and son. But just at the very end, Will is hooked by his father's stories.

Edward's wife and Will's mother, Sandra, is the big fish. Will's wife is the big fish. Will is the big fish. Love is the big fish. Edward's destiny is the big fish. The quest for human significance is the big fish. But mostly, Edward is the Big Fish.

Story-Shaped Lives

Big Fish illustrates how stories provide life with a narrative structure and unity, on which hang human significance. Let us consider story-shaped lives more philosophically. Eschewing the analytic method of argument and counterargument, our approach will be more descriptive and reflective. Understanding, the goal of philosophy, is achieved sometimes by careful argument and sometimes by describing and reflecting on actual human practices. In the case of story or narrative, the descriptive-reflective approach seems best suited to the subject matter. Let us begin with a discussion of the importance of story to understanding ourselves and a clarification of what a story or a narrative is.

In the West, we have two approaches to understanding the self: the way of abstraction and the way of narrative. The way of abstraction seeks the nature of the human self in universal, ahistorical metaphysical essences.[4] The way of abstraction turns away from our particularity and toward the universally or essentially human: humans are featherless bipeds, thinking things, disembodied souls, embodied souls, Homo sapiens or rational animals. This approach seeks the universally common nature of human beings rather than any particular traits that might distinguish one person from another.

The question, who am I? cannot be answered solely by the way of abstraction. The way of narrative seeks to understand the self in ways that distinguish us from other humans—by turning toward the particular historico-cultural circumstances that have formed our unique selves. My self is discovered by reflection on the universally human and by discovery of those unique particularities that have shaped my life. The human self is partly understood through narratives, in all our particularity or individuality.

Our lives are shaped not by stories as such but by the events and circumstances we experience, the people with whom we interact, and the choices we make. But as we try to understand our lives, we throw these events into a narrative structure that makes sense of it all. Not all events in our lives shape us in equally powerful ways, and they don't come with labels: we narratively attach labels that help us to select, construe and evaluate these events. If someone were to ask me who I am, I would answer with stories. The bare recitation of facts— "I am a philosopher, a man, a father, a husband, a soccer player . . ."—provides an impoverished understanding of my self. Perhaps I play soccer to get exercise, or perhaps I play in the (futile) pursuit of vainglory. To clarify, I might tell a story: "I started playing soccer with my son when we lived in Scotland. He loved playing soccer but had no friends in our neighborhood, so I kicked the ball with him every day. When we returned to the United States, I helped coach some of his teams. Then, at forty years old, I started playing on a team. I enjoy the game and the exercise. I hope to be able to play on a team with my son when he gets older." Only when placed within a narrative context can one gain any deep understanding of what being a soccer player means for me.

We are, as Alasdair MacIntyre writes, storytelling animals.[5] The impulse to tell stories is rooted in our desire to understand ourselves and others. We are historical creatures seeking our own (his)story—or (her)story—to make sense out of the apparently disparate events in our lives. Things happen to us and we understand them by placing them in a narrative context. Michael Novak writes that a story is "a narrative that links sequences. . . . It unites past and future. It supplies patterns, themes, motifs by which a person recognizes (or someone else recognizes) the unity of his or her life."[6] In a narrative, the facts must be linked, relationships signified, purposes specified. The tensed order or pattern of experience is made explicit in the narrative. Notice that the linkages are more than tense; we seek a meaningful pattern (this occurred because of that, I became this kind of person because of that). The narrator offers a linkage that she believes is *already there* in the experiences that are linked.[7] They are given, recognized and then proclaimed in narrative. A narrative also states that *this* happened because of *that* (and not because of some other event or simply for no reason at all). The relationships among events, among the people in the events, among people and their desires, needs and purposes are made apparent. In so doing, these relationships are *signified* both in the sense of being signs which point to reality and in the sense of making us aware of the significance, depth or weight of various circumstances or relationships. *These* and not others, the narrative tells us, are the significant facts placed in their proper relationships. The facts are linked and the relationships signified by reference to the goal or purpose of the activities or events.

Narrative seeks the unity of a life amidst the diversity of life-events. It seeks a meaningful pattern or shape to our lives. Meaning searches the muddy little tracks of our existence and locates in them the meaningful path. Significance draws us out of bare sequence into the realm of value: we are recognizing the worth of the actions or events. And purpose points the present or past sequence toward the unrealized future (and to the kind of person we are striving to become). MacIntyre contends that we are seeking the concept of a self, "a self whose unity resides in the unity of a narrative which links birth to life to death as narrative from beginning to end."[8]

Will, the newsman, believes he reports the bare facts. When Edward reminds Will that they are both storytellers, Will demurs, saying, "I'd just like to know the true versions of things. Events. Stories. You." But he fails to see that Edward cannot be found in a bare recitation of events. When Edward asks Will's wife whether Will told her the story of his courtship of Sandra, she says that he hasn't. Edward sighs and says, "Probably just as well. He would have told it wrong anyway. All the facts and none of the flavor." Significance requires reflecting on and conscious ordering of events which give a flavor that both engages the imagination and indicates the meaning of certain events.

Let us now consider the possibility of understanding our lives within the context of grander, overarching narratives—say, religious or ethical narratives—that inform our lives.

Grand Narratives

Philosophy professor Adriana Cavarero, recounting a story that author Karen Blixen was told as a child, places the quest for human significance in a narrative:

> A man, who lived by a pond, was awakened one night by a great noise. He went out into the night and headed for the pond, but in the darkness, running up and down, back and forth, guided only by the noise, he stumbled and fell repeatedly. At last, he found a leak in the dike, from which water and fish were escaping. He set to work plugging the leak and only when he had finished went back to bed. The next morning, looking out of the window, he saw with surprise that his footprints had traced the figure of a stork on the ground.
>
> At this point Karen Blixen asks herself: "When the design of my life is complete, will I see or will others see a stork?" We might add: does the course of every life allow itself to be looked upon in the end like a design that has meaning?[9]

As the man in this story looks out of the window on his past, he sees a design that he did not intend. He simply took one step after another, did one thing and then another. Only upon looking back could he see the pattern of his life—his life story. Cavarero concludes, " 'All sorrows can be borne if you put them into a story or tell a story about them,' writes Blixen. And Hannah Arendt comments: 'the story reveals the meaning of what would otherwise remain an intolerable sequence of events.' "[10]

Insofar as we cannot locate our life within the context of a unified, coherent and complete narrative, we may experience some sort of disintegration. Integration is secured only when one is able to discern the meaningful pattern of experience that links past and present with future, without the loss or betrayal of any of them. One may secure complete self-integration only through sacred or secular grand narratives (often called *metanarratives*) that are sufficiently powerful for understanding one's whole life. C. S. Lewis concurs: "In life and art both, as it seems to me, we are always trying to catch in our net of successive moments something that is not successive."[11] Lewis claims that in our lives we are seeking the eternal; we yearn to connect our time with eternity. We cannot gain the perspective from our finite standpoint within time. This explains why grand narratives are so compelling and their loss so tragic: so much of what we cherish and what makes life bearable, lies, if at all, beyond the realm of immediate experience. We want our finite lives and diverse and divergent experiences to find significance within an overarching, even moral and religious, narrative.

Understanding a self is not a simple recitation of past events; it involves interpretation of the past. How did we get here from there? What were the significant road signs? Where are we going? The latter question recognizes that narratives are essentially goal oriented. We are moving in a direction toward our (chosen?) end. "Men die because they cannot join the beginning and the end," writes Frank Kermode.[12] It is through the end that past and present moments find their significance. Through the end humans find their ultimate meaning.

Some recent thinkers in the West—such as Jean Paul Sartre, Samuel Beckett and Franz Kafka—deny the narrative quality of life, believing that life is nothing more than an unconnected series of events with no purpose or goal: life is just one bloody event after another. This happens and then that happens, and nothing more can be said. There is no overarching rhyme or reason for why this happened after that happened; there is no unifying goal that makes sense of each step along the way. Life is just one senseless step after another on the road to nowhere. Those who project an order on their inherently disordered lives—from the optimistic humanist to the religious—practice various forms of self-deception. Life is not an adventure, which requires a good ending to redeem the pain and sorrow of the journey; life is a tragedy with no redemptive ending, nothing but death. Pain and sorrow are the victors, swallowing up any hope or human significance.

Big Fish, although not explicitly religious, plays with the themes of grand narrative, of adventure and tragedy. Old Edward, lying on his deathbed, worries that he's ended up in Spectre—the land of unfulfilled or lost dreams. In the past, coming home reminded him of his finitude, of his ordinariness. So he retreated to the road, to fulfill his destiny.[13] He had come to view his son as just another giant—one more person whose greatness competes to eclipse his own. His frantic, itinerant activities were designed to make himself big and bright, but as he proceeded through life, Edward felt his light growing dimmer and dimmer. Now, on his deathbed, he wishes to pass the torch to his unwilling son.

We may then ask, How do Edward and Will avoid tragedy?

The Necessity of the Other

We ended the previous section with Edward, tempted to view his life as a tragedy, as the big fish drying out in his deathbed. What turns his life into an adventure? Before dying Edward needs to learn to be loved. In a beautiful love scene, Sandra gets into a bathtub fully clothed with her dying husband and weeps; she whispers through her tears, "I don't think I'll ever dry out." Edward also needs the love, forgiveness and understanding of his son, whom he neglected. The man who wished to be great needed to be an ordinary, flesh-and-blood human being to be accepted and loved. This is precisely the point that connects his temporality with eternity. In the novel, Will says, "Death was the worst thing that ever could have happened to my father. I know how this sounds—it's the worst thing that happens to most of us—but with him it was particularly awful, especially those last few preparatory years, the growing sicknesses that disabled him in this life, even as they seemed to be priming him for the next."[14] Love and forgiveness prime us for the next life. Edward's demise provided the occasion to redeem his dream to be great. This dream had alienated him from what he most wanted, the love of his wife and son.[15] To be loved unconditionally by his son is his mantle of greatness. To accept this sort of greatness, he must renounce his desire to be great. It wasn't his stories that distanced Edward from his son; it was his insistent self-aggrandizement and his absence from home (seeking greatness). Only at the end, when Edward concedes the need for his son to tell his story—to understand his life—does his authentic love for his son come through. For the first time, he comes to Will speechless; nothing in his hands he brings. Only then can he accept Will's offer of his storytelling gift.

Will is also essential to his father's redemption because Edward needs Will to gaze upon, to discern and assemble, the story of his life. The meaning of the man's life comes after the sequence of events in his life—the story puts the man's life into a meaningful pattern. Can Will, in Blixen's terms, discern Edward's stork?

Will, the film's narrator, recounts his father's life after Edward's death. While Edward is living his life, he is not, indeed cannot, be fully aware of his own life's pattern. Though Edward's biography requires information gained from Edward's autobiography, only someone who has gazed upon the entire course of his life has the opportunity to discern that life's story. Edward's life is in Will's hands.

Narrative Deceptions

In telling a story of Edward's transformation I took details and clues of the movie and then organized them, highlighted them, called attention to this and that, and said that this all happened for the redemption of Edward. Or not. Narratives are often self-deceptions, serving to build up one's ego. Think of how much more clever and humorous we are when we recount an event than when we participated in the event. Think of the stories we tell ourselves when someone tells us that they got an A on the exam while we earned a C. Narrative self-aggrandizement is found on a worldwide scale in history textbooks that tell stories that, say, favor Europeans and denigrate Native Americans. And most religions tell cosmic stories that elevate human beings to nearly divine status. Narrative can be just as much or more a tool for self-deception as it is for self-understanding. Events happen, and we interpret them. Events are ambiguous and lend themselves to a variety of interpretations. We include this but omit that; we highlight one portion but downplay another; we say that this happened because of that without being able to see the causal connections; we have selective memories; and we have a natural human tendency to favor ourselves and denigrate others. The delicious and terrifying prospects for narrative are that, from a human perspective, we cannot tell whether we've gained understanding or been deceived.

And the same goes for the film: its clues are tiny, its meaning not explicit, and what actually happened in Edward's life is ambiguous and seldom clarified. We are not granted access to the meaning of the film outside of its various stories.

When Del Ratzsch, my colleague and ex-friend (just kidding), read a draft of this chapter, he claimed not to see Edward's transformation and accused me of cheating by relying on the book at key points. He lamented Edward's self-fascination and self-created distance from his son. But he believed that Edward died with his shortcomings intact and that his son simply played into his hands by telling his father's stories. While I believe that to be a misreading of the film, I cannot deny its possibility.

Let me recount the clues that guide my interpretation. Edward's desire to be great, to become a giant, is seen in his quest to become the Big Fish by leaving the small pond for the bigger pond. But his quest is competitive—in sports, the science project, the "defeat" of the giant and the battle for his wife; whether he views Will as a competitor is ambiguous. He desires to be great but ends with lost dreams. He is on his deathbed, shrinking. I take the metaphor of his drying out to indicate that he is shrinking down to size. His metaphysical discomfort is revealed in the glimpses of his pain that we see when everyone else leaves the room. And, finally, the book casts an interpretive shadow over the film.[16] These and other clues accumulate suggestively around the interpretive narrative that I've constructed—or not. Because of the fallibility of human narratives, I must concede the fallibility of my narrative. Del's and my understandings show how the end, variously understood, transforms the entire story.

Perhaps the most important interpretive clue for any understanding of the film is that Will is the narrator. This requires some understanding of the psychodynamics of his conversion from one who feels aversion to his father's stories to one who completes and delights in his father's stories. If the end transforms the story, then in the end, Will tells his father's story. Will's narration of Edward's story turns it from tragedy to adventure.

Will's Transformation

How does Will go from despising his father's stories and occasionally his father to loving both? Will gives or perhaps shows his love to his father by telling his father's story. As narrator, Will-the-journalist has become Will-the-teller-of-tall-tales. How does Will-the-hater-of-myth become Will-the-lover-of-his-father, whose life is embedded in myth?

When Will rhetorically asks his father whether he knows much about icebergs, Edward replies, "Do I? I saw an iceberg once. They were hauling it down to Texas for drinking water, only they didn't count on an elephant being frozen inside. The woolly kind. A mammoth." Will demands that his dad stop interrupting so he can make his point, cashing out his metaphor: "The thing about icebergs," Will says, "is you only see 10 percent of them. The other 90 percent is below the water where you can't see it. And that's what it is with you Dad. I'm only seeing this little bit that sticks above the water." When Will declares that he has no idea who his dad is because his dad never told him a single fact, Edward counters that his stories contain lots of facts. Will replies, "You tell lies, Dad. You tell amusing lies. Stories are what you tell a five-year-old at bedtime. They're not elaborate mythologies you maintain when your son is ten and fifteen and twenty and thirty. And the thing is, I believed you. I believed your stories so much longer than I should have. And then when I realized that everything you said was impossible—everything!—I felt like such a fool to have trusted you. You were like Santa Claus and the Easter Bunny combined. Just as charming and just as fake." When Edward asks Will whether he still thinks he's a fake, Will answers, "Only on the surface. But that's all I've ever seen." Ironically, Will is speaking in metaphors but is deaf to his father's metaphor. He couldn't see that his father was delivering a gift of himself inside his stories. What would coax Will to accept his father's gift?

Three factors properly dispose Will toward his father. First, Will's heart is softened by the gentle pleas of his mother and, especially, his wife. Although he initially disdains these pleas, their cumulative effect begins to warm him toward his father. Second, Will visits Spectre, where he learns that his father was an extraordinarily generous person who also deeply loved his family. Jenny, the adoring girl who has grown into a longing woman in Spectre, says, "I wanted to meet you for the longest time. I did. I envied you so much. The way Eddie would talk about you when you were at Missouri, that award you won. Congratulations, incidentally. And when you got the job at the A.P., everything, he

was so proud of you. I mean, that's the thing. Every moment he loved you. . . .
And as brightly as the sun would shine when he was with me, every time he
left, it disappeared. I wanted to be as important to him as you were, and I was
never going to be. I was make-believe and his other life, you, were real."

Here the camera changes angle to focus on Will, who is sorting through his
confused thoughts. Jenny asks him, "You knew that, didn't you?" Will does not
know; but he is beginning to learn.

Will's transformation is effected finally when he discovers that his father
needs him. When Will enters his father's hospital room, he finds him awake
and gasping for breath. His eyes are open. He's scared and confused. He invites Will to tell the story of how he dies. Will balks, unsure of how to proceed.
But Edward is increasingly desperate and Will sees that his father needs to be
loved by him. Edward needs Will's life-giving story.

Edward's need for his son comes into focus in that one moment, moving
Will to understand and accept his father. Will comes to value and esteem his
father through grasping and passing on his father's story. His father's desperation, need and impending death move Will to see the shape of his father's life.
It's not surprising that death can so powerfully reorient one's passions and so
direct one's intellect to truths one was previously emotionally prevented from
grasping.

Although Edward went through his life seeking gigantification, he now lies
in bed with his lost dreams and lost loves. As Edward's body fails him and his
life slips away, his story rushes toward a tragic end: he may die estranged from
the one he loves most. His son finally senses his father's need and begins to
understand and appreciate his father's love and life. Will narrates two final adventures of his father's death and funeral, one fictional and one real, that turn
his father's life from a tragedy into an adventure. Of course, the stories don't
rescue the father's life; the love of his son does.

The Big Fish's life is complete. Edward, relieved of the burden of gigantification, finds in his son's love his mantle of greatness. Will's role in the Big
Fish's redemption is clear: Will sees the pattern of his father's life and accepts
him unconditionally. Edward's and Will's redemption are achieved—dare we
say—by grace. Through their life and loves, through their stories and passions,
they reconcile and are redeemed. It would be an odd theology, indeed, that
failed to see grace in the ordinary and extraordinary events that shape and re-
shape our storied lives and thus attributed grace only to the splashy miracu-

lous. Grace is the shaping power that dramatically redirects the story of one's life from tragedy to adventure.

Christian Reflections

Perhaps the most obvious point of the film is Will's learning to honor and love his father. But we can't honor our parents by ignoring or failing to appreciate them. And we can't appreciate them until we come to understand their stories. Only when Will sympathetically listens to and then tells his father's stories does he see the weight of his father's glory.

Unfortunately, it is often death that forces reconsideration of a loved one's glory. Before my grandmother died she lapsed into an irreversible coma. I went to visit her in the hospital with my oldest, but still young, son. As I sat by her bedside I recalled the photo of her I had found a few years earlier and had placed in an antique frame. It was a photo of her as a little girl, twelve years old, in fancy clothes and full of promise. I thought of this little, poor farm girl putting on her special clothes, traveling by horse cart from the farm to the photography studio in Churubusco, Indiana. I told my son that my grandmother's husband died at forty-three, so she had to raise five children on her own with only social security and a few odd jobs providing meager financial support. In spite of her living through the depression and raising five children near the poverty level, I never heard my grandmother complain; I only recall her kindness, gentleness and good humor. I felt a sense of gratitude to my grandmother and was pleased that her blood runs through my veins. And I told my son my grandmother's story so that we could appreciate her in her presence and declare one last time our love for her.

I retell some of my grandmother's story in order to love and honor her. I do so just as Will retells his father's story. And Will does so perhaps as director Tim Burton, through *Big Fish*, mythically declares his love and honor of his own father, who died before Burton made this film and from whom Burton was estranged.

Christians should also appreciate narrative because God's self-revelation comes to us in a story. I don't mean to say that God *is* a story, as some hip theologians are wont to say, but although we recite creeds, Scripture is not a creed. The biblical narrative is an ordered and highly selective retelling of events that attempts to shed light on their significance. And the biblical narrative serves as the grand narrative that is intended to render—to shape and order—our lives. We need to learn to see how our narratives intersect with the grand Christian narrative in ways that integrate our lives with eternity.

Scripture renders a life in two ways. When we understand how our story intersects the story of Scripture, our lives are morally and spiritually reoriented. The second way, more relevant to *Big Fish*, is that Scripture illuminates the ways in which our lives have a pattern or purpose. As we journey through life, the lesson of Blixen's stork story is clear: we often can't see the pattern, meaning or purpose of our own lives. We lack the perspective to see the intersection of our time with eternity. Failed aspirations and relationships or profound suffering and disappointment can often make it difficult to see that our lives have any meaning. Recounting Edward's story, we are reminded of the necessity of the other to help us understand and appreciate our own lives. In a sense, Will is Edward's salvation as he graciously recounts Edward's life in spite of the distance that Edward has created between himself and Will. I have friends who I call "life-givers": they are the people who hear my story without ever standing in judgment. They listen sympathetically, hear my sorrow or my struggles, are slow to offer advice or correction, and yet help me to see the good in my life. They patiently bear me up and help me understand my own story. Life-givers graciously and unconditionally accept us and offer their very own selves to us. Although it nearly takes too long, Will becomes just this sort of life-giver to his father. I also know people who are what I call "life-suckers": they are judgmental and they gossip, put others down, hasten to give advice and seldom offer their shoulder to cry on. The Christian community should seek to be stork-seeking life-givers. They should affirm God's great work in human lives in ways that are neither judgmental nor obtuse to human shortcomings. Everybody needs a Will.

But even the best human life-giver cannot discern the entire pattern of my life. And most times neither can I, even with others' kind assistance. The Christian life is the in-between life, and the end is not seen but only hoped for. And not seeing the end or not hearing the still, small voice of God in the whirlwinds of our lives can be demoralizing and demeaning. In the in-between times, not seeing the end, we can be unsure whether our lives will turn out a tragedy or an adventure. And so we need to hear the story of faith; we need to trust that though we see ourselves through a glass darkly, God sees us face-to-face. The grand narrative of Scripture tells us a story of the shape of reality (within which fit our individual lives) and of the faith necessary to grasp and participate in that reality. When we can't see the pattern of our lives, we need to cultivate trust or faith that there is and will be such a pattern. Our lives don't or shouldn't feel meaningful to us because we've got it all figured out. Rather, we can feel our lives are meaningful because we trust it will all be figured out. We trust that the God who comes to us in a story will, in the end, tell us our story and that it will end in such a way that what, from our perspective, may seem a tragedy is in the light of eternity revealed as part of a grand adventure. That the God, the great Life-Giver, in whose very hand our name is inscribed, will graciously and unconditionally accept us and integrate our lives into eternity. And in our adventure story, and the story of the world, we trust that, as Julian of Norwich writes, "All shall be well, and all shall be well, and all manner of things shall be well."

3

Defining Love Through the Eye of the Lens

Romance, Sex and the Human Condition in
Pretty Woman, Legends of the Fall and *The Bridges of Madison County*

GREG JESSON

● ●

Nothing is so beautiful and wonderful, nothing is so continually fresh and
surprising, so full of sweet and perpetual ecstasy, as the good.
No desert is so dreary, monotonous, and boring as evil.
This is the truth about authentic good and evil.
With fictional good and evil it is the other way round.
Fictional good is boring and flat, while fictional evil is
varied and intriguing, attractive, profound, and full of charm.

Simone Weil,
On Science, Necessity, and the Love of God

If you live to be a hundred years old, you will have lived only 36,525 days. Doesn't seem like very much, does it? And obviously, if you're reading this essay, you've already used up a considerable number of those days. Inescapable questions flash across the darkness of the mind like lightning: What was I doing for all those days? What kind of person did I spend my days becoming? What purpose have I been living for? Often such questions are weighed and carefully measured by graduations, careers and locations. But more significantly, these questions are answered in terms of love: those we loved, those who loved us, those who refused to love us and those we refused to love. Even though many are tempted by the hollow diversions of lust, greed and power, every person must struggle with the reality that our greatest joys and deepest sorrows are tied primarily to love. Consequently, the films concerning love that are being considered here are especially poignant.

Being loved and loving another are the most complex and consuming relationships we can have with another person. Yet despite its immeasurable importance, romantic love is one of the most confused and painful concerns in contemporary life. Although everyone draws the distinction between love and lust, this distinction is almost meaningless since many, if not most, think of love as little more than an effervescent feeling that one is falling into or falling out of. Romantic love is seen as being as undeniable and unavoidable as a glacier, only smaller.

This chapter explores and analyzes this contemporary concept of love and romantic experience in the films *Pretty Woman, Legends of the Fall* and *The Bridges of Madison County*. These films are deeply moving, and even serious, attempts to salvage meaning and hope out of hopeless plights: in *Pretty Woman* Vivian Ward is a golden-hearted prostitute looking for love, with pay, in all the wrong places; Tristan Ludlow in *Legends of the Fall* bears double guilt for seducing his younger brother's fiancée and for the subsequent death of that brother; and Francesca Johnson, feeling unappreciated and disillusioned, waiting for something inspiring to happen, faces endless years of loneliness on an Iowa farm in *The Bridges of Madison County*.

I argue that these situations are dramatically distilled paradigms of the human condition. Because each of us necessarily lives within the subjectivity of his or her consciousness, life is often lonely. The only hope of each person is to discover a private reservoir enabling him or her to truly love another person—but not just any definition of love will suffice. Either we learn to love genuinely, or we wither away in loneliness.

For a film or novel to be more than an entertaining diversion, it ought to address some ultimate issues of life. Since we are not only conscious, but also self-conscious, this allows us to forge our own characters through our choices in an environment that is always complex, at times morally ambiguous and often heartbreaking. We become, whether we intend it or not, precisely what we choose. Within the context of its genetic inheritance, the human personality is structured and determined not by its environment, but by its volitional and reactive activity within that environment. If the unexamined life is not worth living, it would be simplistic to claim that the unreflective film is not worth watching. Perhaps it's more accurate to claim that the unreflective film is not worth watching twice. That said, *Pretty Woman, Legends of the Fall* and

The Bridges of Madison County are not simply entertaining films; they are serious and even profound films.

It is easy to portray human brokenness and the dismantling of the human soul cinematically. Indeed, the world is overflowing with such films. However, what is rare and exceedingly difficult to portray is the wonder of human redemption, the power of unconditional love, the presence of genuine goodness, the reality of hope and the boundless joy of living a worthwhile life. Although these three films do not explore all of these issues, and perhaps no film ever could, they all wrestle with some of these topics. Therefore, these films are worth watching and pondering—even twice.

I have selected these films for their provocative portrayals of love, romance, friendship and sex. Being loved and loving another are the two most powerful and character-transforming experiences of life. So what do these films say about the emotional, intellectual, moral and spiritual development of the characters? The contemporary misunderstanding of love identifies it with an emotion, an inscrutable force that one falls into (or out of) irrespective of thoughts, facts and promises. The immediate issue here is whether we can choose whom we love, but the ultimate issue is whether reason, evidence and objective values such as goodness and selflessness have anything to do with that choice.

Two of the films, *Legends of the Fall* and *The Bridges of Madison County*, deal with doomed romances. In contrast, *Pretty Woman* depicts a lasting but shallow romance. *The Bridges of Madison County* and *Pretty Woman* take place over a few passionate days, whereas *Legends of the Fall* covers five turbulent decades, and by the time it's over, everyone's life has been destroyed—ironically enough, by love.

Pretty Woman

Of the three films, *Pretty Woman* is the least serious and the most unrealistic. It has been described as the ultimate feel-good movie, and many filmgoers, especially women, found the romantic vision of *Pretty Woman* inspiring, even captivating. It always surprises me to hear many people, both religious and nonreligious, say that *Pretty Woman* is their favorite film. Unlike the other two dramas, *Pretty Woman* falls into the hybrid category of romantic comedy. Nevertheless, it raises deep questions about love and romance, but its answers are neither plausible nor deep.

The Cinderella story line of *Pretty Woman* is both simple and simplistic.

Edward Lewis, an ultra-rich, self-absorbed playboy, comes to realize that he needs commitment to more in life than buying companies to break up and "sell off the pieces." Edward finds himself in Beverly Hills for one week, engaged in tough business negotiations to take over a shipbuilding company. Not wanting to be alone but also unwilling to be burdened with "romantic hassles," he hires a streetwalker from Hollywood Boulevard to be his "employee" for a week. Vivian Ward is a charming, fresh-faced prostitute from Georgia; a high-school dropout who doesn't do drugs, she is sensible enough to use dental floss on the job because "you shouldn't neglect your gums." She has a sterling personality in that she is refreshingly vulnerable, bubbly, naive, witty and kind, especially in contrast to almost all the other Beverly Hills women who are haughty, condescending and envious. Vivian wins Edward's heart through her purity of character—despite her chosen profession and Edward's self-absorbed attitudes concerning romantic commitment. Although Edward has become wealthy through the dismantling of companies, his entire professional and personal life is challenged by Vivian's puzzled and penetrating questions: "You don't make anything and you don't build anything?" Predictably, they fall in love and live happily ever after.

In one touching scene, the manager of the Regent Beverly Wilshire Hotel, Bernard, warns Vivian not to come back after Edward leaves for New York, reprimanding her for her inappropriate and trashy clothing. Struggling to retain the smallest sliver of pride, Vivian sobs, "I tried to go get a dress on Rodeo Drive today, and the women wouldn't help me. I have all this money now [from Edward] and no dress. . . . I *have* to buy a dress for dinner tonight but nobody will help me." Vivian, who has experienced little kindness in life, expects the professionally snobby Bernard to call the police, but he is an uncommonly kind man who reaches out to her with unexpected grace. It is a small act. He calls a friend at a boutique to help Vivian find a cocktail dress, telling the saleswoman that Vivian is "a special guest. She is the niece of a very special guest." The lovely but unloved Vivian leaves his office, eyes filled with tears, believing, or maybe just hoping, possibly for the first time in her life, that she is not beyond all hope.

As the poet Bruce Barton says, "Sometimes when I consider what tremendous consequences come from little things, a chance word, a tap on the shoulder, or a penny dropped on a news stand—I am tempted to think that there are no little things."[1]

Life is composed of little things and small events, but these, both good and bad, add up to big things, like human lives, which in turn add up to history. The small things in each of the character's lives have resulted in personalities that are not very different. Edward, the businessman, and Vivian, the hooker, are as Edward describes them, "such similar creatures, Vivian. We both screw people for money." Realizing that they are both emotionally shallow, Vivian says that her approach to business is like Edward's: her rules are "don't get emotional when you turn tricks," "stay numb" and act "like a robot" when working.

The plot deviates further from reality when Vivian is almost instantly transformed into an Audrey Hepburn-like character, overflowing with style, poise and charm. This immediate change and her sudden love of Edward are propelled by the jet fuel of an almost limitless amount of money, designer clothes, a few hundred thousand dollars worth of jewels, a private jet, a private box at the opera, the penthouse suite in a Beverly Hills hotel, a limousine with an armed bodyguard, polo matches, horses and nonstop gourmet meals. Finally, Vivian's childhood dreams of a knight climbing a tower to rescue her come true when Edward, who has a fear of heights, appropriately climbs up the fire escape of her apartment with a bouquet of flowers in his hand to save her from her life.

If Edward has spent his adult life selfishly living only for himself and focused only on making money, is it plausible to believe that he can significantly transform his character and life after missing Vivian for *one* day? His personality restructuring seems effortlessly superficial, even flippant.

And what about Vivian? She correctly claims that once "people put you down enough, you start to believe it," and that "the bad stuff is easier to believe." Can the lifelong rejection experienced by Vivian, which contributed to her becoming a prostitute, be overcome in a week? Is that all it takes for her to overcome the pain from the past and become an emotionally mature person capable of accepting and giving love?

It is possible for romantic films to portray meaningful change. *Breakfast at Tiffany's* offers a nuanced account of character transformation. Audrey Hepburn's character, Holly Golightly, fills her life with diversions to avoid her pain. Nobody ever looked better, but nobody ever looked more forlorn. *Casablanca* also offers a glimpse into the private struggles of the cautious Rick Blaine as he weighs romance against the deeper issues of life. Character transformation is agonizingly depicted in the graphic film *The Unbearable Lightness of Being*, in which a womanizer faces how his pattern of adultery is destroying his wife and confronts who he really is for the first time. However, his redemption is incremental, it threatens his view of himself, and it is incapable of undoing all the anguish he caused. Finally, in *Shadowlands*, Anthony Hopkins plays the famous Oxford professor, writer and Christian apologist C. S. Lewis as he discovers that he is not a loving person. Although Lewis had an uncommonly great mind, he was emotionally immature. Through a complex sequence of events and choices, late in life Lewis married a woman he knew was dying of cancer. He had to be challenged to the core of his identity in order to be capable of such love.

While *Pretty Woman* lacks realism, it has a profound message that tugs at the human heart: character transformation, and thus redemption, are possible. Redemption is not an exclusively religious phenomenon. M. Scott Peck was not quite correct when he argued in *The Road Less Traveled* that emotional maturity is identical to spiritual growth. They are not literally the same: spiritual growth without emotional growth is impossible, but up to a certain point emotional growth without spiritual growth is possible. One's discovery of the exceedingly complex world of emotional growth often opens the door to the spiritual insights beyond the human sphere.

In the film both Vivian's and Edward's lives are saved by loving and being loved, but how does one become capable of truly loving another? How is such love to be distinguished from lust or mere infatuation? One of the great appeals of *Pretty Woman* is the expressed hope that love can be simple and that it is best when it is painless, without challenges and growth.

Lewis argued in *The Four Loves* that there are four different kinds of love: friendship, sacrificial nurturing, sexual intimacy and unconditional acceptance. (What is often and disastrously overlooked is that for any marriage to *flourish*, it must regularly express each of these four kinds of love. *Such inspiring marriages never occur by mere accident.*) Lewis also argued that friendship—the most profound of all loves—has the greatest potential for personal transformation since it goes deepest into the human heart.[2] Since few films are capable of dealing with the long-term complexities and stages of love, the exhilaration and delirium of infatuation are preferred. The definition of the word *love* is completely up for grabs in our age. What does it mean when the single most important word in our language is indefinable? If love is merely a vague, impulsive feeling uncoupled from actions and thus character, then the feeling of love would be compatible with any actions and any character *whatsoever*. Further, one could never ascertain whether he or she is loved merely by observing the other's actions. Unfortunately, this opens the door to massive and painful deception, both of the other person and of oneself. It is not uncommon to hear a man or woman who is unfaithful to or emotionally and even physically, abusive of another still claim to love that person, just as it is not uncommon to hear of someone falling in love not for who the other actually is, but for his or her potential. But are not these views simply the height of absurdity?

Jesus expressed a view of love that identifies love with actions. The feeling of love is subjective and therefore private, as all feelings are, and it is different from love itself, which is objective and therefore public. This just means it is possible that one can fail to feel in love while actually being in love, and that one can feel in love and not actually be in love. In John 15:13, Jesus said "Greater love has no one than this, that someone lay down his life for his friends." We lay down our lives for our friends not only by dying for them, but also by living for them. How is it possible to live for another? The single greatest impediment to living a good life, overflowing with joy, is self-centeredness. Because each person necessarily lives within the subjectivity of his or her consciousness, living for oneself *feels* like the most natural thing to do. Such self-centeredness is always built on the prideful delusion of what happiness consists in, and it guarantees a lonely life without profound and compelling love. Superficial and self-centered concerns only contribute to a character that is superficial and self-centered no matter how sincere one is (see 2 Corinthians 5:15). As Michel Quoist writes in *Prayers*,

> It's a long apprenticeship, learning how to love,
> And there are not several kinds of love:
> Loving is always leaving oneself to go towards others.[3]

Feelings of attraction are an important component of our emotional lives, as are other feelings; but as we know from our own lives and the lives of others, basing decisions predominantly on feelings leads to disaster. Why? Because feelings are not faultless indicators of the way reality is. Feelings can seamlessly percolate on and on independently of what is true, good and beautiful. In almost every other area of life outside of the romantic, we primarily rely on reason and evidence since they are open to examination and correction. To the extent that our feelings are not founded on reason and evidence, they are not open to rational scrutiny; therefore, they can easily lead us away from what is true. The discovery that our feelings have led us astray is always surprising and often devastating. Such insight cannot be accomplished merely by consulting another set of feelings, since no feeling *by itself* is necessarily sensitive to truth and evidence. Only feelings that exist in the context of a careful weighing of the evidence can be trusted to track reality accurately.

Even though Edward and Vivian have feelings of excitement and admiration, mixed with a healthy dose of infatuation, their actions have not sufficiently demonstrated a genuine love that can support a lifetime of commitment and challenges. They just don't seem to know each other well enough. In 1 Corinthians 13:8 Paul says "love never ends"; so if it ends it's not love. Bertrand Russell was perhaps the most famous philosopher and mathematician of the twentieth century. He was a professor at Cambridge University, an engaging and popular lecturer who published over eighty books and hundreds of scholarly articles and received the Order of Merit from King George VI. In his Nobel Prize-winning autobiography, Russell tells how his first marriage ended. Even though he and his wife, Alys, experienced "great happiness" for eight years, the marriage ended abruptly in 1902. "I went out bicycling one afternoon, and suddenly, as I was riding along a country road, I realized I no longer loved Alys. I had had no idea until this moment that my love for her was even lessening."[4] So much for Alys. The simple truth is that he never really loved her. Such impulsive selfishness and heartlessness are tragic for *all* involved, yet this kind of romantic narcissism is considered quite normal by many. Not surprisingly, more than *fifty* years would pass until Russell was romantically happy and stable again.

Authentic love always goes to the core of a person's character, values, hopes and dreams, and it is always a character-transforming reality in one's life. It often involves positive and ecstatic feelings, but not always. *Legends of the Fall* powerfully explores these issues.

Legends of the Fall

If *Pretty Woman* reveals a love that is too easy, then *Legends of the Fall* reveals a love that is too difficult, because it is impossible. Set in the high mountain meadows outside Helena, Montana, and spanning the years from the budding industrial revolution at the turn of the century through World War I and into the mid-twentieth century, this moving epic follows the turbulent lives of the three sons of Colonel William Ludlow. The scenery and music, beautiful beyond all hope and belief, are as majestic as the Ludlow family is dysfunctional. (Unfortunately, because the crucial moments of our lives are not accompanied by heart-stirring music, we often don't recognize when they are occurring.)

The brothers are as different as possible: Alfred, the eldest, is pragmatic and rigid; an aspiring politician, he is the most responsible of the three. Samuel, the youngest, is naive, boyish, idealistic and dutiful; he is a Harvard student and is probably in the glee club. Tristan, the middle son, is as wild as a Montana grizzly bear and loved by everyone; he is larger than life, his father's favorite. One Stab, "an elder of the Cree nation" who narrates the film, says of Tristan, "Some people hear their own inner voices with great clearness, and they live by what they hear. Such people become crazy; they become legends. . . . Every warrior hopes a good death will find him, but Tristan couldn't wait—he went looking for his." Ironically, Tristan's craziness hurts those around him more than it hurts him. His choices are so destructive that he outlives almost everyone else in the film.

As an army officer in the Dakota Territory, the father witnesses the government's deplorable treatment of Native Americans. He tries in vain to help them. Disgusted and disheartened, he resigns from the army "to go his own way. He wanted to lose the madness over the mountains, he said, and begin again." The brothers grow up in this setting without their mother, who retreats to the East Coast to escape the isolation.

In the absence of their mother, Alfred and Tristan "watched over [Samuel] like a treasure." The turning point in their lives is the apparently innocuous arrival of Miss Susannah Fincannon in the summer of 1913. In due course, she becomes romantically involved with all three brothers. Samuel "instantly loved" her when they met at a Harvard Tea. Unfortunately, Susannah's experience was not the same—at least not with Samuel. Instead, on her first trip out to Montana to meet Samuel's family, she falls for the restless Tristan *the moment* she sees him, even though she is engaged to his younger brother. (Never underestimate the power of riding up on a horse with a dead deer to win a woman's heart.)

Samuel's concern over German aggression leads him, despite his father's strenuous protests, to join the Canadian Expeditionary Force fighting in France. Both of his brothers also volunteer, and Tristan promises that he will protect Samuel from harm. The night before their departure to the war Tristan has a brief, but intense, romantic interlude with Susannah. After this, there is simply no way for things to end well.

Samuel is fortuitously spared the inevitability of a broken heart by getting himself killed in the war, at a moment when Tristan briefly neglects his promise to protect his brother. Bearing the crushing guilt over his brother's death and the seduction of his brother's fiancée, Tristan's life unravels as he descends into madness. Of course, none of this deters Susannah in the least, because her feelings for Tristan have nothing to do with his character and integrity. Although he is a lost and selfish soul, she is drawn to him like a moth to a bonfire. The rest of the film depicts the consequences of Tristan's choices and how life disintegrates for everyone around him.

This hauntingly beautiful film powerfully depicts romantic determinism in all its passion and torment. Romantic determinism is the view that love is an overpowering attraction that has been programmed into the individual by heredity and environment. Charlie Young, a character in the TV series *The West Wing*, gives this perfect one-sentence summary: "I don't think that you have any control over who you fall in love with." Of course, if you don't have any control over whom you fall in love with, you also don't have any control over whom you fall out of love with. Not only does this deny romantic volition, but it also renders the character, values and actions of the beloved irrelevant because they can always be overridden by irrepressible feelings for that person. In isolation, feelings are not open to correction, because they cannot be supported or challenged by evidence. Such "love" is compatible with any kind of behavior. Consider Tristan's brotherly "love" for Samuel: he will risk his life to protect his brother in the war, yet he finds this compatible with wooing Samuel's impulsive and vulnerable fiancée. Of course, the default excuse is that one can't help it, because, after all, one can't choose one's feelings. Or consider Tristan's short, self-centered letter to Susannah after she has waited years for his return: "Susannah, All we had is dead, as I am dead. Marry another." Doesn't Susannah deserve a little more of an explanation? Is such a letter consistent with authentic love?

The deepest principle in the human heart, contrary to all the insanity of the contemporary world, isn't sex—it's love. But not just any definition of *love* will do. Genuine love is not a mere feeling; rather, it is the expression of one's complete character, which includes values, aspirations, thoughts, preferences, feelings, habits, conscience and actions. In every relationship, if it lasts long enough, character emerges sooner or later as the *decisive* issue. (Since character ends up as the decisive issue, shouldn't every relationship begin with it being consciously considered?) Character is revealed in how one interacts with the deeper issues of life. Although the connection between sex and love is a powerful reality in the human psyche, we are presently witnessing the incongruity of a scarcity of love amidst a surplus of meaningless and thus unfulfilling sex. Many desperately base their romantic lives primarily on sex, simply because they can't imagine that there is anything more substantial. Apart from death, disease and war, nothing in this world has caused more pain, suffering and tears than so much contemporary "love" and sex. No matter how great sex is, if it is not accompanied by sacrificial nurturing, unconditional acceptance and deep friendship, there will not be a genuinely loving relationship. The impossibility of basing love on sex alone is compelling evidence that the human person is more than merely a sensate entity. Romance and sexual attraction are important and even magical parts of our conscious lives, but like every good thing, they can easily be distorted and idolized. They are not nothing, but they clearly are not everything either.

The connection between sex and character is easily missed in our culture. Philosopher Immanuel Kant said that most people don't desire to be evil; they just want to take a moral holiday. The new and widely advertised motto of Las Vegas sums it up perfectly: "What happens in Vegas stays in Vegas." Of course, this means only one thing: sex without the hindrance of friendship or future. It is ridiculous to claim that what happens in Vegas stays in Vegas, because choice and character are reciprocally related, and one's character necessarily follows one home from Vegas—or from anywhere else.

Love is not a perfectly unwavering attraction toward another; there is no such thing. Nevertheless, this is the myth presented by *Pretty Woman* and *Legends of the Fall*. Unlike all the hollow substitutes, real love is about gaining, through sacrifice, the ability to see the world through another's eyes. It's about learning to know another even as we are known. It's about triumphing over daily inconveniences and conflicts, not merely surviving them. It's all about emotionally growing together. And it's about participating in the redemption of another, even as we are being redeemed. Such love touches and challenges every part of one's life. In summary, love is learning to respect, adore and cherish the other (cf. 1 Corinthians 13:1-13). True love is always a life-transforming friendship, and such friendship has nothing to do with a constantly overpowering attraction. The danger of hoping for such attraction is that it is impossible to obtain—or to sustain for any length of time, no matter who you're with. Those who seek it, then, are wasting their lives. A strong component of the current popular myth concerning love is that the most challenging part of romance is finding the "right" person; yet this is false. The most challenging, and the most fulfilling, part of romance is learning how to love another selflessly over the long haul. While such attraction is initially blissful and effervescent, it is like the tide, always ebbing and flowing, tempered by our histories, choices and frailties.

The Bridges of Madison County

One of the greatest joys in this world is the joy of being loved by another person for who we are, in spite of our faults. Nevertheless, few can imagine, before they get married, how lonely a bad marriage can be. Of course, nobody expects that his or her marriage will be joyless and soul grinding. *The Bridges of Madison County* thoughtfully explores the tragedy of discovering late in life that one's marriage is not much of a friendship and therefore is not much of a marriage.

During World War II, young Francesca meets Richard Johnson, an American soldier, in Naples, Italy, and becomes a war bride, anticipating a new life in America. Isolated on a farm outside of Winterset, Iowa, for two decades, Francesca's life is profoundly lonely as she is unappreciated and barely noticed by her husband. She had dreams of romance and hopes of deep companionship, which she now realizes will never come true. She faces a lifetime of silent and lonely evenings sitting with her husband in front of the moronic television. During four days when Francesca's husband and children go to the Illinois State Fair to show a prize steer, her life unexpectedly changes forever when Robert Kincaid, a photographer from *National Geographic*, drives down her driveway seeking directions to the Roseman covered bridge. Each is surprised to find that the other notices and cares. Love begins with attention, and in a world with people who often do not notice and therefore do not care, this should never be underestimated.

We are given the impression that Robert and Francesca communicate more profoundly in four days than she and her husband have during their entire marriage. Not surprisingly, they become romantically and sexually involved, and as the State Fair is ending, Francesca must make the most heart-wrenching decision of her life. She must decide whether she is going to stay in a boring, unfulfilling marriage or travel the world with an adventurous man who finds her enchanting in every way.

It is not surprising that viewers reacted in two different ways to this dilemma. On the one hand, Francesca's actions were almost universally condemned by religious people—she commits adultery and adultery is wrong. On the other hand, many people find the story of *The Bridges of Madison County* inspiring. (The novel, the bestselling hardcover book of all time with over twelve million copies sold, was on the *New York Times* Best Seller List for 150 weeks.) It's not that all these readers think adultery is good; rather, they find the hope of a caring and fulfilling relationship, after so much unhappiness, compelling. *The Bridges of Madison County* has captured the imagination of millions of people who think that there must be something life-transforming and even miraculous about love.

It's important to understand that Richard Johnson is not a bad man. He's just a bad husband. He is not mean, he never hits his wife, and she never lacks food or shelter. However, he never sacrificially loves his wife *"as Christ loved the church and gave himself up for her"* (Ephesians 5:25). As a result, Richard does not consciously try to make Francesca's dreams come true. It's not that their relationship has always been devoid of affection, but that season of affection was over long ago. In this respect, a romantic relationship is like riding a bicycle: if it's not moving forward, it's foundering. The love of yesterday is never sufficient for today.

Near the end of his life, Richard apologizes to Francesca: "I know that you had your own dreams; I'm sorry I couldn't give them to you." The fact is that he never tries. Unfortunately, he doesn't understand his wife, even though they have lived together for eighteen years and have raised two children. Often it is difficult to discern the difference between mere inattention and selfishness, but the outcome is always the same. If Richard had been told he was leading a self-centered life that made real love for his wife impossible, he would never have believed it.

Many confuse love of self with love of another. The exact definition of selfishness is *always* doing whatever one wants to do whenever one wants to do it. The essence of every closed and unloving person is the relentless insistence, however subtle, on having one's own way. Such people do not have relationships; they only have strategies.

It is also important to understand that Francesca does not set out to have an affair. She has sacrificed everything for her husband, without his reciprocating, until she has almost no life left. When she meets Robert, she takes incremental steps toward him without initially entertaining the possibility of adultery. But it is no accident that she ends up committing it. If Richard and Francesca had loved each other by living for each other, they would gradually have become the very best of friends. And if this had happened, Francesca probably never would have given Robert a chance to win her interest and admiration. But outside of God, the human personality is the biggest thing in the universe. People are immensely complex, and one of the most important truths about people is not what they do, but what they would do if the circumstances were different. Like an iceberg, most of the human personality lies beneath the level of consciousness, and often what is beneath that level is only revealed by new circumstances. This is why one can be surprised by one's own actions. If Francesca had been told the week before that she would be unfaithful to her husband, she would never have believed it.

Does *The Bridges of Madison County* reveal an impasse between two equally disastrous alternatives? One common response is to stay together for the sake of the children. But is this really a solution? When grown, Richard and Francesca's children have serious marital problems: the son neglects his wife's needs, and the daughter's marriage is at its end. Each alternative—just staying or just leaving—is inadequate, because neither confronts the underlying issues.

What is often overlooked is that Francesca's husband had been committing adultery long before her affair with Robert. Admittedly, Richard had not had sex with someone else, so how could he have committed adultery? There are many ways to destroy a marriage. In the Sermon on the Mount, Jesus presented an ethic that is more profound than one that merely prohibits certain acts. Jesus challenges what he called the righteousness of the scribes and Pharisees (Matthew 5:20). Simply refraining from doing certain actions never captures what makes an action good, so it never gets to the heart of what goodness is. Just because one avoids bad actions, it does not follow that one is moral. The scribes and Pharisees mistakenly thought that as long as they did not kill anyone or did not have sexual intercourse with a woman married to another they were virtuous. One can follow all the rules and laws and yet be immoral. Bill Clinton maintained that since sex means only sexual intercourse, one can engage in any other sexual activity without committing adultery. Clearly, this self-deceiving sophistry is not what makes a person good.

The word *adultery* has the same root as the word *adulterate*, which means to poison or spoil the purity or strength of a substance. If one adulterates a pond, that pond is being poisoned, and if it is adulterated enough, it will be unable to sustain life. Jesus said that "everyone who looks at a woman with lustful intent has already committed adultery with her in his heart" (Matthew 5:28). To treat another person merely as an object for sexual gratification is already to be involved in the psychological process of poisoning one's own soul (cf. Jeremiah 3). Richard was adulterating his marriage for years by not loving his wife, by not laying down his life for her. Whether they could sustain their marriage as more than cordial roommates is unclear. Richard's poisoning does not justify Francesca's unfaithfulness, but it does explain her feelings of loneliness and hopelessness. Francesca's affair does not arise from nothing; people are not that uncomplicated. Immoral acts are pure poison to the human soul, and as one persists in such acts, one becomes increasingly incapable of seeing the difference between what is authentically good and what is actually evil. To be sure, the Johnsons have a deeply hollow marriage, but Francesca's affair makes a bad situation infinitely worse and makes the possibility of reconciliation and healing far more difficult.[5]

The Bridges of Madison County depicts the heart-rending consequences of not living for another in marriage, and it reveals that withholding sacrificial love permanently affects everyone involved. The presence or absence of love, both received and given, is as powerful a force in any person's life as anything else in this world. Given the quality of their marriage, there are not just two options open to Richard and Francesca. They could fight to save their relationship by facing the inadequacies of their marriage. Only they can determine whether it is too late to save it. Never underestimate the power of personal repentance to contribute to reconciliation and redemption, but also never underestimate the intractable mystery of selfish freedom to harden the heart by making one incapable of seeing and hearing reality. Marriages are gradually poisoned by those oblivious to the needs and hopes of their spouses. Here is a perfect formula for a disastrous marriage and a lonely and miserable life: live only unto thyself. Every married person should, from time to time, introspect and ponder, what is it like to be married to *me?*

Conclusion

Real love is the most radical and the most beautiful thing in the whole world. It is also surprisingly rare. It doesn't require much to begin the process of learning to love by seeing the emptiness of selfishness, but sadly the little that is required is often more than many are willing to give. The cost of Christian discipleship and of learning how to love is not nearly as high as the cost of self-centeredness and of not learning how to love.

Authentic love, unlike all its hollow substitutes, is always a transforming reality in the lives of both lover and beloved. Such love always perceives a glimmer of sadness and vulnerability veiled in the other's eyes. It grasps that each person has a history, strengths, weaknesses, hopes, fears, needs, wants, dreams, potentialities and vulnerabilities. It understands that an authentically loving relationship is of incalculable worth, a refuge from so much of the insanity and loneliness of life. Martin Buber explains that "every person longs to be confirmed in their deepest being by others, and wishes to have a presence in the being of the other. . . . Secretly and bashfully he waits and watches for a Yes which allows them to flourish, and which can come to them only from one person to another."[6] And, as Matthew Arnold writes in his poem "Dover Beach,"

> Ah, love, let us be true
> To one another! for the world, which seems
> To lie before us like a land of dreams,
> So various, so beautiful, so new,
> Hath really neither joy, nor love, nor light,
> Nor certitude, nor peace, nor help for pain;
> And we are here as on a darkling plain
> Swept with confused alarms of struggle and flight,
> Where ignorant armies clash by night.

Such a love would not only revolutionize the lives of both lovers; it would also be a blazing beacon of hope to all who come to know them.

The central characters in each of these films are profoundly lonely and yearning to have a life encompassed by heartfelt love. For that reason they are open to startling possibilities: asking a prostitute to be one's wife, taking the fiancée of one's younger brother in one's arms and contemplating leaving one's husband to run off with a photographer from *National Geographic*. This loneliness and yearning for love reveal a pivotal fact of human existence: *genuine love always uncovers a spiritual dimension to reality.* Attempting to honestly live for another will disclose truths about oneself that are not particularly attractive. Every individual must choose whether or not to live humbly, by facing his or her selfishness. "The question, How is love to God or to [others] possible if as a fact I do not have it?" writes William Ernest Hocking, "would be answered if there were, as the moving spirit of the world, an aggressive lover able and disposed to break in upon my temper of critical egoism and win my response."[7]

One's pride and selfishness, if honestly faced, reveal the need for a fixed fulcrum of transforming power outside oneself, since the self is the source of the problem. Thus our need for grace.

PART TWO

MIND AND KNOWLEDGE

Escaping into Reality

What We Can Learn from *The Truman Show* About the Knowledge Enterprise

R. DOUGLAS GEIVETT

●　●

MERYL. Truman, I took the "hypocrite" oath.

TRUMAN. I bet you did.

The film *The Truman Show* is named after a fictitious television program featuring Truman Burbank, a man whose name oozes with oxymoronic significance. The show's creator, Christof (Ed Harris), thinks of the protagonist as the "true man," a rare exemplar of human authenticity. Truman's surname, Burbank, alludes to that city of celluloid, Burbank, California. The television show is broadcast live and via satellite from a studio there. Truman is the unsuspecting star of the show, and the film depicts the final days of the broadcast.[1]

Truman himself is for real. Though he's an orphan adopted by the multimedia giant, Omnicam, he's not an actor. As far as he's concerned, he lives a comfortable, though increasingly banal, existence in the town of his birth, an island village called Seahaven Island Township. Even at age twenty-nine, he radiates childlike innocence. He's sincere to a fault. His wife, mother and best friend are actually actors paid to play these roles. Others play bit parts: neighbors, coworkers, a newspaper vendor, shoppers, telephone operators, radio disc jockeys. A cohort of technicians manipulates Truman's physical environment from an unseen location, training cameras on Truman 24-7. Millions of viewers around the world are complicit in this charade. Their indefatigable voyeurism keeps the program on the air, making millions of dollars for the show's greedy sponsors.

We're introduced to Truman in a scene with him standing before a bathroom mirror in his pajamas. With cheerful self-confidence, he performs a ritual. He impersonates an adventurer, talking of his latest exploits, as if before a television audience. His revelry is interrupted by a shout from his wife, Meryl, telling him he's going to be late for work. Subsequent scenes reveal Truman's larger surroundings. We see his neighborhood, meet his neighbors, follow his trek to the office. Everything is quaint and pleasant but somehow surreal. His life is superficially enviable but hauntingly trite, repetitious, commonplace. Truman, born for adventure, is an insurance salesman.

Truman is good-natured and resigned. But we sense that his powerful impulse to embark on risky adventures in exotic places has been abandoned with melancholy reluctance. He seems fated for an inauthentic form of life. All efforts to pursue his dreams have been thwarted. A flashback shows Truman scampering to a hilltop with boyish curiosity, and being scolded by his father for taking such chances. Another portrays a budding romance with a young woman, Lauren Garland, abruptly ending in mystery and confusion. On the rebound, Truman has married an attractive and gentle woman—with whom he has little in common. His one and only friend, Marlon, is intensely loyal but obtuse and indifferent about life. Truman's acts of genuine self-determination are limited to the mundane: what he reads, what he listens to on the radio, where he goes about town, the chores he does around the house. He orders the same meatball sandwich at the local Italian deli every day.[2] He's become a painfully predictable creature of habit. Wherever he goes, Truman is greeted by name and treated with utmost courtesy; but all of his relationships (with the possible exception of his friendship with Marlon) are shallow.

How can such a humdrum life be the backdrop of a film that is at once comedic, heart-rending and, yes, philosophically stimulating? Screenwriter Andrew Niccol and director Peter Weir make this happen with an ingenious narrative trick. Truman's mundane existence is punctuated with odd events. Anomalies accumulate to a point that attracts Truman's attention and galvanizes his curiosity. Finally, he's faced with the most critical choice of his lifetime—a choice entirely within his power. This film, *The Truman Show,* traces one ordinary man's opportunity to discover the truth and embrace reality. If we're attentive, we may discern vital lessons for our own lives.

Truman's Plight

Truman is a tragic figure. He's deceived with systematic precision. His movements and opportunities are controlled with preternatural consistency. His plans are frustrated at every turn. His privacy is a figment of his imagination. His passions are deflated by feelings of inferiority. The embers of dejection are stoked by the cynicism of friends and family. Truman's closest relationships are fraudulent. His long-term ambitions are subdued with artificial dangers calculated to instill fear, dread and even guilt. Paranoia threatens. He hankers for things beyond his reach. He pines for the only woman ever to kindle his love and self-confidence, and he languishes in a marriage void of affection. He grieves the loss of his father and blames himself for the sailing accident that took his life. The behavior of the townspeople is an elaborate ruse. His physical surroundings are artificial. The very buildings he passes every day are mere façades. And every puzzling feature of Truman's life is trivialized or explained away by those he consults.

The irony is that Truman could leave Seahaven, at will, anytime. But Truman is imprisoned within a thick shell of conviction, beliefs that seem perfectly justified but happen to be utterly false. He believes that his life is normal and that he should be satisfied with his personal relationships, even if they're not very fulfilling.

We could easily miss the most important aspect of Truman's predicament and overlook the significance of the most promising avenue of escape. After all, *The Truman Show* is for us a form of entertainment. Jim Carrey's portrayal of Truman is endearing. The drama of Truman's estrangement from Lauren—Truman's creative efforts to keep her memory alive and disappointed strategies for going off to find her—infuse the plot with a romantic twist. Meryl's panic grows as Truman's behavior becomes more and more unpredictable, fueling our curiosity about how this will threaten the show's continuity. Marlon's submission to Christof's directions during his most emotionally taut encounter with Truman is heart wrenching. We're lured into an emotional connection with Truman.

Our hearts go out to Truman. We're saddened at the exploitation of his innocence. We feel contempt for Christof, who dictates everything that happens in Truman's life. We resent Meryl and Marlon, and all the others, for their lifelong role-playing, with feigned intimacy and friendship. Viewers worldwide who tune in to be entertained by Truman's life are repugnant to us. We lament the isolation and artificiality of Truman's existence. We are *for* Truman. We want him to wake up to reality; we want him to escape. The odds are against it. But we're prepared for him to emerge, by the end of the film, a kind of hero—someone who has prevailed against the odds. But everything depends on this: Truman must come to a *knowledge of the truth.*

Our emotional engagement may divert our attention from the cognitive aspect of Truman's plight. We realize that Truman must discover the truth if he's to escape his bonds. But do we understand the real nature of his bonds? They're not purely social and psychological. They're also *epistemological.* In fact, they're most fundamentally epistemological.

What Is Epistemology?

Epistemology is a branch of philosophy. The word *epistemology* comes from the Greek word *episteme,* meaning "knowledge." Epistemology is the study of knowledge. In epistemology, we seek knowledge about knowledge.

Clearly, we prize knowledge; knowledge matters to us. But why?

For starters, we care because knowledge has *instrumental* value for us. We use knowledge to navigate our way in the world. Knowledge keeps us alive when we think of crossing a busy street. It's what keeps us from becoming a bumper sticker on the front of a Mack truck. We count on knowledge to keep ourselves fit and healthy—and for innumerable other purposes.

We rely heavily on the knowledge of others. We can't know everything firsthand. Much of what we know is on the say-so of people around us. We trust people to know things that we don't know and can't know. For example, we depend on the expertise of dentists and surgeons, generals and elected officials, lawyers and judges, automobile manufacturers and airline pilots. For most of us, these are people whose knowledge serves and supports us in important ways. And we may have specialized knowledge that contributes to the well-being of others. Even if most of what we know is common knowledge, it's important to others that we have such knowledge. When I'm driving my car, it's not enough that I know the traffic laws, the meaning of the signage and the rules of etiquette. The other drivers I encounter had better know these things, too.

This suggests that *part of being responsible is having knowledge and acting on the basis of the knowledge we have.* It also suggests that our acquisition of knowledge should not be haphazard. There are certain things we feel we must know. There may also be things we would very much like to know, even if such knowledge is beyond our reach. But in many areas of life we're pretty good at getting knowledge when we need or want it.

We also prize knowledge for its *intrinsic* value; that is, we value knowledge for its own sake. This makes more sense when we unpack the concept of knowledge.

It isn't very controversial that knowledge includes *true belief.* And truth is intrinsically valuable. Truth is intrinsically valuable to someone who cares to know the truth even if the truth is inconvenient. It is valued intrinsically when it is desired, however unpleasant it may be and regardless of the burdens it places on the one who has the truth.

We prefer people who are truthful over people who are not, even if their character and their behavior have no direct bearing on our lives. Our disapproval is roused when we become aware of dishonest dealings between people, even when they remain perfect strangers to us—even, I should say, when the characters are fictional (or not "true to life"). This is further evidence of the intrinsic value truth has for us.

We also want our own existence to be "true." Nearly all of us so crave authenticity that we would not be willing to trade an authentic existence, even suffused with anguish and disappointment, for a contrived existence that is thoroughly artificial but relentlessly pleasurable. Our instincts are to favor reality over virtual reality as the fundamental framework of our lives. (Yes, we love fiction. But really great fiction illuminates the human condition and mirrors our experience in ways that enable us to see who we are and what we might become.)

True belief is not all there is to knowledge. To believe is to hold that some proposition or statement is true. The believer naturally thinks he has the truth, or he wouldn't believe. So if he believes when he might not, why does he? He may simply be caused to believe. But causes of belief don't generally give the believer anything to go on. A belief may be caused any number of ways and not be true or even most likely true. What the believer needs, if he would believe responsibly, is some indicator that what he believes is true.

Believing responsibly has double significance. First, it means to believe because there is some reason to think that what is believed is true. That is, the belief is *reasonable.* Second, it means to believe in ways that can be the basis for responsible action in the world. In other words, the belief is *actionable.* In both cases, the believer must possess the truth a certain way. He must have some means of getting in touch with the truth. This is the role of *evidence.*[3]

Knowledge, then, is true belief that is both reasonable and actionable because it is grounded in adequate evidence. Epistemology is about the nature of knowledge, the conditions under which we have knowledge and the scope of knowledge.

So knowledge is both instrumentally and intrinsically valuable. But having knowledge is also a fundamental condition of human flourishing. This is a huge topic, reaching into areas beyond the limited scope of this chapter. But we can relate this concept of flourishing to the significance we attach to knowledge. Some rivals to happiness are rooted in the scarcity of knowledge and in false ideas about knowledge. It may be fruitless to mount an *argument* that knowledge is essential to human flourishing. The cogency of this claim may be more aptly reinforced by concrete representations of its truth. One virtue of art is that it captures inarticulable features of the human condition and shows us how these features crop up in our own lives. Dance, sculpture, music, painting, poetry, fiction and film are all effective ways of showcasing aspects of the human situation. They teach by illumination—by throwing light on those contours of human existence that lurk within the shadows. Some reflect light on the human *cognitive* condition in instructive ways.

Truman's Deliverance

The connection between flourishing and knowledge is ingeniously illuminated in *The Truman Show*. Truman's life is relatively comfortable and free of pain. His physical needs are amply met. He lives in society with pleasant individuals. His surroundings are maximally picturesque. Despite all this, something is missing. Superficially, the problem is disappointment in vocation and romance. Truman is stuck selling insurance when he would prefer gallivanting around the globe. He would rather be luxuriating in the presence of Lauren (AKA Sylvia) than be tied down in a zestless marriage.[4]

Truman senses that his life is artificial. But his perception of this is partial. Initially, it's just a matter of boredom and unrequited love. In fits and starts he plans his escape. He calls information services seeking a phone number for Sylvia in Fiji. There is none. He looks into flights, tries for a bus and sets off in his car. None of it works. The only escape route he does not pursue is by sea. He's simply too terrified of the water that has taken his father.

As we'll see, Truman's determination eventually pays off. But before this can happen, he must grasp more fully the extent of his predicament. He must discover that his life is false at the very core. When he does, his obsession with leaving Seahaven acquires a new urgency. He's no longer preoccupied with a sense of adventure. Though he doesn't realize it for some time, Truman's ultimate ambition is to *escape into reality*.

· · · · ·

I've suggested that Truman's plight is most fundamentally epistemological. Social and psychological factors contribute to Truman's condition as well. He values fulfillment in his vocation, something sadly missing from his life. This hole, he thinks, can be plugged only by the infusion of greater adventure. He also values connection with Sylvia, but she's inaccessible. Since Sylvia is, as far as Truman knows, living in Fiji, these two values come together for him. His willingness and determination to act for the realization of these goals is an indication of the degree to which he values them. We find that he values them greatly. This is reflected in the action he's prepared to take.

Truman is stymied by two kinds of obstacles. Invariably, an event or a person interferes with his plans. He visits a travel agent about passage to Fiji and he's told that everything is booked solid. He boards a bus, determined to leave Seahaven, and the bus breaks down. In countless situations, people deliberately distract his attention from important realities. All of these are circumstances beyond his control. These obstacles to Truman's ambitions are *external*.

Other obstacles are *internal* and more subtle. Truman oscillates between fatalism and renewed enthusiasm for a more fulfilling life. His double-mindedness is artfully induced by his guardians and his peer group. With cultivated indifference, his social circle challenges his belief in possibilities for self-development. He's surrounded by polite but shallow individuals. Friendly conversation with his neighbors is reduced to exchanges of inane pleasantries. Truman's bosom buddy, Marlon, isn't any help either. His entrepreneurial aspirations top out with his own job—stocking vending machines. He thinks Truman has it made because he at least has a desk job.

Meryl's conjugal attentions are exaggerated and phony. Her behavior is eccentric, even bordering on the bizarre. We know that she's playing to the camera and advertising commercial products, but Truman is oblivious to this. At times, she seems downright kooky. There's a scene where Truman is gardening and Meryl rides up on her bicycle. "Hi, honey," she says. "Look what I got for you at the checkout. It's a 'Chef's Pal.'" Quoting the packaging, she adds, "It's a dicer, grater, peeler. All in one! Never needs sharpening . . . dishwasher safe!"

She says this with inordinate intensity accompanied by a broad smile and a contrived look of amazement. Truman replies with simulated gusto, "Wow! That's amazing."

As Truman matures, the instruments of deceit become more sophisticated. Eventually, extravagant attempts to keep Truman in the dark begin to unravel. This, actually, is where the movie begins. In an early scene, Truman is in his driveway, about to get into his car, when a large object crashes from the sky. The scene is important to the whole development of the story. There's a pattern here that will be repeated: (1) something unusual, attention getting and initially inexplicable happens; (2) Truman notices the event or circumstances; (3) Truman is surprised and confounded by what has happened; (4) Truman looks for an explanation, sometimes checking with others who are present; (5) Truman concludes that none of his hypotheses is satisfactory.

In this early scene, a light fixture has fallen from the sky, some apparatus used to create the special effects of Truman's environment. Truman hears the crash, is startled and sees the object lying in the street. It doesn't look like something that would naturally fall from the sky. Truman's instinctual response is to study the nearby streetlights in search of an explanation. Everything is intact.[5] Meanwhile, his neighbors have vanished into their homes. At a loss for other ideas, Truman shrugs and loads the thing into the trunk of his car.

Several scenes later, Truman is discussing the incident with Marlon. Truman asks, "You really think it could have dropped off an airliner?" Marlon's reply would be comical if he didn't sound so sincere: "Sure. It's halogen. Shame it didn't hit you—you could've sued." Marlon then changes the subject.[6]

In another scene, Truman is caught in a rainstorm. There's a technical malfunction and the "storm" becomes extremely localized, with the rain falling only on Truman as he walks along. When Truman notices, he playfully experiments with dancing in and out of the shaft of falling water. Truman is amused, but he doesn't make much of it.

A sequence of lesser oddities come his way—events that have little significance until something else happens. For example, while alone in the park, eating his lunch, Truman is approached by a transient in a wheelchair. Truman hands over his sandwich. He vaguely notices that the man's shoes are embossed with the letters T.S. (as in "Truman Show").

In a hilarious scene, Truman is driving his car, listening to the radio. It goes berserk. First, the DJ's voice, during an announcement, slips into a mode that sounds more like a worn-out cassette tape than a live broadcast. Then, when Truman, somewhat puzzled, punches to another station, he hears a detailed report of someone's driving itinerary. Before long he realizes that it's an exact match of his own route across town. After a loud and obnoxious screech that has all in the vicinity covering their ears, the broadcaster makes one more weird remark, and the radio goes dead.

Immediately following this freakish incident, Truman begins to act erratically. It's part of a strategy. He's testing a hypothesis, seeking to confirm his suspicions. He won't figure things out right away, but he'll make it harder for conspirators—whoever they are—to anticipate his moves and respond accordingly. Truman attends more carefully to his surroundings. Perched on a park bench, he studies the details of his environment. Things appear normal. Then he notices a jogger. He's wearing the same shoes with the initials *T.S.* It's the transient Truman had seen before in a wheelchair!

Truman leaves and rushes unpredictably into an office building. None of the actors are prepared for his arrival. He presses the button for the elevator, the door opens, and there's no back wall. He sees through the "elevator" into a gallery where people are milling about, having refreshments. (Meryl has a doozy of an explanation for this later the next morning.)

For a time, Truman is suspicious about everything. He has paranoid moments. He has misgivings about the world around him and then misgivings about his misgivings. But he gathers his composure and concludes that there are too many things that "don't fit." He resolves to leave Seahaven, no matter what. His attempts will compound the problems for the Omnicam Corporation as their frantic efforts to keep one step ahead of Truman grow more and more clumsy. Each instance reinforces Truman's suspicions.

Matters climax when Truman exposes Meryl's cover as a "nurse" who has taken "the hypocrite oath." He takes Meryl hostage in a zany attempt to escape the city in their car. Truman demonstrates that the traffic is "beautifully synchronized" to block their exit. He resorts to more dangerous tactics to flee Seahaven; Meryl fears for her life and becomes hysterical. Once again, Truman's plan for escape is foiled. But he will not give up.

Finally, sailing out of the harbor is the only option that remains. In the end, Truman must conquer his fear of the sea. He still doesn't know the full extent of his situation, but he knows enough to want out and to do whatever it takes. He goes for it and nearly loses his life. But he will not turn back. Lightning strikes the mast. It seems all hope is lost. On the verge of capsizing, the vessel suddenly collides into . . . a wall, a painted backdrop made to look like the sky.

This is the crowning moment, the culmination of Truman's quest. He reaches out and touches the "sky." Moments later he spies a staircase against the wall. It leads to a door. As he reaches for the handle, Christof speaks, out of view and with a booming voice:

CHRISTOF. Truman. You can speak. I can hear you.

TRUMAN. Who are you?

CHRISTOF. I'm the creator, of a television show that gives hope and joy and inspiration to millions.

TRUMAN. Then who am I?

CHRISTOF (with passion). You're the star.

TRUMAN. Was nothing real?

CHRISTOF. *You* were real. That's what made you so good to watch.

Truman is confused but not amused. In a last-ditch effort to talk Truman out of leaving, Christof says, "Listen to me Truman! There's no more truth out there than there is in the world I created for you. Same lies. The same deceit. But in *my* world, *you* have nothing to fear. I know you better than you know yourself."[7] Truman screams back, "You never had a camera in my head!" "You're afraid. That's why you can't leave," says Christof.

What We Can Learn from Truman

Christof urges Truman to remain inside the bubble that's been created for him. The master manipulator betrays his own cynicism about reality and truth. Christof's desperate appeal is rebuffed. As Truman walks through the door into the real world, viewers worldwide clap their approval. (Their hypocrisy is palpable.)

This film illustrates key features of the human cognitive condition. The challenge to believe responsibly on matters of great significance is one part of the human predicament. Truman's predicament matches our own. His capacity for authenticity depends on his fundamental beliefs. For nearly thirty years he has been oblivious to the source of his frustration with life. His treadmill existence is linked to a sophisticated deception that has him trapped in a world of make-believe. His freedom depends on the apprehension of truth.

Let's explore several aspects of the human cognitive condition as illustrated in the film and relate them to dimensions of religious belief. For at the heart of religious belief are questions of ultimate concern and the project to know the truth about ultimate reality.

The quest for knowledge is stimulated by curiosity. We're naturally intellectually curious. This doesn't mean that we all want to be intellectuals. But we're all interested in having knowledge. There are many forms of intellectual curiosity. Literature and film play on our natural curiosity. Once our attention is hooked by the plot of a story, we want to know how things will turn out. (In the film, Sylvia's sweater, kept by Truman, has a button that reads, "How's it going to end?")

We're curious when we encounter puzzling phenomena, things that don't fit our ordinary experience. If I return to the parking lot at the end of the work day and my car isn't where I left it, I'm going to want an explanation. And I'm going to have some ideas about what might explain this unexpected circumstance. We also seek explanations for things that don't comply with our understanding of the laws of nature. This is how science progresses.

Cognitive dissonance is a natural spur to intellectual inquiry. This dissonance may come from your awareness of some inconsistency or incoherence in your belief system. It may arise out of a clash between what you believe and what you prefer to believe. It may emerge in behavior when you're uncomfortable acting in accordance with what you believe. And dissonance may turn up as you begin to wonder whether your beliefs are adequately grounded.

This phenomenon of cognitive dissonance figures prominently in Truman's experience. The total sequence of events and what they reveal rocks his world. Near the end, he realizes that his life may be more fiction than fact. This is for him the height of existential angst. Often, when fundamental beliefs are shaken, a religious or spiritual element is involved. But Truman never seems to contemplate the divine. He appears to be thoroughly secular in his outlook. Christof has no doubt planned it that way.

The moment precipitating Truman's escape coincides with a quick cut to Sylvia. She's poised in front of her TV, watching Truman's antics as he stands on the threshold of reality. She looks skyward and prayerfully whispers, "Please, God," then back to the screen at Truman. "You can do it," she says, earnestly. It's natural to think of this as a petition for Truman's salvation. Certainly, Truman must be maximally curious about what lies beyond the threshold. Is he eager enough to take that important step? In that moment the stakes have an almost spiritual significance. We expect a reunion with Sylvia, who has now done two things for Truman: she has tried to tell him the truth about the world, Truman's world, and she has prayed for his escape. What will happen if they meet again?

Questions about ultimate reality are inherently most absorbing. Answers to these questions have weighty implications for human nature and human significance. We should like to know the truth about the things that matter most. Unfortunately, various obstacles discourage people today from investigating the possibilities and exploring relevant evidence. First, many people are so absorbed with responsibilities and commitments that they have little time or energy for labor-intensive inquiries about ultimate reality. Lamentably, the responsibilities and commitments that steal their attention are routine and unremarkable. By force of habit, people drift into a pattern of trodding through life that suffocates their natural desire to know the most fundamental truths. Consequently, they have little experience with the *pursuit* of truth. Second, people carry on within an atmosphere toxic with cynicism about knowing truth. There are obvious parallels between these obstacles and the ones obstructing Truman's path to truth.

We don't always understand what we know. Recall the incident with Truman driving his car, radio on. The announcer says, "Don't forget to buckle up out there in radioland." Suddenly, the rest of the report becomes garbled. Truman reacts to this aberration by punching the button for a different station. He hears a conversation and soon realizes they're talking about him, apparently aware of his every move. A male voice says, "He's heading west on Stewart. Stand by all extras . . . OK, he's making his turn onto Lancaster Square." Truman glances up and sees the street sign for Lancaster as he rounds the corner. Distracted, he almost strikes a pedestrian. The male voice exclaims, "Oh, my God! He nearly hit Marylyn!" Then, "Change frequencies!"

Truman *knows* he's being watched. He doesn't know *why*. What he knows is unnerving. What he doesn't know makes matters worse. This circumstance is galvanizing. Truman rightly senses the urgency of his need for knowledge. This is the tipping point. Shaken by this development, Truman becomes especially proactive in his quest to understand.[8]

This is the sensible response. Truman should begin to wonder who in his community can be trusted. He should embark on a more careful investigation of his circumstances. He should develop a strategy to turn up evidence that will either confirm or falsify what he's used to believing.

This is appropriate in religious contexts, as well. It comes naturally to many people of faith, during a certain period in their intellectual and spiritual development, to wonder about the sources of their fundamental beliefs. At this stage they're more reflective than before and they know more about the world. What they know does not always harmonize easily with what they understand of their faith.

What is the appropriate response when this happens? Many believers at this junction in their personal development consult leading figures in their believing community. They ask the questions that confound them. Countless people have been told at this point that they should simply believe on the basis of faith. Some have even been counseled against the sin of doubt. And recently there has been a movement to understate the importance of belief and to stress the greater significance of communal life.[9] The value of evidence is derided and people are left to flounder in a sea of confusion about what to believe or whether belief even matters.

But if what we believe matters—and we will believe something, one way or the other—then we must take the most responsible path in our belief-forming practices. This is the path that improves our chances of believing what is true. And for that we need evidence. We also must have suitable ways to collect and assess evidence that is relevant to our fundamental questions. Then the knowledge that led to greater confusion may lead us on to the doorstep of greater knowledge—and confidence in the things we believe.

Cognitive success depends on the intellectual virtues. What accounts for Truman's cognitive success, given the conspiracy of deception he must overcome? How is he finally able to discover the truth about his situation and escape into reality? Truman's *character* is pivotal. He's modest, good-natured, innocent and full of goodwill. These are endearing qualities. But he has *intellectual* virtues as well. These are virtues that improve a person's belief-forming practices. They're signs of intellectual responsibility and they make conditions for the acquisition of knowledge more favorable.

What are Truman's intellectual virtues? He's interested in truth. He also desires to be reasonable. He trusts those around him to be reliable in their testimony, unless there is some special reason why he should not. He tests his own ideas against the ideas of others. He appears to be open-minded but not gullible. He's a careful observer and pays attention to detail when this will improve his chances of acquiring true belief. His curiosity is itself a virtue. He doesn't allow the apathy of others to infect him with indifference. He is not only proactive but also persistent in his quest for truth. And he's intentional about developing strategies for acquiring truth. He's thoughtful in his collection and assessment of evidence and also in his formulation and testing of possible explanations when he's puzzled.

Above all, Truman is intellectually courageous. He's able to resist the blandishments of his community when it seems that they're mistaken, and he's willing to take personal risks to discover the truth. He's remarkably alert to social anomalies given his upbringing. He recognizes when members of his intellectual community lack important intellectual virtues.

Truman is not the perfect embodiment of intellectual virtue. He suffers misgivings when we feel he should be resolute. He may not be as persistent in solving problems as we think he should be at times. He is perhaps a little slow in connecting the dots, if we count all the clues from his childhood, his dramatic encounter with Sylvia in college and the barrage of offbeat circumstances that he encounters. He becomes morose and self-indulgent when the chips are down, though he never quite gives up. Some of his strategies for determining the truth are zany and ineffectual—like clapping his hands loudly in the supermarket and drawing rash conclusions based on the reaction of shoppers. For much of the time, Truman is propelled by fear. At one point, his actions endanger Meryl's life. For all of these imperfections, Truman is, on balance, an admirable figure. And he's admirable for his intellectual character.

We might even say that Truman is heroic. But we might attribute this impression to his praiseworthy endurance of physical challenges and his final decision to cross the threshold into the real world. Let's remember, however, that Truman is propelled by a craving for authenticity and a desire for truth. His heroism is rooted in these internal states.

For a while, we pity Truman. This strong feeling of pity recedes, though, as we watch Truman take responsibility for his cognitive condition. Our pity shades into admiration as we see him taking steps that improve his chances of finding out the truth. Our admiration increases with every show of determination.

While Truman may not be a paragon of intellectual virtue, his character and the conduct that stems from his character are exemplary and laudatory. The pursuit of religious truth also calls for practices that accord with intellectual virtue. Open-mindedness, persistence and invulnerability to the subtle pressures of society are critical to religious knowledge. There may come a time when religious inquiry yields strong support for religious truths. But the investigator may not come to believe these truths unless he is prepared to act in accordance with the truths indicated by the evidence. In other words, he may need to perform a kind of devotional experiment, where he makes an existential commitment before making a belief commitment. But he may do so for the sake of coming eventually to believe what is indicated by the evidence, as far as he's able to discern. And whether he's willing to do so is a question of character. This is reflected in the next point.

Sometimes the truth hurts. Truman's quest for authenticity drives his quest for truth. But the more he finds out, the more painful the quest becomes. He learns that he's somehow in the center of mysterious circumstances. He grows anxious and mistrustful. He senses that he's being watched by everyone. He suspects that Meryl doesn't love him, that she's part of a conspiracy. He feels that circumstances have been deliberately orchestrated to stifle his ambitions. He's misunderstood by his best friend. He feels imprisoned and fears that there is no way out.

These are painful truths. Truman's quest has made them evident. However unwelcome these truths may be, Truman—the "true man"—believes them, and he acts in accordance with what he believes. His commitment culminates when he shouts defiantly into the storm, "You're gonna have to kill me!" He's prepared to die in pursuit of reality. Ultimately, this leads him to knowledge of a solution to his predicament. And his practice of acting boldly in accordance with the painful truths he discovers is a necessary precondition of his knowledge of what is most important and liberating.

There is a false impression that Christian belief is a crutch, that it's too easy, that it's for weak-willed and soft-headed people. But in a very real sense, Christian belief has been the source of much personal heartache among believers. Innumerable believers have been ridiculed, physically abused and even martyred because of their convictions. Christian truth claims offend many nonbelievers. Some would not believe no matter how strong the evidence. It would simply be too costly. (Jesus said that those who look for a sign of his authority would not believe even if they witnessed his resurrection from the dead; see Matthew 12:38-40 and Luke 16:30-31.)

Our determination to believe what's true, however unpleasant or unwelcome it may be, is a reflection of our character. Christian belief should be consistent with intellectual virtue. And we should explore more fully ways that Christianity may inform our conception of the intellectual virtues.

We rely on each other for much of our knowledge. Truman spends the first twenty-nine years of his life believing that his environment and the people around him are genuine. If asked, he would have said that he knows many of the things he believes. He knows that Seahaven is a town in its own right. He knows that Marlon stocks vending machines for a living. He knows that the woman he calls "mother" is his mother. He knows that the salt water that laps the shoreline in Seahaven is part of a massive ocean. He knows when the sun sets and when the sun rises. He knows that his father died in a sailing accident. The thing is, he doesn't know any of these things. He *can't* know them because *they aren't true.*

Even though Truman does not know many of the things he thinks he knows—because they aren't even true—he is justified in believing them. He has evidence that supports his beliefs, good evidence. It's the sort of evidence we all depend on for much of the knowledge that we have.[10]

As it is for us, testimony is a core component in the total evidence that Truman has for his beliefs. All of the beliefs listed above are either directly or indirectly grounded in *testimonial evidence.* They depend to varying degrees on the say-so and attitudes of other people. Some of the testimony grounding his beliefs we may call *explicit* testimony. This includes whatever Truman has actually been told, by parents, teachers, neighbors, coworkers and strangers. It includes much of what he has read or seen on TV or heard on the radio. But Truman also depends on what I call *complicit* testimony: the testimony of a community that reinforces what we believe by means of social expectations, assumptions and behavior. These things contribute to our belief-forming and belief-maintenance habits through our membership and participation in a community.

Some commentators linger on this point and fret about the problem of skepticism it raises.[11] But here I want to focus the issue differently. I want to emphasize the key role that community plays in our belief-forming habits. We must be thoughtful about the credibility of members of our community. We must also recognize the responsibility we have for each other, living in community and sharing in the quest for truth and authenticity. Truman's community actively misleads him into false beliefs. In this way, members of his community wield considerable control over his values, desires and actions. As we've already seen, the knowledge enterprise depends on growth in intellectual virtues. Now we see how important it is that those around us—those who influence our beliefs about the things that matter most—also have these virtues. And it explains why, for the sake of others, we should nurture these virtues in ourselves.

This has obvious significance for Christian belief. Christians constitute a believing community. Members of this community absorb ideas about what to believe and why. They imitate habits of mind modeled by those in leadership, often without knowing anything about their true character. Christian belief may be reinforced or undermined through participation in community. The proper nurture of Christian belief is part of what the Apostles' Creed means by "the fellowship of the saints."

Christian thinkers have a responsibility to serve the church with their expertise. They need to consider carefully what this means. They should exercise caution—and what I would call compassion—when displaying their wares before an unwary laity. Scholarship has an experimental aspect. This is risky business. Christian philosopher Alvin Plantinga writes that "the method of true philosophy, unlike that of liberal theology and contemporary French thought, aims less at novelty than at truth."[12] Intellectual representatives of the Christian knowledge tradition should resist the temptation to impress others with their erudition and the impulse to propose experimental theories for the sake of originality. The lure of prideful posturing is an occupational hazard for those of us who work in the academy. Christian intellectuals are not immune to the desire for celebrity status; intellectual hubris joined with spiritual elitism is an especially deadly concoction. And members of the believing community are vulnerable to its poison.

Evidence matters in the quest for truth. Truman's cognitive success depends crucially on his sensitivity to evidence. He acquires evidence that his environment is not normal. Studio lamps fall from the sky, radio announcers monitor his movements, the rain behaves unnaturally, the same people pass in front of his house on a continuous loop.

Initially, the only evidence Truman notices is that which is more or less thrust upon him. He then pays closer attention to his environment and is supplied with additional evidence that things aren't right. There's a scene where Truman is looking over his wedding photos. By chance he notices the odd

configuration of Meryl's fingers in a picture of them embracing. Using a mag-
nifying glass, he sees clearly that Meryl's fingers are crossed. He's startled, and
he infers from this that she may not actually love him. Later, as she leaves for
work to assist in an amputation at the hospital, she says, "Wish me luck." Truman says, "I'll cross my fingers for you." Here Truman is testing the quality of
his evidence. He's looking for a response from Meryl that will confirm what
he suspects.

As time goes on, Truman takes more and more elaborate steps to accumulate evidence. He discovers that he is somehow the center of attention in his
community. Eventually, he learns that he's been the unwitting star in a television show. He's no sucker. On the contrary, he proves that he's perfectly capable of determining when members of his community are no longer to be
trusted.

This emphasis on evidence is a unifying thread in all the lessons of this section.[13] We are exquisitely sensitive to evidence. We are evidence gatherers by
nature. This is because of our truth-interested aims. Curiosity stimulates a
quest for knowledge, but the immediate effect is to search out the evidence.
We may have evidence for beliefs when there are dimensions of the things believed that we do not fully understand. The knowledge we acquire through
stages advances in accordance with our collection and assessment of evidence.
The intellectual virtues include dispositions to handle evidence responsibly.
The evidence may indicate truths that are unpleasant and unwelcome. And
much of our evidence depends on the reliable testimony and the intellectual
virtues of others in our believing community.[14]

*　*　*　*　*

I've suggested that these lessons are effectively illustrated in the film *The Truman
Show*. Truman Burbank lived in the shadow of reality. His beliefs were the
source of his imprisonment. Knowledge was his only avenue of escape. Truman
Burbank is not the "true man" that Christof imagined. But Truman does discover the truth that turns his life around and paves the way for genuine authenticity. Jesus Christ, who called himself the Son of Man, offered the promise of
life everlasting—the best kind of life we could hope for. That kind of life, he
promised, is available to anyone who believes in him, for he is "the way, and the
truth, and the life" (John 14:6). In conclusion, it is fitting for us to recall his
words: "you will know the truth, and the truth will set you free" (John 8:32).[15]

The Sleeper Awakes

Gnosis and Authenticity in *The Matrix*

DAVID P. HUNT

* *

A young man, to all appearances typical of his species, is vaguely dissatisfied with life. He can't shake the nagging suspicion, embedded in his consciousness "like a splinter in the mind," that something is seriously wrong with the world. Left to his own devices, there is little hope that he can resolve his worries, if indeed they aren't entirely baseless.

Then one day, out of the blue, he gets a call from an underground group claiming to possess answers to the questions that have been plaguing him. As they gradually initiate him into the truth, he begins to understand why things didn't make sense. The familiar world of the young man's experience—its values as well as its sheer concrete reality—is a cosmic illusion, a "prison house for the mind." The essential purpose of this vast deception is to keep human beings ignorant of who they really are, thereby making it easier to enslave them. Knowledge of humans' true nature and situation is therefore the most important condition for liberation.

The road ahead is fraught with difficulty. Our young man, who used to think that he was in control of his own life, has reluctantly come to appreciate the power of fate. Moreover, the evil deity who created the cosmic prison is not alone: there are various superhuman agents who must be contended with, gatekeepers who must be defeated if one is to pass through to the other side. Nevertheless, ultimate success against these forces is assured, owing to the intervention of a more-than-human, messiahlike "anomaly" who is destined to break the power of the forces of darkness.

Most readers will recognize in the foregoing narrative the underlying premise for the blockbuster film *The Matrix,* together with its two sequels, *The Matrix Reloaded* and *Matrix Revolutions.* What fewer readers will recognize is that this narrative also constitutes, with equal accuracy, a thumbnail sketch of the leading ideas of Gnosticism, a religious movement active during the first few centuries of the Christian era, often as a parasitical growth on Christianity itself. I would like to begin by saying a bit more about the Gnosticism connection, before going on to look at some of the philosophical issues raised in the films.[1]

The Gnosticism Connection

The name Gnostic comes from *gnosis,* a Greek word for knowledge. It is an apt name for a religion that regarded *knowledge* as the key to salvation. What sort of knowledge? A formula originating with Valentinus, a second-century Gnostic leader, sums up the matter this way: "What liberates is the knowledge of who we were, what we became; where we were, whereinto we have been thrown; whereto we speed, wherefrom we are redeemed; what birth is, and what rebirth."[2] Of course Christians, too, have typically maintained—to one degree or another—that *holding the right beliefs* is of the utmost importance. But Gnostic belief differs considerably, in content and salvific role, from Christian belief.

What did Gnostics believe? Modifying Valentinus's series of questions, let us organize the answer under three subquestions: Where are we from? Where are we now? Where are we going (and how do we get there)?

Where are we from? The Gnostic system begins with a unique supreme reality, a Source that possesses many of the classical theistic attributes but that is exceedingly remote. This primal reality gives rise to a collection of spirit beings that together constitute the "Pleroma." The Pleroma is an unstable mix, not under the complete control of the Source, and it is their feckless attempt to produce, as they were produced, that leads ultimately to the material world. Wisdom (Sophia), a feminine principle in the Pleroma, turns away from the Source, reproducing on her own initiative. Her offspring, Ialdabaoth—ignorant of the true scheme of things and thinking himself the supreme being—undertakes to create a world over which to exercise dominion, but he can only fashion it out of matter, a metaphysically inferior principle opposed to the spirit. ("Christian" Gnostics identified this defective creator-deity with the Yahweh of the Old Testament.) Fragments of divine light are rounded up and compelled to animate the fleshly bodies that are part of this material cosmos. We are those sparks of divine light, whose true origin is in the Source.

Where are we now? We are "strangers in a strange land," our exile so profound that we have forgotten who we are. Ignorant of our origins, we lack the wherewithal to stand against the systems of control constituting *heimarmenē,* or universal fate. The world conspires to persuade us that material objects are the paradigms of reality and that our concerns should be all about them; thus materialism, in both the metaphysical and valuational senses, is part of the system that enslaves us. So is conventional morality, with its this-worldly, social orientation. (Gnostics rejected the Old Testament Law along with its creator.) Gnostic texts speak of the "noise of the world"[3] that drowns out any discordant messages coming from deep inside us; by accepting the dream-world around us, we live life as though asleep rather than fully awake. And should anyone come to doubt that things are as they seem and endeavor to discover the truth, escape would seem out of the question: the entire universe constitutes a maximum-security prison, guarded by Ialdabaoth's agents. Yet alongside the mass of unenlightened humanity are some who claim, against all odds, to have found a way out.

Where are we going (and how do we get there)? Human destiny is to free ourselves from our gross material surroundings and rejoin the spiritual world from whence we came. Fulfillment of this eschatological hope requires *knowledge*. Because the system is set up to reinforce itself and prevent awareness of radical alternatives, this saving knowledge can only come from outside the system. Here the Gnostics introduce a divine emissary, called the Alien Man, to correct the misinformation that is promulgated and reinforced by the world-system. (Christian Gnostics naturally identified this messianic figure with Jesus Christ.) This divine initiative is experienced as the Call: a general exhortation to wake up from the sleep of earthly existence and face the human condition head-on. If effective, the Call should lead to a renunciation of the worldly powers (Christian Gnostics generally approved St. Paul's warnings about "the world") and enlistment in the Gnostic movement. The latter provides access to further knowledge of a "technical" nature: for example, passwords or spells designed to secure passage through the cosmic exit gates. Eventually, all the sparks of divine light will be reunited in the Pleroma, and the world will come to an end.

One way to see the *Matrix* trilogy as a cyber version of the Gnostic epic is to consider how the same three questions would be answered if asked by a character in the films.

Where are we from? As the charismatic rebel leader Morpheus explains in the alternative history lesson he gives to the films' hero, Neo, "At some point in the early twenty-first century, all of mankind was united in celebration. We marveled at our own magnificence as we gave birth to A.I. [artificial intelligence] . . . a singular consciousness that spawned an entire race of machines." But our hubris is misplaced; realizing too late that our creation has a "mind" of its own, we try to pull the plug but fail, and the machines we thought we controlled end up controlling us. Like the Gnostic Pleroma, the machine world includes a diverse cast of characters, some of them exhibiting considerable independence from A.I.; but these are computer programs, not superhuman spirits. They include Seraph, Merovingian, Persephone, Trainman, the Keymaker, the Rama-Kandra family and the Agents (notably Agent Smith, Neo's nemesis). The most important, however, are the programs to which A.I. has entrusted the task of creating a suitable prison cell for the defeated human race: the Architect (a program enamored of mathematical perfection and personified as a white-bearded male) and the Oracle ("an intuitive program, initially created to investigate certain aspects of the human psyche. If I am the father of the Matrix," the Architect explains, "she would undoubtedly be its mother"). The solution arrived at by these programs is to impose on human consciousness a global illusion, called the Matrix, in which things seem very much as they did around the year 2000, before the machines took over. The solution is ingenious: ignorant of their true situation, humans have no basis for resisting.

Where are we now? In fact, it is hundreds of years after the year 2000. (Even Morpheus does not know the exact year or even century.) Far from leading the normal lives of their experience, human beings are actually confined to pods of goo, a coaxial cable attached to a plug in the back of their heads feeding them the dream world of the Matrix, while a tangle of tubes and wires keeps them alive and siphons off their body heat and electromagnetic energy, which are used by the machines as a power source. "The Matrix is everywhere," Morpheus explains to the incredulous Neo. "It is all around us. Even now, in this very room. You can see it when you look out your window, or when you turn on your television. You can feel it when you go to work, when you go to church, when you pay your taxes. It is the world that has been pulled over your eyes to blind you from the truth . . . that you are a slave, Neo. Like everyone else, you were born into bondage . . . a prison for your mind."

"Billions of people living out their lives, oblivious," Agent Smith exults. But not quite everyone is oblivious. Alongside the majority living in illusion, there is an alternative society living in the real world. At some indeterminate time in the past a human being arose who had the mysterious power to see through the Matrix and escape from it. This anomalous individual, known as "the One," succeeded in freeing a handful of others and establishing a city of refuge, Zion, deep underground, beyond the reach of the machines. From this base of operations teams in hovercrafts, like Morpheus's ship *Nebuchadnezzar,* ascend through tunnels to "broadcast level" where they hack into the Matrix and seek further recruits. Protecting the system are Agents, programs designed to enter the Matrix and actively thwart the rebels' efforts. "They are the gatekeepers," Morpheus explains. "They are guarding all the doors. They are holding all the keys." Some, like Morpheus, believe that the only hope for humanity is the prophesied return of the One.

Where are we going (and how do we get there)? It's at this point that the action of *The Matrix* begins. We first meet Neo running a computer search. It is answered not by Google, but by a hacker from outside the system: "Wake up, Neo. The Matrix has you." This is the Gnostic Call in a nutshell. Indeed, in the first film, no other aspect of the Gnostic myth is better realized cinematically than the Call. It comes to Neo the first time over the phone lines connected to his modem; the second time it is via a cell phone delivered to him at work in a FedEx package, leading Neo to a test of faith on a window ledge. Throughout the films, telephone connections allow our heroes, with their saving knowledge, to travel in and out of the Matrix. And the first film ends with Neo in a phone booth announcing humanity's liberation from the machines. Enlightenment is, quite literally, a (phone) call away.

Neo is the Gnostic Everyman whose existential search leads him first to Trinity—the purveyor, like Eve, of forbidden knowledge (the Gnostics made the serpent the good guy in Genesis 3)—and then to Morpheus, who provides Neo with the red pill that enables him to cross over from the dream-world to the real world (Morpheus being the Greek god of dreams). But Neo is also the Alien Man or Gnostic messiah, the One (an anagram of "Neo") whose advent is announced by Morpheus in his role as John the Baptist, the forerunner. Both identities are contained in the name Neo bears in the world of the Matrix: Thomas Anderson. He is Doubting Thomas ("I don't believe it," he reacts in horror, when Morpheus shows him the "desert of the real") and Ander-Son (the Son of Man). At the critical moment during Neo's confrontation with Agent Smith in the subway station, when he moves beyond doubt and accepts his identity as the One, he disavows his "slave-name":

SMITH. Goodbye, Mr. Anderson.

NEO. My name is Neo.

The Matrix ends with Neo's death, resurrection and ascension. But further salvific work awaits him as Smith mutates into more powerful forms in the two sequels. Physically blind but now able to perceive the luminous essence of things, Neo enters the machine world itself (on a hovercraft named the *Logos*, no less) and offers A.I. a deal. Cruciform, he is pierced with a coaxial cable and jacked back into the Matrix for a final confrontation with Smith. Paradoxically, it is by suffering and dying that he vanquishes Smith, thereby redeeming humanity. "It is done," the machine god intones as Neo is released from his cross and dragged away.

The parallels with Gnosticism are hardly perfect. Perhaps the most significant difference lies in the films' portrayal of what is ultimately important. For the Gnostics, the spirit is more real than the flesh and is the object of our deepest longings, whereas the body with its senses is a snare and a delusion. Matter, in short, is evil—a position consistently rejected in orthodox Christianity. The films appear at times to approach this view, as when Morpheus declares that even gravity is just a "rule" that can be bent or broken, or when he explains Neo's physical injuries from a computer-simulated jump on the grounds that the "mind makes it real." But what we're *shown*, as opposed to what we're *told*, points strongly in the other direction. Morpheus's maxim is true (if at all) only in the Matrix, with its purely mental reality. In the *real* world—the world of Zion and the *Nebuchadnezzar*—the laws of physics reign supreme. Far from advocating transcendence of the body, Mouse declares (apropos the Woman in the Red Dress) that "to deny our own impulses is to deny the very thing that makes us human." And if there is any doubt about where the films stand on this question, it is settled by the temple gathering in *Matrix Reloaded*. As the machine army digs inexorably toward Zion, the entire community comes together to celebrate Zion's civic religion, the expression of its core values. Drums throb throughout the immense cavern as the "worshipers" start to dance, the camera entering the undulating throng to linger lovingly on sweaty, semiclothed bodies; meanwhile, Neo and Trinity, having found some privacy, make love under an arch, the symbol of eternity. We are clearly meant to understand the physicality and sensuality of this scene as a healthy assertion of human nature against the machines. It's everything that Agent Smith abhors:

"I *hate* this place. This *zoo*, this *prison*, this *reality*, whatever you want to call it. I can't stand it any longer. It's the *smell*, if there is such a thing. I feel *saturated* by it. I can taste your *stink*, and every time I do, I feel that I've somehow been infected by it." The Gnostic attitude toward the body is held not by the "liberated" humans, but by the machines.

I don't see that this counts much against a Gnostic reading of the films, however. The films' creators and directors, Larry and Andy Wachowski, have simply played up the cool aspects of Gnosticism and downplayed the uncool bits. "Free your mind" and "just believe" are very much part of the spirit of our age, while serious body-denying asceticism is not. Gnosticism as a richly drawn and credible alternative to the value system of the average moviegoer is simply not on the films' agenda. *The Matrix* has other business to transact, which it does very, very well.

While Neo, Trinity and Morpheus, with their designer shades and balletic moves, are the very quintessence of eye candy, the *Matrix* trilogy is clearly more than just an entertaining series of action movies; it triggers thought as well as adrenalin. At the heart of the films' Gnostic narrative is the question of appearance versus reality, of error versus truth. The films take up these themes at several levels, making the *Matrix* trilogy a virtual primer in all three of the major areas of philosophy: epistemology, metaphysics and ethics. Let's take them in that order.

Epistemology: How Can We *Know* What Is Real?

"Ever have that feeling where you're not sure if you're awake or still dreaming?" Neo asks Choi. This feeling is a common one. It usually gets resolved one way or the other: it turns out we were awake, or it turns out we were asleep. But Neo's question about dreaming versus waking life anticipates a deeper question he is about to confront. The Matrix is a superduper dream machine, capable of generating experiences that are indistinguishable from ordinary waking experiences. If the Matrix has you, as Neo's computer informs him just before Choi arrives, it's hard to see how you could know that the Matrix has you, since your experiences would be just the same as if the Matrix did *not* have you.

Neo's beliefs, when we first meet him, include the following: that the year is 1999, that he lives in a cramped one-bedroom apartment, that he owns a computer, that he has trouble sleeping, that he is employed by a software company and so on. These beliefs are in fact false, as he will soon discover. That

Neo holds some false beliefs is not itself of much philosophical interest. What *is* of interest is that he could be so thoroughly wrong about *these* beliefs. Suppose, for example, Neo also believed that the Atlantic is larger than the Pacific, that horoscopes have predictive value and that it's okay to break promises when keeping them is inconvenient. These beliefs would also have been false. The difference is that these mistakes are ones that Neo could have avoided by taking greater care. He had what it took to acquire better beliefs than these and he failed to do so. In contrast, he had the best reasons in the world for his first set of beliefs. In adopting the belief that he owned a computer, for example, he was relying on the clear testimony of his senses. He wasn't being credulous or perverse; he wasn't engaging in wishful thinking or succumbing to Alzheimer's. And yet he was wrong about this belief, as he was about all the beliefs he had acquired in a similarly unimpeachable manner.

This isn't a problem just for Neo, in the fictional world of the *Matrix* films; it's a problem for us. We have beliefs very much like Neo's—for example, your belief that you are reading a book right now. And these beliefs rest on the same sorts of grounds: your belief about the book, for example, like Neo's belief about his computer, rests at least in part on perception. If Neo could be wrong about his beliefs, we can be wrong about our corresponding beliefs. But if even our most scrupulously formed beliefs can turn out to be false, how can we claim to know *anything?*

The most influential treatment of this problem is found in the *Meditations on First Philosophy* by René Descartes (1596-1650), often called the father of modern philosophy. To dramatize the problem, Descartes conjured up a "universal doubt-maker," a sort of theological (or demonological) version of the Matrix. It is possible, Descartes maintained, that all his beliefs and other conscious states (sensations, perceptions, desires, etc.) are produced in him by a powerful demon bent on deceiving him to the maximum extent possible. But if this is possible, how could Descartes know, when he experiences himself sitting by the fire in his dressing gown, that he really is sitting by the fire in his dressing gown, rather than being deceived by the demon?

A radical solution to this problem is *skepticism:* one can just give up on the possibility of knowledge. But Descartes was not a skeptic. We can know such things as that we're sitting by a fire, and any credible epistemological theory must account for this fact. Descartes approached the problem he had raised as a puzzle to be solved, not as a counsel of despair.

Since sensory evidence cannot refute his demon hypothesis, Descartes had to look elsewhere. His surprising move at this point was to offer two proofs for the existence of God, versions of the ontological argument, which relies on nothing but the *idea* of God. With the existence of God thus ensured, Descartes believed that the prospects for knowledge had undergone a tectonic shift. It is part of the very idea of God that God is perfect and therefore is a *nondeceiver.* In proving the existence of this nondeceptive deity, Descartes thereby secured a guarantee that the world would not be arranged in such a way that we would be routinely and systematically deceived when using our cognitive faculties in a responsible manner. We might still have legitimate doubts on particular occasions (is that a lake in the middle of the desert, or a mirage?), but the threat of universal doubt was broken.

It would probably be a mistake to dismiss Descartes's general strategy out of hand, especially since there aren't a lot of alternative strategies waiting in the wings. Nevertheless, few have found Descartes's solution entirely convincing. One way to bring this out is to imagine Neo reading the *Meditations* while in the Matrix. If Descartes's argument is successful, Neo is entitled to conclude, on the basis of that argument, that he isn't the victim of a global deception. But he *is* the victim of a global deception, Descartes's assurances to the contrary notwithstanding. Something has clearly gone wrong. I leave it to the reader to decide whether Descartes's argument can be revised so that it doesn't have this consequence.

What solution do the *Matrix* films offer? Neo takes the red pill, bursts out of his pod and sees his true situation for the first time; Morpheus then receives him onboard the *Nebuchadnezzar* with the words, "Welcome to the real world." Well, that was easy: the red pill is the answer! But of course it isn't. Neo's evidence that he has now joined the real world is the same kind of evidence he used to have for thinking that the Matrix was the real world, namely, experiential confirmation (he sees it, touches it and so on). But why suppose that his new experiences aren't just as deceptive as his old experiences? The films *could* have ended with Thomas Anderson waking up in his cheap apartment and finding that his adventures as the heroic Neo, with the glamorous Trinity and unflappable Morpheus as sidekicks, were all a dream. Audiences would undoubtedly have felt cheated by such an ending, but they couldn't complain that the resulting story line would be less consistent than the films' actual story line.

Perhaps no philosopher has had so much influence on science fiction as Descartes, and no film has raised the problem of Cartesian doubt quite so effectively as *The Matrix*.[4] What it does not do is offer a serious solution to that problem—unless that solution is to be found in a suggestion to be explored in the next section.

Metaphysics: What Is It for Something to *Be* Real?

"This . . . this isn't real?" Neo asks, as he begins to realize the horrible truth. Morpheus, like a good philosopher, kicks the question upstairs: "What *is* real? How do you *define* real? If you're talking about what you can feel, what you can smell, what you can taste and see, then real is simply electrical signals interpreted by your brain." Morpheus appears to be suggesting that, when it comes to perceptible objects, at least, reality is *mental* ("electrical signals interpreted by your brain").

This is a position most famously associated with George Berkeley, an eighteenth-century Anglo-Irish philosopher. Berkeley's central maxim is *esse est percipi:* to be is to be perceived. According to Berkeley, there are no "material substances" lying behind and causing our perceptions of things; there are only the perceptions themselves, together with the "mental substances" that are engaged in the perceiving. Thus, Berkeley's position is more radical than the one suggested by the famous question, if a tree falls in a forest and no one is there to hear it, would it make a sound? Berkeley would not only deny that it made a sound, he would deny that the tree even existed. This assumes, of course, that *no perceiver at all* is present. But Berkeley, who was also an Anglican bishop, believed in the existence of an infinite perceiver, God, in addition to finite perceivers like you and me. Since *esse est percipi,* if *God* perceives the tree falling in the forest, it exists (and makes a sound) even if no *finite* perceiver happens to be present. Indeed, God creates the world by perceiving it into existence.

To understand the implications of the Berkeley-Morpheus proposal, let us return to the problem from the preceding section. When we wonder whether our beliefs put us in touch with reality, there must be some idea of reality with which we're operating, some standard with respect to which reality measures up and unreality falls short. What is it for something (anything) to *be* real in the first place? Few questions in philosophy are more basic (or abstract). Fortunately, we can delimit the question a bit. Though Descartes *tries* to doubt everything, he finds that some things just can't be doubted: for example, his own existence ("I think, therefore I am") and the content of his own consciousness. Consider, then, some occasion on which Descartes experienced an ovoid patch of red in his visual field, followed by a tactile sensation of smoothness and hardness, followed again by the gustatory quality of sweetness with a hint of tartness. It isn't these conscious experiences, or the existence of the experiencing subject, that he questioned; what *was* subject to doubt was whether these experiences provided adequate grounds for believing that he was in the presence of a real apple (first viewed, then grasped and finally tasted). He has a problem with his knowledge of reality only because he assumes that there is a reality apart from his own thoughts about it. This *metaphysical* assumption—that reality is, for the most part, extramental—is precisely what Berkeley denies.

The *Matrix* films also question this assumption about reality, if they don't deny it outright. The best confirmation from the first film is the scene with the "potentials" at the Oracle's apartment. Neo notices a boy with a shaved head who is manipulating a spoon telekinetically. When Neo's attempt to imitate the boy fails, he turns to the boy for help:

SPOON BOY. Do not try and bend the spoon—that's impossible. *Instead* only try to realize the truth.

NEO. What truth?

SPOON BOY. There is no spoon. . . . Then you will see, it is not the *spoon* that bends, it is only yourself.

Neo tries again and this time succeeds. Whatever is going on here, it appears to be more than Berkeley would endorse: he never suggested that reality could be manipulated in this fashion, except by God. This is Berkeley on steroids; better, it is Buddhism. There is much that a Buddhist reading of the films might make of this scene; for purposes of our Gnostic reading, however, the important point is that Spoon Boy's philosophy does appear to solve—or better, *dissolve*—Descartes's problem. There is no spoon "out there" to stand in judgment of the spoon in my head.

Let's pause to take stock. The *Matrix* films raise the epistemological question—how can we tell the difference between reality and illusion?—in a particularly powerful way. At the same time, there are suggestions throughout the films that the correct metaphysics is one in which reality is fundamentally dependent on the mind ("there is no spoon"). This leaves it an open question how there can *be* an ultimate distinction between reality and illusion, as presupposed by the epistemological question. Certainly this distinction can no longer rest on mind dependence versus mind independence, and the films do not suggest an alternative way of marking the distinction (such as Berkeley's appeal to the way God perceives things). Do the films then mean to reject this distinction? That's doubtful, because this distinction is all-important when we come to the last of the three philosophical questions raised by the films, namely, the moral significance of embracing reality and rejecting illusion.

Ethics: Why Does It *Matter* What's Real?

The key scene in the first film is arguably the meeting between Cypher and Agent Smith, when Cypher's agreement to betray Morpheus is finalized. The rendezvous takes place at a restaurant in the Matrix, and Cypher reveals his motive while biting into a thick steak: "I know this steak doesn't exist. I know that when I put it in my mouth, the Matrix is telling my brain that it is juicy and delicious. After nine years, you know what I realize? Ignorance is bliss." Notice that Cypher does not rest his case for ignorance on the claim that since there is no difference between "reality" and illusion anyway, there's no reason to prefer knowledge over ignorance. It isn't his endorsement of a radical metaphysical theory that has brought him to this pass. Rather, Cypher is reaffirming the difference between knowledge and ignorance, and he is choosing ignorance— because living in the full knowledge of the truth is so unpleasant.

The film shows us enough of the real world—the blasted surface of the Earth, the Spartan living conditions and constant danger aboard the *Nebuchadnezzar*—that we understand Cypher's wish to be reinserted into the Matrix. We understand, but we do not condone: we are clearly meant to recoil from Cypher, while admiring and identifying with the hardy band of rebels who embrace reality despite its hardship. But why? When truth and pleasure conflict, what's so bad about opting for pleasure?

An interesting approach to this question is taken by philosopher Robert Nozick with the help of a fictional device called the Experience Machine. Like the Matrix, the Experience Machine produces a complete set of experiences indistinguishable from real life in the person hooked up to it; unlike the Matrix, a person *chooses* to go on the Experience Machine for the sake of these simulated experiences. These can range from simple physical pleasures, like an expert back massage, to more complex experiences, like discovering and exploring a new continent, performing at Carnegie Hall to a standing ovation or loving (and being loved by) the ideal mate. Unpleasant experiences, like headaches, broken legs, the hurt of rejection or the tedium of waiting in line, can be reduced or eliminated. The only catch is that once you're connected, it's impossible to disconnect: you're on the machine for life. So if you had the opportunity to go on the Experience Machine, *on this condition*, would you do so?

Nozick was confident that virtually no one, upon reflection, would agree to go on the Experience Machine. If Nozick was right about this, it tells us something important and perhaps surprising about our ultimate values. We must value more than just our subjective mental states. What's missing from the Experience Machine, Nozick opined, is this: "First, we want to *do* certain things, and not just have the experience of doing them. . . . [Second] we want to *be* a certain way, to be a certain sort of person. . . . Is [someone floating in a tank] courageous, kind, intelligent, witty, loving? It's not merely that it's difficult to tell; there's no way he is. Thirdly, plugging into an experience machine limits us to a man-made reality, to a world no deeper or more important than that which people can construct."[5] Let's pursue these doubts about the Experience Machine under the rubrics *doing* and *being*.

Doing. What is it *to do* something, as opposed to having something *done to* you? Most important, the action must flow from one's own choices. "Choice. The problem is choice," Neo tells the Architect in *Matrix Reloaded.* This is true from the beginning of Neo's journey (the choice to get back in the car taking him to Morpheus, the choice of the red pill over the blue) to its end ("Why do you persist?" asks Smith. "Because I choose to," answers Neo). But what *is* choice? The walls of the room where Neo is interviewed by the Architect are covered with monitors displaying Neo's possible reactions to the Architect's revelations; at the end of the interview Neo must exit through one of two doors. This is one way to think of choice: two or more responses are genuinely open to me, and I'm the one who settles which of these possibilities is to become actual. But choice, so understood, is under assault throughout the films.

One critic is the Merovingian, who delivers the following minilecture in *Matrix Reloaded:*

MEROVINGIAN. You see, there is only one constant, one universal, it is the only real truth: causality. Action. Reaction. Cause and effect.

MORPHEUS. Everything begins with choice.

MEROVINGIAN. No. Wrong. Choice is an illusion. . . . This is the nature of the universe. We struggle against it, we fight to deny it. . . . Our only hope, our only peace is to understand it, to understand the "why."

The Merovingian assumes here the truth of *causal determinism*, the position that all events (including human actions) are the necessary causal consequences of prior events over which we have no control. He also assumes, not implausibly, that causal determinism rules out free choice. Finally, his *response* to these assumptions is similar to that of certain ancient Stoics, who likened human beings to a dog tied behind a moving cart. The dog has no choice about where it's going—that's determined by the cart. But it *is* up to the dog whether to trot compliantly behind the cart or to be dragged. Once we understand that we are in the same situation as this dog, the Merovingian suggests, it's best to accept this rather than engage in futile resistance.

Another challenge to free choice comes from the Oracle, a considerably more sympathetic figure than the Merovingian. There's an obvious allusion here to the oracle at Delphi: the motto over her kitchen door, "Know thyself," was also inscribed on the shrine at Delphi, and she advises Neo while sitting on a kitchen stool inhaling the aroma of freshly baked cookies, just as the priestess at Delphi prophesied while sitting on a tripod breathing in the hallucinogenic fumes issuing from a crack in the ground. The future is fated, and the Oracle knows what it holds in store; when she declares that such and such will happen, it *must* happen. This fatalistic necessity is even stronger than the causal determinism to which the Merovingian appeals. Trinity, for example, has been told by the Oracle that she will fall in love with the One, and she has in fact fallen in love with Neo; she therefore infers, when Neo dies, that he can't remain dead—and she's right. When the course of nature (fatal gunshots causing the heart to stop beating) conflicts with the edicts of fate, it is nature that must give way.[6]

If either determinism or fatalism is correct, then the monitors in the Architect's room do not represent a *real* diversity of responses open to Neo; insofar as choice requires genuine alternatives, choice is therefore an illusion. There is little evidence, however, that the films mean to endorse this conclusion. How then do they escape it?

One suggestion is that what looks like fate might instead be *providence*. Notice the difference this makes to Morpheus as the parts of a complex mission into the Matrix fall into place: "Tonight is not an accident. There are no *acci-*

dents. . . . I do not believe in chance. When I see three objectives, three captains, three ships, I do not see coincidence; I see providence, I see purpose. I believe it is our fate to be here; it is our destiny. I believe this night holds for each and every one of us the very meaning of our lives." If Morpheus is right in discerning the hand of providence in these events, his enthusiasm is understandable. It's not clear, though, how this serves to rehabilitate choice. I'd rather be a character in a script composed by an intelligent author than in one produced by twelve monkeys pecking away at twelve typewriters, but it's not because the first scenario delivers more freedom. The problem of finding a place for free choice in a world ruled by blind, impersonal fate has simply been replaced by the problem of finding a place for free choice in a world governed by providence.[7]

The films are at their best when they raise questions about free choice, but the temptation to provide answers (however enigmatic) is too much for the filmmakers to resist. The Oracle, who might be expected to offer some insight into how fate can coexist with choice, is given the last words of the final film: "I believed. I believed." That's not a solution, to this or to any of the problems raised in the films; it's just magic—and a disappointingly flabby ending for a series that is, at least intermittently, more rigorous than this.

Being. The second moral Nozick derives from the Experience Machine is that we want to *be* something. But how is this missing for someone hooked up to the Experience Machine? There is something you are when you are on the machine—or in the Matrix, for that matter. You are a blob floating in a tank. But this is no way to be. Why not?

At the beginning of *Matrix Reloaded*, Neo laments: "I just wish . . . I knew what I'm supposed to do." Freedom is only a start; it also matters how we use our freedom. When we act, we do so as particular beings (humans, not cats or corkscrews) in a particular context. There are two touchstones here: who *we* are and how the *world* is. The norms guiding free choice must take both of these into account. Let's call this dual norm *authenticity*. Neo aspires to an authentic life, one that is true to the facts about himself and the environment in which he lives; Cypher, on the other hand, no longer cares.

The films are quite clear that authenticity begins with a thing's function or *purpose*. "Every program that is created must have a purpose," Neo is told by Rama-Kandra in the train station; love, for example, is just "a way of saying 'what I am here to do.'" This is the position Aristotle develops in his *Nico-*

machean Ethics. Aristotle notes that what it is to be a good flute player or sculptor depends on the *function* of flute playing and sculpting, and he suggests that what it is to be a good human being might likewise depend on the function of human life. What could this be? Simply being alive is shared with plants, perception is shared with other animals—"but what we are looking for," Aristotle writes, "is the special function of a human being." He concludes that this must involve "some sort of life of action of the part of the soul that has reason."[8]

One implication of Aristotle's approach is that it makes sense to speak of an owner's manual for human beings. The owner's manual for a washing machine explains what it can do, how to operate it, how to care for it and how to troubleshoot when something goes wrong. These instructions are all predicated on there being something that this thing *is*. A washing machine is not a cement mixer; using it as a cement mixer means *not* using it to do what it's made for and can do well, and it risks damaging it so it *cannot* do what it's for. Likewise a human being is not a dog, a daffodil or a DVD player. Aristotle devotes a lot of attention to the various virtues, like courage and truthfulness, that equip us to function well and be all that we can be. The *Nicomachean Ethics* is, in effect, Aristotle's owner's manual, as the Bible is for Christians.

The supreme good for human beings, according to Aristotle, is *happiness*. This is not a subjective mental state, like a feeling, though it is ordinarily *accompanied* by desirable mental states. It is instead an objective condition in which a person's activity fits harmoniously into the nexus of facts about that person and the relevant aspects of the environment. Real happiness, in this sense, cannot be achieved through activities that run counter to who we are (e.g., taking advantage of others) or that exemplify nothing higher than what we share with plants or animals (e.g., a life devoted to fine dining), no matter how pleasurable they may be. Happiness can even be undermined by facts of which we are completely unaware. Imagine an elderly woman, contented with life, whose joy rests on the belief that her only child is prospering in a distant country; imagine further that this belief is false and that she never discovers the truth: her son is in fact childless, divorced, indigent and homeless, sobering up only long enough to write the weekly letters in which he tells his mother what she most wants to hear. For Aristotle, this woman is not happy, even if she thinks she is—her situation is simply sad, no matter how good she feels.

The same is true of people stuck in the Matrix. There's something sad about imagining oneself a talented artist, successful entrepreneur or beloved spouse, while in reality one is immobile in a tank of goo. It matters how things are, not just how they seem.

Wake Up, Neo

The Matrix is the story of a sleeper who wakes up. This is a very powerful metaphor. Saint Augustine, the great Christian Platonist, uses it to express the difficulty of breaking free from old habits and bringing his will into sync with his intellectual acceptance of Christianity: "I was held down as agreeably by this world's baggage as one often is by sleep; and indeed the thoughts with which I meditated upon You were like the efforts of a man who wants to get up but is so heavy with sleep that he simply sinks back into it again."[9] Descartes echoes this passage from Augustine when describing his own efforts to awaken from the sleep of doubt.[10] "There is no one who wants to be asleep always," Augustine adds. This is the moral of both the Experience Machine and *The Matrix*.

At the end of the first film, when Neo emerges from the phone booth, the people crowding around him look like sleepwalkers, moving robotically toward meaningless destinations, as though on autopilot. Neo seems the only person truly alive. Here's someone who has found out what it's all about, what it is that we're *for*, and it's exhilarating. We want to be like Neo, not like the oblivious crowd. It's true that the films are short on details, such as what it is we should be waking up *from* and *to*. The boundary between authenticity and inauthenticity can get drawn in many different ways. (Is there a cosmic struggle in which viewers should enlist? What is it?) They're also vague about what one should actually do in order to "wake up." ("Free your mind?" What's that?) This is a vexing practical problem, with which Augustine struggled at length in *The Confessions*. But what the first film, at least, does very effectively is stir the viewer with the thrill, wonder and transformative power of waking up to . . . whatever it is that the real world has to offer. There is more to life—on any account of what that "more" might be—than simply drifting along, unreflectingly, from one experience to another. With this much of *The Matrix*, at least, the apostle Paul would surely agree: "Awake, O sleeper, /and arise from the dead, /and Christ will shine on you" (Ephesians 5:14).

Consciousness, Memory and Identity

The Nature of Persons in Three Films by Charlie Kaufman

GREGORY E. GANSSLE

• •

Suppose you are flipping through the newspaper and you see an unusual ad.

Ever want to be someone else?
Now you can!
Visit JM Inc.

What would you think? Would you pay to be someone else for, say, fifteen minutes? What is so intriguing about the possibility of being someone else? I wonder, do we actually want to *be* someone else, or do we want to be ourselves while having elements of the lives of other people? It is a common experience for people to feel stuck in their lives and long to break out. This, novelist Walker Percy observes, explains the pervasive use of amnesia in television and film.[1] To wake up completely forgetful of one's past is to be given a new life altogether. The future is a blank slate on which anything can be drawn. "Blessed are the forgetful for they get the better even of their blunders."[2] But *can* you become another person? What are the limits and possibilities for such adaptation? The question collides with deep issues in metaphysics. What *is* a person? What is it that makes a particular person *that* particular person? What makes a particular person the same person throughout her life? Are there limits to the degree to which people can change?

Our question of what it means to be a human person is one of the large themes found throughout the history of philosophy. Such an issue, to be sure, is not limited to philosophy. Poets, playwrights and novelists, as well as psychologists and other thinkers in the social and physical sciences, have taken up the same question.

In the twentieth century the new medium of film emerged, and with it came the possibility of a new method of investigation. Film, like literature, raises universal questions in the context of particular characters and stories. As a result, there is a different sort of emphasis in a film than there is in a philosophical essay. The contribution of film to philosophy is that the particularity of the stories and characters brings clarity and seriousness to the philosophical issues in a way that can be missed in more abstract discussion.

Three films written by Charlie Kaufman pay considerable attention to the nature of human persons: *Being John Malkovich* (1999), *Adaptation* (2002) and *Eternal Sunshine of the Spotless Mind* (2004).[3] These stories each show what happens to people as they bump against the boundaries of identity.

Being John Malkovich and the First-Person Perspective

In *Being John Malkovich*, Craig Schwartz enters the mind of John Malkovich. Schwartz enters Malkovich's mind but retains his own consciousness. He encounters the world through Malkovich's body. He sees through Malkovich's eyes and hears with Malkovich's ears. He does all this while remaining conscious that he himself is Craig Schwartz. When he tries to explain his first experience within Malkovich to his coworker, Maxine Lund, he describes it as something that he himself remembers experiencing.

There are two distinct persons within Malkovich's body with little blurring of perspective. Neither Schwartz nor Malkovich has access to the other's thoughts. So while Schwartz can hear Malkovich talking, Schwartz does not experience *himself* speaking those words. Presumably, Malkovich later remembers his conversations as things *he* experienced. At the time, he was not aware of Schwartz's presence. Each participant retained his own first-person perspective. In a sense, Schwartz has *eavesdropped* on Malkovich's conversation.

If we reflect on Schwartz's experience, we may gain some insight into the nature of the human person. The first-person perspective is that perspective from which we experience everything. It is, in some sense, the way my experiences are experienced by me and your experiences are experienced by you. There is a vast difference between watching you experience the pain of a stubbed toe and my experiencing that pain myself. In each case, there may be the same amount and kind of pain in the room. I sense your pain only from a third-person point of view. My own pain I experience from the first-person perspective. It hurts me and that is why it is my pain and not yours.

Philosophers have been both intrigued and troubled by the first-person perspective. Some have thought that the first-person was the key to having certainty. In the seventeenth century, René Descartes proposed the most famous thought in philosophy: "I think, therefore, I am."[4] Descartes was especially concerned about knowledge. He wondered, is it possible to know anything with certainty? He answered that I, as an individual subject, can know my own existence with certainty because it is impossible for me to doubt that I exist. Descartes attempts to build a complete structure of certain knowledge from his foundational certainty about his own existence.

The success of Descartes's project depends on our certainty about the contents of our own minds. If it looks to me as if I am seeing a brown table in front of me, then while I may not know there actually is such a table there before me, I do know with certainty that it looks as if there is one. I know that I am having an experience as if there is a brown table. This idea about the content of our own minds can be called *the transparency of the mind*. The transparency of the mind indicates that the content of a person's mind is transparent to that person. This notion in Descartes and in subsequent philosophers has helped produce the conviction that there is a substantive difference between the first-person and the third-person perspective. When I say "I see a table," the sentence involves both the first- and the third-person perspectives. It involves the first-person perspective in that it is a statement about my experience. It involves the third-person perspective in that it is about things in the world. If there is really no table, then my statement is not true. I can be mistaken about third-person claims. Perhaps I am dreaming. When I say "It seems to me that I see a table," I am not making any claim about what exists outside my experience. This sentence involves only the first-person perspective. The first-person perspective is immune from the skeptical challenges that threaten third-person knowledge claims. Even if I am dreaming and there is no real table, I cannot be mistaken about the fact that it seems to me that I am seeing a table.

In the twentieth century, many philosophers rejected the philosophical significance of the first-person perspective. This challenge comes from two general directions. The first is *behaviorism*.[5] Gilbert Ryle, for example, has argued that we understand the mind best by grasping how *mental terms* function in our language.[6] When we observe how we use mental language, we see that the meaning of such language is cashed out in terms of behavior. A sentence such as "Malkovich knows French" does not mean that Malkovich has some kind of mental thing called "knowledge of French." It means that he behaves or he is disposed to behave in certain ways. If you ask him a question in French, he will answer in French. If you ask him what languages he speaks, he will include French in his answer. All of our mental language, behaviorists maintain, can be expressed in behavioral terms.

The advantage of behaviorism, it is thought, is that we do not have to think that we have some kind of mysterious mental life that is fundamentally out of reach to other people. I have as much access to your mental life as you do. I can say with confidence that, for example, you are confused because what it means to be confused is a perfectly public item that is accessible from the third-person perspective.

The second major challenge to the first-person perspective comes from *identity theory*.[7] Identity theorists hold that our mental states are identical to our brain states. So my worry about missing my son when he goes to college is nothing more than some sequence of neural firings in my brain. This identity is similar to other theoretical reductions in science. For example, it turns out that heat is simply mean molecular energy. All of the causal influence that the heat of some system has can be explained in terms of the mean molecular energy of that system. The word *heat* often carries the connotation of the sensory feel we associate with touching hot things. This feeling is one of the effects of the molecular energy. Heat, properly speaking, is not the feel but the molecular energy itself. The identity of heat and mean molecular energy provides an instructive analogy for the identity theory of the mind. My worry about missing David when he goes to college is identical to some set of chemical reactions in my brain. If it is true that my worry causes me to do certain things, then it is the chemical nature of those reactions that does all of the causal work. The content of those reactions (what I experience as *worry* and as worry *about missing David*) does not play any role in the causal story.

Identity theory grants the third-person perspective nearly as much priority as behaviorism does. I can know by looking at your brain that you are angry or worried. Of course, I might have to open your brain and subject it to some rather precise chemical testing in order to determine what specific brain state you are experiencing. But in principle, the third-person perspective is as accurate and well grounded as the first.

Both behaviorism and identity theory hold that the nature of our mental life can be investigated thoroughly from the third-person perspective. The former investigates the mind through the behavior of the person, while the latter does so through the chemistry of the brain. Since the middle of the twentieth century, when these theories were launched, there have been many versions of each. Some of the strengths of some of these versions have been combined into a family of theories called *functionalism.*[8] The basic functionalist thesis is that what makes a particular mental state the state it is—that is, what makes what is going on in my mind a case of my worrying about my son—is the function it plays. Some functionalists claim that a mental state is identical with whatever series of neural firings in the brain serves to play the right causal-functional role in the person. This sort of functionalist takes up themes from identity theory by identifying mental states with brain states. The functionalist takes up some of the strengths of behaviorism by identifying the causal-functional role of the mental state in the behavior of the person. For example, it seems to me that my worry causes me to think a lot about what next year will be like when David is off at college. What is my worry, then? That is, what particular *thing* is it? The functionalist will maintain that it is whatever functional role my brain states play in the right causal relation to my thinking about next year. Like behaviorism and identity theory, functionalism minimizes the importance of the first-person perspective.

It is not an exaggeration to characterize the philosophy of mind in the last hundred years as an attempt to undermine the primacy of the first-person perspective. There has been a widespread aversion to the first-person perspective because, many think, only the third-person perspective fits neatly into a scientific worldview. Views which claim that all of a person's mental life can be explained either in terms of the person's behavior or in terms of the chemistry of the brain fit more easily into the world of scientific theories. If our notion of the mind requires something that cannot be so explained, then human beings stand outside of what science can explain. Many thinkers, as a result, try to show that the first-person perspective can either be eliminated or reduced to items that can be explained within a third-person perspective.

In contrast with many contemporary philosophers, Descartes argues that the domain of science covers only one of the distinct kinds of substances in the world. The two substances, he believes, are matter and mind. Matter includes everything that is extended in space and can be measured with geometry. The essence of mind, however, is thought. Mind is not extended and it is nonphysical. A person's mind interacts with her body. The resulting theory is a kind of interactive dualism. Although Descartes aims to give the new sciences a firm philosophical grounding, he does not think that this task required rendering *everything* part of the subject matter of physical science. He is content that human minds, God and morality should remain outside the domain of scientific inquiry. Descartes and other dualistic thinkers see no need to try to reduce the first-person perspective to a third-person perspective.[9]

As we look into Kaufman's exploration of perspective in *Being John Malkovich*, we see that there are fixed boundaries around a person's first-person perspective. As I noted, in the first few trips into Malkovich, there is a clear distinction between Malkovich's own self-consciousness and that of the person who enters him. As Schwartz learns how to move Malkovich's arms and to speak with his voice, Malkovich experiences the sense of being possessed by another mind. Once Schwartz learns to control Malkovich effectively, Malkovich's own self-consciousness is rendered ineffective. In some minimal sense, he retains his own first-person perspective. It is now Schwartz in Malkovich's body. Note well that Schwartz cannot yet *be* John Malkovich. He can only be Craig Schwartz. He does not merge or blend with Malkovich's consciousness. He does not have his memories or his aspirations. Schwartz remains completely Schwartz even as he inhabits and manipulates Malkovich's body. So although Kaufman has one person take over the body of another, he does not have one person take over the *mind* of another. Minds are things that cannot be invaded. In the end, no one else can *be* John Malkovich.

Adaptation and the Stability of Persons

Adaptation is the story of Kaufman's struggle to adapt Susan Orlean's book *The Orchid Thief* for a script.[10] Orlean's book focuses on John Laroche's arrest for harvesting orchids from a state preserve. In the film, Kaufman's research leads him to discover a darker story. Laroche introduces Orlean to a drug that he can extract from the Ghost Orchid. They become sexually involved. Laroche and Orlean catch Kaufman spying on them and decide to kill him in the swamp. Instead, Kaufman's brother and Laroche are killed. Orlean breaks down as she sees her life unraveling around her.

This film explores the nature and limits of adaptation on four major levels. The first is the level of the media. Kaufman's character is trying to adapt a work produced in a text-based medium (a book) to a work in an image-based medium (film). The difficulty of doing so creates one of the deep ironies of the film. "Why can't there be a movie about flowers?" he asks.

The second level concerns the portrayal of real people in a highly fictionalized manner. It is difficult to discern where fact stops and fiction begins. The most severe treatment is reserved for himself. He heaps layers of insecurity on his own character and then exploits a method he repudiates in the story itself—that of the split personality. Charlie Kaufman's brother, Donald Kaufman (also played by Nicolas Cage), is what Kaufman would like to be but cannot.

Third, throughout the story, we learn about the nearly infinite adaptability of orchids. There is no end to the variety that can be found or produced in the greenhouse. Any environment, even the most remote and difficult, is fertile ground for the flower.

The last level is the most crucial to the film. This is the adaptation of human persons. Laroche moves from obsession to obsession without a trace of regret. He is the supremely adaptable human being. Orlean wants desperately to feel passionately—about anything. She is trapped by who she thinks she is or ought to be. Laroche confesses, as he is driving Orlean around Florida: "You know why I like plants? Because they are so mutable. Adaptation is a profound process. Means you figure out how to thrive in the world." Orlean responds, "Yeah, but it's easier for plants. I mean, they have no memory. They just move on to whatever's next. With a person, though, adapting is almost shameful. It's like running away." She looks out the window. She is afraid to adapt but she longs to. Laroche, in this sense, is more like a plant than a person. He moves on from obsession to obsession and drops each without a trace. He does so to figure out how to thrive. It is almost as if he, too, has no memory.

During World War II, philosopher and novelist Jean Paul Sartre delivered a lecture titled "Existentialism and Humanism." His aim in this lecture is to defend existentialism against some criticisms. He describes the starting point of existentialism as the premise that if God does not exist, everything is permitted—a perspective best illustrated by Ivan Karamazov in Fyodor Dostoyevsky's *The Brothers Karamazov*.[11] While Dostoyevsky intends for this announcement to be received with dread, Sartre thinks it was the foundation of true freedom. It gives credence to the summary of Sartre's existential vision: *Existence precedes essence.*

What Sartre meant by this is best seen in contrast with Saint Augustine and the Christian Platonists. Plato and his followers hold that there are eternal universals that explain the nature of the particular things in the world. Augustine and other Christians argue that Plato's "forms" are eternal and unchanging ideas in God's mind. They do not exist independently from God, but they exist as eternal universals in God's thoughts. When God created, he did so in accordance with his ideas. So the idea of what it means to be a human being was in God's mind before he created any actual human beings. The idea of a human being was God's idea of what the nature of persons ought to be. He then created people to be this way. Sartre rejects this picture. Because there is no God, he argues, there is no idea of what a human being must be that constitutes a common human nature. There are existing persons and each person creates her own nature. People exist before they have any essence. In this way, my nature is up to me. Sartre calls this a radical freedom. There are no moral or divine boundaries limiting how I create myself. My only obligation is to choose. Not to choose—to unconsciously allow the culture around me to mold me into its own image—is to live in bad faith. Whatever life I live, I must choose it, and in doing so, I create my nature. To choose my nature is my great dignity. I am responsible for what I am and what I become. For Sartre, real external values that might limit what I ought to be have disappeared along with God. Human beings are free. We are, in Sartre's words, "condemned to be free." We *must* create our own values as we create ourselves.

The high degree of adaptability that Laroche embodies is a good picture of Sartre's view of human existence. There are no moral or metaphysical constraints on individual persons. Laroche simply must choose whom he will be. Orlean and Kaufman are examples of persons living in bad faith. They do not and, it seems, cannot take responsibility for what they have become. They feel trapped in who they are and long to break out. Orlean finally attempts to do so but she destroys her life in the process with drugs, pornography and, eventually, murder.

Adaptation is also a study in how individual people *place themselves* in the world. Walker Percy has described how people navigate their interactions with the world.[12] The flourishing of a self depends on its understanding of itself and its relation to the world. Percy notes that in the postreligious world, there are two postures from which the self attempts to understand itself. The first is through *immanence*. The self is identified as a consumer of the goods of life. These goods are not limited to food and drink. They include the goods of the self, such as the many strategies to improve the self that are open to a discriminating consumer. The immanent self is the consumer self. The second mode of identifying the self is through *transcendence*. Transcendence is achieved by the ability to step outside of the world and view it from a privileged position. Two domains of transcendence in our culture are science and art. The scientist, Percy thinks, occupies a Godlike position because she objectifies the world and masters it through knowledge. The scientist pronounces on all of reality. The artist's transcendence is achieved by her ability to diagnose and name the maladies of the age. The artist, then, tells a different sort of truth than the scientist does. The truth of the scientist is a generalizing truth while the writer's is a particular truth. It is the truth about particular persons in particular situations.

Both strategies encounter difficulties. The immanent self is always somewhat of a problem to itself. Each particular consumer strategy becomes exhausted and must be replaced by a new one. Each new strategy appears to hold the promise of real peace or freedom, but no strategy can work for long. A person's life will crash if he runs out of strategies before he runs out of time. Another possibility is that he will come to realize that the strategy of the discriminating consumer is doomed to fail. He may lose hope or try to achieve some kind of transcendence.

The difficulty with transcendence is reentry. Neither the scientist nor the artist can escape the fact that she is a human person herself. The scientist renders the world tolerable through discovery of generalities. When the scientist develops a theory that explains everything about persons, how does she then live? She, the individual, is lost in the theory. When the artist grasps and articulates the ills of the age, what does she do next? The efficacy of art as a strategy for transcendence and for identifying the self is, in the long run, minimal. Percy observes that the transient effect of art explains why so many writers drink and wind up as suicides.[13]

In the film, Orlean is a failure at placing herself in the world. She longs for the immanent passion of Laroche, yet she approaches Laroche from the transcendent posture of the writer. Her own life seems pale and insignificant in comparison with Laroche's. The brief experience of transcendence that articulating Laroche's life gives her soon dissipates, and she is left in her New York life, passionless and alone, a discriminating consumer who has run out of things to consume. It is no surprise that she returns to Laroche and enters the world of drugs and pornography. Drugs and promiscuous sex represent, for Percy, the last feeble attempt to salvage a decayed life of immanence. Laroche is correct when he hurls this accusation at her: "You are just like everybody else—leeches. You attach yourself to me and you suck me dry, spit me out. Why don't you get your own life—your own interests?"

Laroche is almost totally immanent. He moves from one object of obsession to the next without regard for the past or any attempt to find meaning. He is much like the plants he seeks: an organism in a world. Although he attains a level of expertise in his knowledge of orchids, this knowledge barely affects him. There is no hint of whether or not he will run out of obsessions before he runs out of time. The tragedy of Laroche's immanence is that the orchids—with all of their natural history, beauty and delicacy—get used up and forgotten. The world is forgotten. It is lost. Orchids become mere preludes to Internet pornography. The Ghost Orchid becomes a source of drugs and nothing more.

The deeper message of the film is that there are limits to human adaptability. Because we are conscious selves, there is a continuity to our lives. Because we have memory, we have some stability. Stability and unlimited adaptability are not, in the end, compatible. Near the closing of the film, Orlean cries out, "I want my life back. . . . I want to be a baby again. . . . I want to be new!" Some adaptations exact a terrible cost.

Eternal Sunshine of the Spotless Mind and the Persistence of Personal Identity

Joel Barish decides to have his former girlfriend, Clementine Kruczynski, erased from his memory after he finds out that she has done the same. As he sleeps, technicians attach a memory-wiping device to his head. During the procedure Joel realizes that he wants to retain the memories. So in the recesses of his mind he runs with Clementine to hide from the memory wipe. Everywhere they turn, the memories get erased. Finally, she whispers to him, "Meet me in Montauk." This one memory escapes detection. Joel wakes with no recollection of Clementine. But as he heads for work, Joel finds himself jumping suddenly onto a train heading for Montauk. He sees Clementine, and although neither has any memory of the other, they begin to talk.

Eternal Sunshine of the Spotless Mind focuses on personal identity as both problematic and fragile and as resourceful and stable. Identity is fragile in that the memory-wiping process is shown to be very costly for those who undergo it. The resourcefulness and stability of the self is expressed through the fact that Joel and Clementine are the same people after the memory-erasing procedure as they were before it. The wiping process does not change them either in a metaphysical way or in a deeply psychological way. They have the same dispositions to be attracted to each other afterward as they did before.

It is important to distinguish two different senses of the term *identity*. The first is what philosophers call *qualitative identity*. An item is qualitatively identical with another if it has all the same properties the other has. For example, we own a forest green 1999 Plymouth Voyager. There are a lot of forest green Plymouth Voyagers on the road. These are all, more or less, qualitatively identical. In parking lots, I often have to check the license plate to make sure I am getting into the right one. The second sense of the term *identity* is what we call *numerical identity*. An item is numerically identical with another if they are one and the same item. Each thing in the universe is numerically identical with itself and with nothing else. Where this notion is important is when we think about identity across time.

In psychology, identity is often thought of as qualitative identity. It makes sense, in psychological contexts, to say that you are not the same person you used to be. Philosophers mostly worry about numerical identity. In this sense, I am always the same person that I was. Numerical identity across time is related to survival. Some changes that a thing can undergo are trivial enough that the object survives the change. For example, my car would still exist if we washed it or painted it. It would survive these changes. There are other changes that my car would not survive. If the temperature rose to about ten thousand degrees Celsius, the car would not survive.

When it comes to persons, the philosophical questions get turned upside down in a sense. It is not that we wonder *whether* my son Nick now is numerically identical with Nick as he was when he was ten years old. We know he is the same person. What we want to know is what *makes* him the same person. We know that most of the cells in his body have been replaced since he was ten. So his being the same person cannot be because he is made up of exactly the same physical parts.

Many philosophers have thought that one of the more important features indicating or grounding numerical identity has to do with consciousness. If there is a continuity of consciousness, then there is identity across time. John Locke, for example, holds that to be a person is to be a "thinking intelligent Being, that has reason and reflection, and can consider it self as it self, the same thinking thing in different times and places."[14] The concept of personhood, for Locke, is connected to issues concerning praise and blame. I cannot rightly be blamed for some past action unless I am the same person who performed the action. There must, then, be continuity of personal identity across time if there is to be a system of moral praise and blame.

Locke affirms continuity of personal identity over time. What grounds this continuity of identity, he argues, is continuity of consciousness. Locke remains agnostic about whether there is an immaterial substance (or soul) to which consciousness is attached. Consciousness itself can uphold personal identity, whether or not there is some kind of immaterial substance. If I am conscious of myself having performed some action yesterday, then it is truly the case that I performed the action.

Locke's view is confronted with the problem of memory loss. When I fall into a deep sleep and cannot remember the day's activities, do I cease to be me? Do I go out of existence each night and come back into existence each morning? Locke denies that normal, everyday forgetfulness is a threat to the stability of our personal identity. If there is a traumatic memory loss with no possibility of recollection, however, then there is no basis for thinking that the past person and the present person are the same person. A person's consciousness accumulates experiences in the form of memories throughout her life. As far back as the memory goes, there is a continuity of personal identity. Locke thinks that it is at least possible that an entirely different person can be attached to the same human body. If there is a completely discontinuous consciousness, there is a new person.

Locke does not hold that identity *consists in* memory. Rather, memory is the best test available for verifying the presence of that in which identity does consist: namely, consciousness. Personal identity is a matter of consciousness at a given time. Whether the time is present or past, identity is still a matter of consciousness at that time. If at some time (T_2) we ask who performed an action that was performed previously (at time T_1), the answer does not involve memory. The answer is that the one who at T_1 had a present consciousness of doing the action is the one who owns the action. Personal identity, considered ontologically, is always a matter of present consciousness. Memory plays an epistemic role. In most cases, it is the best test for determining whether there is a continuity of consciousness.

Eternal Sunshine can be seen as an exploration into Locke's theory of personal identity. The memory-wiping procedure as a cure for bad relationships raises the deepest questions about the role of memory in identity. The memory wipe, as portrayed, is a good case of having one's consciousness stripped beyond the power of recall. Joel wakes with no memory of Clementine or their two years together. If anything counts as a disruption of the continuity of personal identity, this procedure does.

After the procedure, there are three periods in Joel's life. For the sake of convenience, we will call the individuals persisting through these periods different *persons*, and we will investigate whether any of these persons is numerically identical with any others. So while there may be as many as three different persons, it also may turn out that there are only two distinct persons or that all three periods are episodes in the life of one person. The periods are the time before Joel meets Clementine (this is person Joel A), the period of Joel's relationship with Clementine (Joel B) and the period after Joel's memory wipe (Joel C). We want to know whether any of these three is numerically identical with any (or all) of the others and, if so, which ones are numerically identical.

If we adopt Locke's memory criterion for tracking continuity of identity, we see that Joel B and Joel A *are* numerically identical. After all, during his relationship with Clementine, Joel remembers his life before Clementine. There is no problem here. Are Joel C and Joel B numerically identical? It seems as though they might not be. Joel C has no memories of any of Joel B's life or experiences. There is a radical break in the continuity of identity.

The challenge comes when we ask whether Joel C is numerically identical with Joel A. It seems that he is. After all, Joel C remembers being Joel A. Joel C remembers things that happened to Joel A as having happened to *him*. In Locke's view, this fact is enough to establish continuity of identity. Now we have hit a wall. If Joel B is identical to Joel A and Joel C is identical to Joel A, then Joel C must be identical to Joel B. This formula is called the *transitivity of identity*. Either we need to reject the transitivity of identity or we have to think that continuity of memory is not necessary for continuity of identity—and therefore not a fully reliable guide to determining continuity of identity. Given this choice, the more reasonable position is to hold that memory is not necessary for continuity of personal identity. The transitivity of identity is a fundamental principle and cannot be rejected.

Kaufman, then, appears to agree with Locke that memory is not necessary for continuity of identity. Notice what happens when Joel listens to the tape he made before he had the memory wipe. He cannot remember making the tape, but he does recognize his own voice on it. He knows, then, that he made the tape and therefore that he told the stories that were on the tape. The tape provides a link between Joel C and Joel B other than that of memory. As a result, Joel C knows that he is the one who had the relationship with Clementine. Personal identity is deeper than memory even if memory is generally our most reliable guide to continuity.

That personal identity is deeper than memory is further indicated by the peculiar experience of characters who have had the memory wipe: they each find themselves still deeply attracted to the same people as before. Joel and Clementine are willing to create again a relationship they know will be difficult. What makes a person the particular person she is cannot be so easily erased.

Theism and Human Nature

The films of Charlie Kaufman explore the boundaries of human nature and identity. While every attempt is made to portray persons as permeable, the boundaries of human identity are shown to be more resilient than the viewer expects. In *Being John Malkovich*, the first-person perspective of another person could not be entered. Schwartz could enter the *body* of Malkovich, but John Malkovich, the *person*, was immune from such invasion. In *Adaptation*, persons are found to be quite unlike orchids. Fruitful human adaptability has definite limits. Those who attempt to abolish the limits of mutability wind up decayed or destroyed. In *Eternal Sunshine*, even the precise removal of every memory of a deep relationship does not dent the nature or dispositions of the people involved.

The picture of human persons that emerges from these films includes a self that persists through time and that has a stability that is deeper and more secure even than bodily stability. The self is resistant to strategies that aim to reduce it to something else. This nonreducibility of human personhood is prevalent in all three films. The person Malkovich is not reducible to his body, the persons Orlean and Laroche are not indefinitely pliable like the flowers they pursue, and Joel's identity is deeper than his memories. If these are glimpses into the reality of human nature, then there is a metaphysical challenge lurking in the region: the stability and resilience of the human person require a metaphysical foundation.

The nature of human persons must be explored in the context of competing metaphysical stories. We saw this link between a particular view of human nature and a broader metaphysical position with Sartre. His claim that there is no human nature is based on and deeply connected to his rejection of the existence of a God who created persons. If Sartre turns out to be wrong about human nature, it does not automatically follow that God does exist. It is worth exploring, however, how theistic positions can bear on our observations about the nature of the self.

Traditional theism holds that human beings have been created in the image of God. There are several salient implications of this view. First, essence *does* precede existence. God had in mind what sort of thing human persons were to be before he created any particular people. The burden of inventing our nature does not lie with us. There is a human nature. This nature provides both the limits of adaptation and the grounding for persistence through time. An individual person cannot be eliminated simply through a memory wipe.

Second, the notion that there is a human nature that is invented by God implies that there are purposes for human beings. If theism is true, the resources for human flourishing expand exponentially. Objective moral values that transcend human beings and that contribute to our good are perfectly at home in a theistic world. Furthermore, traditional theism does not minimize the value and even the centrality of a rational grounding for its most central claims. God, who created the universe, gave us cognitive faculties fitted to the task of knowing. The invitation to think hard about all that God is and all that we are and all that is made is deeply woven into the theistic story.

Christian theism, in particular, goes further in its implications. The divine incarnation grounds the value of every aspect of the truly human life. The doctrine of the incarnation holds that God became a human person in Jesus of Nazareth. God took on human nature and became fully human. If God became fully human, then every aspect of a fully human life is taken up by God. God's concern extends to all that is truly human. Life, love, art, music, knowledge, play, sorrow, joy and death are all given deeper meaning in that God himself experienced them. If God became fully human, then all that is human has meaning.

Charlie Kaufman's three films compel us to think hard about the deepest notions of what it means to be a human person. Kaufman brilliantly explores the boundaries of memory, the mind and personal identity. In the end, however, we see that the human person is more stable and resilient than we may have first surmised. It appears as if there is a human nature and that the self persists through time. What we see in Kaufman's films turns out to be a confirmation of the view of the person found in traditional theistic metaphysics.[15]

What Would Have Been and What Could Be

Counterfactuals in *It's a Wonderful Life* and *Run Lola Run*

JAMES S. SPIEGEL

• •

What if? We have all used this expression in some context or another: What if Babe Ruth had never been sold to the Yankees? What if JFK hadn't been shot? What if my kids grow up to be hoodlums? And we have all made assertions based on the fictional conditions entertained in such questions: "The Yankees would not have become a baseball dynasty." "The sixties would have been a more peaceful decade." "I would feel like a failure in life." Such "what if" questions (and the answers we offer) are called *counterfactuals*, as they regard states of affairs that are merely possible and contrary to actual fact. Despite their hypothetical nature, we find counterfactuals deeply interesting. Who is not stimulated by considering how twentieth-century history might have looked if the Treaty of Versailles had been more satisfactory to the Germans or if the South had won the U.S. Civil War?[1] But for most of us, the most interesting counterfactuals are those that concern our own personal lives. I consider how my life might have turned out if I had had a different mate. And I wonder how things would go for me if I had taught at a different school.

In recent years, a number of films have entertained just these sorts of counterfactuals in their plots. Most of these (e.g., *Frequency, Groundhog Day, Sliding Doors* and *Twice Upon a Yesterday*) have taken the form of comedies or light melodramas. The "what ifs" posed in the plotlines are mere vehicles for dramatizing human relationships or creating comic setups. Here I will discuss two films whose uses of counterfactuals not only raise substantive philosophical questions, but also posit answers to these questions. These two films, *It's a*

Wonderful Life and *Run Lola Run,* come from very different cultures and eras in filmmaking, and the way they treat the subject of counterfactuals reveals some differences in worldview.

What Would Have Been in Bedford Falls

The story of *It's a Wonderful Life* centers on George Bailey who lives in the humble community of Bedford Falls. George has aspirations to travel broadly and experience the world. "I want to do something big and something important," he says. But the need to run his family's building and loan keeps him in his home town. The Bailey Brothers' Building and Loan is upstanding and faithful to the community, in contrast to the avaricious town banker, Henry Potter, who is (in George's words) "the richest and meanest man in the county." Things take a dire turn when George's bumbling uncle Billy misplaces $8,000, putting the already struggling loan office in deep jeopardy. When Potter learns of this, he accuses George of misappropriating funds and has a warrant issued for his arrest.

Seeing no way out, George contemplates suicide. At this point George encounters his guardian angel—Clarence, "Angel, Second Class." George rebukes Clarence for interfering, saying "it'd been better if I'd never been born at all." Undeterred, Clarence proceeds to show George just what things *would have been like* had he never been born. George is then transported to an alternative world, where he learns what it would have been like in Bedford Falls had he never existed. In this world, his brother Harry dies young, since George is not there to save him from drowning. The pharmacist for whom he worked as a boy has become a panhandler, since George is not there to prevent his accidental poisoning of a customer (a tragedy that leads to the pharmacist's depression and chronic unemployment). His wife, Mary Hatch, never marries and, of course, never gives birth to their four children.

George's absence has even broader implications. Main Street is now chock full of casinos, strip clubs and other seedy businesses. The building and loan is dissolved, leaving Bedford Falls to Potter's control. In fact, Bedford Falls has become Pottersville, and the mean spirit of its namesake has infected everyone. George's kindhearted, jovial friends are now malicious and rude. After glimpsing Bedford Falls in this counterfactual situation, George is finally returned to the actual world. Naturally, he rejoices to be back among his friends and family, and his joy is multiplied when he learns that the community has pitched in to cover the debt created by Uncle Billy's blunder. So Potter's plan fails. Good triumphs over evil. And George (with the audience) is reminded that his is, indeed, a wonderful life.

What Could Be for Lola and Manni

The frenetic atmosphere of Tom Tykwer's *Run Lola Run* is a sharp contrast to the tranquility of *It's a Wonderful Life*. Unlike the latter, *Run Lola Run* is in color, enhanced with special effects and animated sequences, and it features a pulse-pounding techno-music soundtrack. The two films also differ fundamentally in their approach to the counterfactual scenarios they depict. Rather than considering just one account of *what would have been* in the past, *Run Lola Run* presents us with three different versions of *what could be* in the future. Interestingly, the plot of this film also is launched by misplaced cash. The neon-redheaded Lola receives a phone call from her panicked boyfriend, Manni. After a major drug deal, he has lost 100,000 deutsche marks while riding the subway to deliver the money to his boss. They are to meet in just twenty minutes, and if Manni doesn't have the money, he's a dead man. Lola tells him, "I'll get the money somehow," and hangs up the phone. She stands wide-eyed for a few moments contemplating her options. Finally, she decides to seek help from her father, a bank executive. Lola begins her race against time, exploding out of her apartment and down the stairs. Here is where the three scenarios diverge.

In the first scenario, Lola sprints to her father's bank and bursts into his office to find him deep in conversation with his mistress, who, he has just learned, is pregnant. Oblivious to all of this, Lola begs him for 100,000 marks, but he demurs, ushering her out of the bank and declaring that he intends to run away with his mistress. Though shaken by this revelation, Lola is no less determined to save her boyfriend. She sprints to their rendezvous point only to find that Manni has begun to hold up a grocery store. Lola joins him. They collect the loot and then run out of the store. But they soon meet an ensemble of policemen, guns pulled and aimed. In despair, Manni throws the bag of money into the air, prompting one of the cops to fire his gun accidentally. The bullet hits Lola, and she drops to the pavement. Dying, she murmurs, "I don't want to leave. Stop." That's when the curtain closes on the first scenario.

The entire narrative is then rewound. Suddenly, Lola is back in her apartment, pondering Manni's frantic appeal, and she's off to the races again. The second scenario features small permutations that bring about radically different outcomes. This time a boy on the stairs trips Lola, slowing her progress. She doesn't make it to her father's office in time to interrupt his conversation with his mistress. Consequently, the woman has time to inform him that he is not the father of the baby she is carrying. He is crushed by the news, and when Lola bursts in, she finds them quarreling. When Lola appeals to him for money, her father becomes irate, slaps her and throws her out. In her desperation and anger, Lola takes the gun from the bank security guard and robs the bank for the 100,000 marks. She makes a lucky escape when the cops arrive and assume she's an innocent bystander. But luck runs out for her and Manni when they rendezvous near the grocery store. She gets there in time to prevent him from holding up the store, but as he turns to walk toward her he is hit by a speeding ambulance. Now it is Manni lying bloodied on the pavement. As he's fading, he says, "No." The story rewinds for one last round of possibilities.

In the third scenario, Lola makes for the stairway and is startled by a barking dog. She quickens her pace, and the ramifications are significant. In the first two scenarios, a sprinting Lola distracts a driver, who then collides with another car. The accident keeps the man from making an appointment—with Lola's father. But in the final scenario she actually runs into the man's car, causing him to stop and thus preventing his collision with the other vehicle. This means that the man can make the appointment. But this also means that Lola's father is called out of his office before she arrives. So Lola doesn't learn of the affair, and her father doesn't learn of his mistress's pregnancy. Moreover, Lola must look elsewhere for help. So she utters a frantic prayer and soon afterward she looks up to see what appears to be God's answer: a casino. She purchases some chips and plays two rounds on the roulette wheel, both winners, yielding a total of 100,000 marks. Meanwhile, through a series of events ultimately connected with Lola's choices (and some good luck), Manni accosts the homeless man who happened to pick up the lost cash on the subway car. Manni gets his money back and returns it to his boss just in the nick of time. So when he meets Lola moments later, their troubles are over, and the two of them are on easy street, prepared to live happily ever after.

The Basics of Counterfactual Conditionals

Before mining these films for their philosophical content, a quick primer on counterfactuals is in order. Counterfactual conditionals, like all conditional statements, have two basic components: an antecedent and a consequent. Here is an example:

> conditional statement: *If the Yankees acquire Babe Ruth, they will win the World Series.*
> antecedent: *The Yankees acquire Babe Ruth.*
> consequent: *They will win the World Series.*

What makes *counterfactual* conditionals especially interesting from a philosophical standpoint is that the antecedent is always false, as in these examples:

> counterfactual conditional: *If the Yankees had never acquired Babe Ruth, then they would not have won a World Series in the twentieth century.*
>
> antecedent: *The Yankees never acquired Babe Ruth.*
>
> counterfactual conditional: *If George Bailey had never lived, then Harry Bailey would have died young.*
>
> antecedent: *George Bailey never lived.*

From a grammatical standpoint, these statements are in the *subjunctive* mood, as opposed to the *indicative* mood. That is, they refer to what *would be* the case given certain nonactual conditions, as opposed to what in fact *is* the case. But there arises a significant philosophical question: in what sense, if any, can counterfactual conditionals be true? Normally we think of truth in terms of correspondence to reality. An assertion is true if and only if the state of affairs it describes corresponds to the way the world actually is.[2] The statement "Mary is a soprano" is true only if Mary's vocal range is sufficiently high to qualify her as a soprano. But counterfactuals do not refer to the actual world, so it seems they cannot be true (or false) in the usual sense of the term. This assessment, of course, is counterintuitive, as we all routinely use counterfactuals to affirm and deny certain things.

To complicate matters, from a strictly logical standpoint all counterfactuals are true. Logic is the study of how to distinguish between good and bad inferences. An inference is essentially an if-then statement, where one statement is claimed to follow from another. And an inference is said to be *valid* if it is impossible for the antecedent to be true and the consequent false. For instance, "If Socrates is a man and all men are mortal, then Socrates is mortal" and "If this figure is a triangle, then this figure is three-sided."

Notice that in each of these propositions the truth of the antecedent guarantees the truth of the consequent. Thus, they must be valid inferences. That is, in each case the conditional as a whole is *true*. Now this includes instances in which the antecedent is contrary to actual fact, as in "If Dr. Doolittle is a man, then Dr. Doolittle is mortal" and "If George Bailey had never lived, then Harry Bailey would have died young."

By definition, counterfactual conditionals have false antecedents. And since an inference is valid just in case it cannot contain a true antecedent and a false consequent, it follows that counterfactual conditionals are always true. This, too, might seem counterintuitive, but our ordinary speech often reveals that we affirm this fact about "truth-functional" logic. For example, someone might proclaim, "If Hillary wins the election, then I'm a monkey's uncle" in order to suggest that there is no way that Hillary can win the election. The absurdity of the consequent is intended to show that the antecedent is impossible. For, again, conditional statements with false antecedents are always true.

Although in a broadly logical sense all counterfactual conditionals are true, there is a more narrow sense in which we ordinarily distinguish reasonable from unreasonable counterfactuals. So we might say that the statement "If the Yankees had never acquired Babe Ruth, then they would not have won more than twenty World Series titles in the twentieth century" is more likely to be true than "If JFK had not been elected president, then he would have become manager of the Boston Red Sox." But the question that begs to be answered is this: since the antecedent in each case is false, by virtue of what factors is one conditional more or less likely to be true?

This problem may be addressed by noting two significant assumptions made by counterfactual conditionals.[3] First, counterfactuals make circumstantial assumptions. They assume that a number of different relevant conditions would hold which are crucial for the events described in the consequent to follow from the state of affairs described in the antecedent. So we may ask, just what conditions would need to obtain in order for George Bailey's absence to result in Bedford Falls' moral degeneration? Director Frank Capra's counterfactual history assumes that no other morally courageous individuals would have stepped forward to arrest the community's moral slide. Also, it presupposes that persons in charge of key institutions were morally weak enough to allow the degeneration to occur. In short, the film's counterfactual scenario assumes that George Bailey was an exceptional person in Bedford Falls by having sufficiently strong moral fiber to stand up to Potter's corrupting influence. But this assumption is dubious, given everything we know about the community, especially the great generosity of the people as demonstrated by the story's climax. While every town has its share of swindlers and greedy folk, it is implausible to suggest that one such person (or even a few) could completely redirect the community's moral course within a single generation. In *It's a Wonderful Life*, then, Capra takes fictional license to make a point, namely, that an individual life is profoundly significant.

Similarly, each of the three counterfactual scenarios in *Run Lola Run* makes a number of circumstantial assumptions. The first scenario makes assumptions about how all of the people at the grocery store would respond to Manni's holdup. It also critically assumes that the policeman would respond to Manni's throwing the bag into the air by inadvertently pulling the trigger of his gun. The second scenario makes assumptions regarding how the people at the bank would respond to Lola's holdup and how the policemen would respond when they see her exit the bank with loot in hand. The third scenario makes a number of assumptions about how the casino employees would respond to Lola's wagering choices. It also makes assumptions about how the homeless man would respond when Manni confronts him. And the first two scenarios make assumptions about how Lola's father would respond to various elements of the conversations with his mistress and his daughter. Given the countless free choices involved in any single scenario, we can conclude that Tykwer has selected three narratives within a virtually infinite set of possible narratives. If at the moment of decision a person may make any one choice among an enormous variety of choices—and the sequence of events set up by Lola and Manni's problem presents just a few of these—then the possibilities increase exponentially at each critical juncture (e.g., Lola's interaction with her father and his mistress, her joining Manni at the grocery store, her noticing the casino, etc.). Given certain constraining conditions pertaining to the freedom of individual choice, the possibilities may be restricted somewhat. Even so, the scenarios that might unfold once Lola hangs up the phone and begins her dash down the stairs appear to be incalculable.

Counterfactuals, Causality and Human Freedom

The narratives presented by Capra and Tykwer also illustrate how counterfactuals make a further assumption, one regarding the nature of causality. Each scenario traced in these films is highly specified, showing us how various decisions and events at early stages of the story bring about particular later situations and events. No person or circumstance is isolated, but each is causally conditioned in diverse ways. The slightest difference of timing of a personal encounter, as Tykwer shows us, might lead to entirely different fates for those involved. And the absence of one individual within a community, suggests Capra, may lead to its having a radically different historical course.

But why must this be the case? Why assume that changing some single choice or event must alter the course of history or even the slightest detail of a single life? The answer regards a basic, commonsense intuition that all of us share. Specifically, we assume that causal relationships in the world are *lawlike*. That is, they are universal (they apply in all cases) and necessary (they cannot be otherwise). This intuition, which is as old as philosophy itself, has been expressed in diverse ways, both positively and negatively. Here are examples of each, respectively:

1. There is an explanation for any being or positive fact in the world.[4]
2. Something cannot come to be purely and simply from nothing.[5]

The essential idea here is that events must have causes. When an event occurs, we can be confident that there is some causal explanation as to why it occurred, even if we are unable to discover the cause or in any way account for it. This is sometimes called the *law of causality*.[6]

Notice that the very concept of "would be" or "would have been" presupposes such causal necessity. To assert "If George Bailey had never lived, then Harry Bailey would have died young" is to declare that George's absence (given certain other circumstances, as noted above) *guarantees* that Harry dies young. The conditional indicates necessity, not probability, at least in Capra's mind. Similarly, Capra (or at least Clarence) is telling us that the good will and strong work ethic of George Bailey was a key causal component in keeping Bedford Falls morally upright and that without his presence it was a *certainty* that the community would become a den of iniquity. Without George's influence, good institutions (such as Martini's restaurant, the building and loan, and Bailey Park) would go bad or disappear altogether. Also, individual lives would take sad or tragic turns. Mr. Gower would go to prison and become a homeless alcoholic on his release. George's flirtatious friend Violet Bick would become a prostitute. And George's uncle Billy would go insane when his efforts to run the building and loan fail.

The point here is that Capra's narrative assumes that given George's ab-

sence *there is but one possible history of Bedford Falls*—the one that Clarence
shows George. Now there is a controversial assumption here regarding human
freedom. It is that given certain preconditions, a person will necessarily choose
certain courses of action. Or, put another way, the law of causality applies to
human choices just as much as it applies to other events in the world. This
view is known as *determinism*, and it comes in two forms.

Hard determinists take such universal causation to imply that human beings
are not genuinely free (and therefore not really morally responsible).[7] On the
other hand, *soft determinists*, also known as *compatibilists*, believe that human
beings are nonetheless free and responsible, despite their being subject just as
fully to the law of causality.[8] Compatibilists typically say that a person's choice
is itself determined and that what determines a person's choice in any particular instance are factors internal to the person's psychology, such as her interests, desires, motives and moral character. And they define freedom as the
ability to choose or act *according to* such factors. Whereas if a person is constrained by external forces such that she cannot do what she wants, then she
is not free.

In telling us that there is just one way things would have gone without
George Bailey, Capra's perspective appears to be deterministic. But the story
also seems to assume that morality is not an illusion, that people like George
really are good and that greedy swindlers like Henry Potter really are wicked.
Even though all of the characters necessarily make certain choices given certain preconditions, both external and internal to their own minds, they are all
responsible for what they do. If this is Capra's view of the matter, then it appears that *It's a Wonderful Life* presents us with a compatibilist view of human
freedom.

Run Lola Run, on the other hand, does not seem to take a deterministic
view. Presumably, the main point in having three different narratives is to suggest that the events they depict are all possible. Perhaps Tykwer believes this
is because the causal relations between people and objects are not so strict.[9] For
example, the freedom of the characters might be such that their wills are not
entirely determined by the preconditions of their choice. If so, then the law of
causality does not entirely apply to their free choices. They enjoy what is called
the *power of contrary choice*. That is, when they freely choose *X* it is always possible that they might have chosen *not-X* instead. This view, known as *libertar-
ianism*,[10] is exemplified in *Run Lola Run* early in each scenario. In one sce-

nario, the boy on the stairs sticks his leg out to trip Lola, while in the others he does not. Presumably, there were no varying preconditions that guaranteed his choosing (or not) to trip Lola. So why did he choose to do so in the one case and not in the others? According to the libertarian, the only reasonable answer here is that nothing determined the boy's choice but his own will. While influencing factors (desires, motives, etc.) are involved in any choice, they do not combine to *ensure* any particular choice.

But Tykwer's narrative is far from being anarchical in its assumptions about causality and human choice. He suggests that we are all subject to subtle causal nuances that are entirely beyond our control. For instance, through a series of Polaroid snapshots, Tykwer shows a woman who later becomes a kidnapper or a faithful Catholic—depending on whether she is bumped or merely brushed by Lola. To Tykwer, it seems, different circumstances may alter one's choices. In nearly every case, the film's characters do not make different choices when they face precisely the same situation for a second time. The lone exception is the boy who is a character in one of the film's animated sequences and is, in this way, figuratively removed from the world of real human beings and their choices. Could it be that Tykwer's point here is that such libertarian freedom really is make-believe, like the world of cartoons, where the law of causality does not apply as it does in the real world?[11]

The Counterfactual Bedford Falls and Divine Knowledge

Now let's address a critical question posed earlier in this essay: how, if at all, can counterfactuals be true (beyond the trivial logical sense of truth, where all conditionals with false antecedents must be true)? According to the above line of thought, counterfactuals are true or false depending on whether the conditions described (and assumed) in the antecedents are such that the law of causality *would dictate* that their consequents come to pass. This seems to be the approach taken by Capra (and Clarence) in *It's a Wonderful Life*, where the message is that without George the town would have become corrupt. This seems evident in the fact that Capra and Clarence give us just one scenario of life without George. The causal nexus in Bedford Falls is such that, given George's absence (among other circumstances), his brother *must* die young, the building and loan *must* go out of business, Potter *must* assume complete control of Bedford Falls, and the town *must* morally degenerate. Thus, the fundamental counterfactual assertion concerning George's life is true.

But must we take this deterministic approach to counterfactuals, particularly given the worldview expressed in this film? Surely it is an approach that would be favored by many naturalists—those who affirm that only the physical world exists and that there are no supernatural beings. This is because most naturalists see the world in essentially mechanistic terms. According to them, everything that happens, including human volition, is simply the result of matter moving in space. But why should Capra or Clarence see things this way, especially considering their apparent theism?[12] Why assume that our world, though subject to the law of causality, could not be supernaturally redirected in various ways?

Indeed, Clarence's own intervention is already a case of supernatural redirection. But, to press the point, in the absence of George Bailey, couldn't God alter circumstances in Bedford Falls such that evil does not triumph? Couldn't God have arranged for someone else to save the drowning Harry Bailey and thus enable him to take over the building and loan? And couldn't God have used some other means to thwart Potter's malicious plot to rule Bedford Falls? Surely an omnipotent God could have intervened to save the town in countless ways. So, it seems, Capra's (or Clarence's) counterfactual scenario is somewhat at odds with a theistic view of providence, which affirms that God can and does intervene in the world to achieve certain ends. And to suggest that Bedford Falls would have been this way or that without George Bailey makes tenuous assumptions about God's providential choices, namely those regarding what God would or would not do given certain counterfactual conditions.

Some theists who favor a libertarian view of freedom would not endorse this approach. They worry that such meticulous providential manipulation precludes human responsibility. Yet they would nonetheless want to affirm God's complete control over the history of Bedford Falls—and the whole universe, for that matter. An alternative view, known as Molinism,[13] was devised to reconcile a high view of providence with a libertarian conception of freedom. On this view, prior to creating the world God considered all of the possible worlds he could create. Within these worlds, God knew what every free creature *would* do under any particular circumstances. Among these innumerable possible worlds, God chose to create that world in which the free choices of his creatures would best bring about his aims. Notice that this special divine knowledge of the counterfactuals of freedom falls somewhere between God's knowledge of the actual world and his knowledge of all possible worlds. Thus, it is called divine *middle knowledge*. The advantage of this doctrine is that, as Molinist philosopher William Lane Craig puts it, "by creating the appropriate situations, [God can] bring it about that creatures will achieve his ends and purposes and that they will do so *freely*."[14]

So how, according to Molinism, can counterfactuals be true? By virtue of the fact that for any set of circumstances in which free creatures find themselves there is some way that they *would* behave. God is perfectly aware of all such counterfactuals, and this supplies the logical and epistemological bases on which God elects to create the world he does. Clarence, a Molinist Capra might claim, simply has access to that aspect of divine middle knowledge. He knows how all of the citizens of Bedford Falls would choose, given the absence of George Bailey. This explains both how Clarence can show this counterfactual scenario to George and, given its dismal contents, just why God did not choose to actualize that world. It just did not sufficiently harmonize with the divine aims.

Despite these benefits of a Molinist account of providence, there are major problems plaguing the view. Keep in mind that the chief aim of the doctrine is to reconcile a high view of providence with the libertarian view of human freedom. However, in divine middle knowledge God knows what any free being—such as you, me or George Bailey's uncle Billy—*would* choose in any set of circumstances. But the very meaning of the term *would* implies the sort of necessity that the libertarian rejects. Essentially, *would* equals *if* plus *must*. So if God knows that Billy *would* choose to run the building and loan in George's absence, then *if* George never existed it *must* be the case that Billy makes this choice. So Billy does not have the power of contrary choice if God has middle knowledge. And this means that Molinism is inconsistent with libertarian free will.[15]

Molinists deny this implication, insisting that there is no such necessity in the choices of free creatures. The world envisioned in God's middle knowledge is, after all, a hypothetical one and the choices of the free beings involved in those possible worlds are indeterminate until they are actually made. But this introduces a different problem. If there is no determinate fact of the matter regarding Uncle Billy's choice, then just what is the object of God's knowledge? Assuming that truth is correspondence to reality, how can it be *true* that Billy would choose to run the building and loan in George's absence? It seems that God cannot have middle knowledge of such counterfactuals precisely because they have no truth value. Knowledge of any kind must be grounded in some state of affairs. But, by the Molinists' own admission, middle knowledge has no determinate object and so lacks such grounding.[16]

Lola, God and James Dean

Now where is the theistic libertarian to turn if Molinism is an unsatisfactory way of accounting for the truth value of the counterfactuals of freedom? One option is to say that such counterfactuals have no truth value, due to the nature of human freedom. Moreover, for this reason counterfactuals are in principle unknowable. So, looking at Lola's situation at the time of her departure from her apartment, we might ask, which scenario *will* ultimately unfold? To this many would reply, "God only knows." But on the view under consideration, even this isn't true. God does *not* know precisely what will happen because the choices of free (in the libertarian sense) people are not perfectly predictable. William Hasker, a Christian philosopher who takes such an approach, maintains that there is an "inconsistency between infallible divine foreknowledge and free will for human beings."[17] And philosopher Richard Swinburne says, "If our universe is created by God and the human beings in it have free will, then the limitation that God cannot know incorrigibly how those humans will act will be a further limitation which results from his own choice to create human beings with free will."[18]

While this appears to contradict the Christian understanding of divine omniscience, these philosophers point out that they do not reject the doctrine but merely qualify its meaning. God knows everything *that can be known.* The counterfactuals of freedom are just not the sorts of things that can be known. God has exhaustive knowledge of other facts aside from future human choices, and this enables him to know much of the future. But he can only make well-informed predictions about those things he doesn't infallibly foreknow.

Such *free-will theists,* as they are sometimes called, would strenuously object to the premise of *It's a Wonderful Life,* insofar as it offers just one counterfactual scenario premised on George Bailey's nonexistence. Indeed, the free-will theist would say that there are innumerable scenarios that could have played out, each featuring a unique combination of choices by the people involved. So *Run Lola Run* would be a much more accurate representation of this perspective. As for what Lola will do when she hangs up the phone, there is no *must, will* or *would* regarding her courses of action. Rather, she *might* or *prob-*

ably will run to her father's bank. And she *might* or *probably will not* run into a casino and win 100,000 marks. And so it goes for each step (or stride) along the way in Lola's path. And even the smallest decision or hesitation before deciding can mean the difference between life and death.

While the action of *Run Lola Run* is especially dramatic and intense, Tykwer intends to make a point that applies to all of our lives, however mundane our daily affairs might be. I might (or might not) decide to have dessert after dinner tonight. I might (or might not) go to bed before 11:00 p.m. I might (or might not) climb right out of bed when my alarm clock goes off in the morning. Some of these decisions might make little to no difference regarding my future. But others might have the sorts of ramifications illustrated in *Run Lola Run*. If I get up at 6:30 a.m. as opposed to 6:35 a.m., this might mean the difference between my driving safely to work or having a fatal car wreck—whether fatal for myself or others.

Speaking of fatal car wrecks, consider this historical case in point. I live in Fairmount, Indiana, which happens to be the hometown of the celebrated actor James Dean. After concluding work on his last film, *Giant*, the young star left Hollywood for Salinas, California, where he was to enter an auto race in his newly purchased Porsche Spyder. Along the way, Dean and his passenger, Rolf Wutherich, stopped to refuel. Dean also bought a soda and some apples, which turned out to be his last meal. After some brief conversation, they jumped back into the car. A little while later they saw a Ford sedan coming the opposite way, which began to turn left across the divided highway. "He'll see us," Dean told Wutherich. But the other vehicle lurched out in front of them, and Dean's Porsche broadsided it at about 70 miles per hour. Not wearing a seatbelt, Dean was killed instantly, while Wutherich was thrown forward about one hundred feet, badly injured but alive.

It is interesting, even eerie, to note how so many of the details surrounding the circumstances of Dean's death were "just right" for the accident to occur. The Porsche had an especially low profile and, therefore, low visibility, particularly at dusk when the accident occurred. Dean and Wutherich stopped for gas and lingered just long enough for the collision to occur. The driver of the other car, Donald Turnupseed, arrived at the intersection at just the right time—a few seconds earlier or later, and Dean would have lived. Of course, there were hundreds, perhaps thousands of little decisions made by Dean, Wutherich, Turnupseed and many others that culminated in this tragic event.

And, as intimated in *Run Lola Run,* there seem to be thousands of alternative directions that things might have gone.

So it is with all of us, as we make multiple decisions per minute for most of our conscious lives. But now consider the God of free-will theism, who does not know future human choices nor, by implication, their consequences. If world history is essentially the sum of human choices and their consequences, then this prompts the following question: how much of our future does God know? Could he have known the fate of James Dean long in advance, decided as it was by so many free choices? Now extend this across generations, even many centuries, inclusive of the billions of procreative events involved—each one of which would have resulted in an entirely different human being (or none at all) with just a variation of a few minutes (or even seconds). So the predictability of any events in the long-term future of human history vanishes even for God, given the assumptions of free-will theism.[19]

The Compatibilist Alternative

So where does this leave us? As we have seen, Molinism and free-will theism face serious difficulties. But the root of the problems plaguing each of these views is the same: that is, the assumption of a libertarian conception of human freedom. A compatibilist perspective offers much more promise in dealing with the issues we have discussed. It allows us to affirm the traditional Christian high view of providence, which states that God's control over the world is complete. On this view, history is truly divine narrative, not the mere result of human choices. God does use human free choices to accomplish his will, but he is the ultimate author of history. And his sovereignty is perfectly compatible with human freedom and moral responsibility, however difficult this might be for us to comprehend.[20]

From a compatibilist perspective, then, what are we to say about the counterfactuals of freedom as represented in *It's a Wonderful Life* and *Run Lola Run?* A few options are available to us. On the one hand, we might reject the notion that the counterfactuals of freedom can be known, since the world goes as it does ultimately because of God's decrees and he can direct history any way he wants. So to ask what would have happened if *X* had been the case is essentially to pose a question about God's purposes and possible choices. We might grant that there is indeed some truth there regarding the matter, such as whether God would have allowed Potter to ruin Bedford Falls. However, being a matter of private divine counsel, the truth would be inaccessible to us (unless God made it known to us). From a human perspective, given a high view of providence, we can simply say that the counterfactual scenario in *It's a Wonderful Life* is a mere fiction. While God could have made the world envisioned by Clarence in the film, he did not. And since God could have intervened at many different junctures in the George-less world, there is no reason to think that things would have gone the way they did in that scenario. From this perspective, it seems that Capra actually applies some naturalistic or at least deistic assumptions to his ostensibly theistic film. To affirm with confidence that Bedford Falls would have turned out a particular way without George assumes that God would not have intervened to do anything about it. But why should we assume this?

Now consider an alternative compatibilist approach that would enable Capra to save face, metaphysically speaking. We might recognize that the operation of the law of causality is decreed by God and that there are always sufficient reasons for people choosing and acting the way they do. We, therefore, can and properly do appeal to such factors to explain and even predict people's behavior. So based on these considerations we might say that counterfactuals of freedom are true (or false). But this interpretation significantly assumes a lack of special divine intervention. If this is a proper approach, then what we find in *It's a Wonderful Life* appears more faithful to the facts of the human condition than what is presented in *Run Lola Run*. Life in Bedford Falls without George Bailey would have been just one certain way (contingent on the characters involved and God's will). The same is also true in the life of Lola. Either she will rob her father's bank, she will help Manni rob the grocery store, she will win big at the casino, or some other state of affairs will come to pass. But given the characters of all the persons involved, combined with God's providential aims and purposes, there is just one way that things will go down—which, of course, God only knows.

Scripture indicates that God knows all of future human history. The Lord says, "I am God, and there is none like me, declaring the end from the beginning and from ancient times things not yet done" (Isaiah 46:9-10 ESV). If so, then God knows in advance what Lola and Manni will do, and there can be really only one scenario awaiting them. The multiple scenarios really only reflect human ignorance of the future, not its actual indeterminacy. Yet Lola, Manni and the others involved are free and responsible, notwithstanding their days having been written in God's book long before one of them came to pass.

Conclusion

As we have seen, Frank Capra's *It's a Wonderful Life* and Tom Tykwer's *Run Lola Run* invite a variety of philosophical questions through the counterfactual scenarios they present. Some aspects of these films are self-consciously philosophical, of course. Surely it is no coincidence that Lola plays the roulette wheel at the casino or that she dashes through a group of nuns on the sidewalk. Tykwer wants us to consider Lola's journey in light of these symbols of chance and divine purpose. Capra's philosophizing in *It's a Wonderful Life* is much more transparent, as are his views on the issues he raises. With this film he declares, among other things, that life is purposeful, that there are real moral goods and that there are supernatural powers at work behind the scenes of our lives. Yet it is unlikely that either director was thinking about the truth value of counterfactual conditionals, let alone the metaphysics of causality or the possibility of divine middle knowledge. But their films nevertheless invite us to ponder these subjects, and they invite attention to particular views pertaining to each. What they give us are stories that demonstrate well the potency of a simple question—*what if?*

PART THREE

THE MORAL LIFE

Liberation Through Sensuality

Cinematic Moral Vision in an Age of Feeling

DALLAS WILLARD

· ·

My aim is to cast light on the moral vision—the vision of what is good and what is obligatory—that governs many motion pictures produced in the United States these days. I especially have in mind productions such as *Pleasantville*, *The Cider House Rules* and *American Beauty*, and I will give special attention to these three films in what follows. But the *phenomenon* I'm identifying extends far beyond these cases. The basic idea governing these films is now a widespread and deep-seated conviction in the contemporary American soul. It is that *moral rules and rigorous moral order in life, as traditionally understood, are meaningless or pointless at best and really are repressive of the best aspects of human relationships, individuality and creativity.* What would traditionally have been thought of as moral propriety and human goodness is now considered arbitrary and harmful to life—perhaps even vicious (at least in its effects)—largely because *moral rectitude eliminates or represses human feelings*, the true elixir of life.

Pleasantville

Let us start with *Pleasantville* as a fairly simple case. This film is a fantasy. The opening frame of the film contains the written line, "Once upon a time." No claim to realism for its primary subject or content is made. The claim to truth (which it certainly *does* make) emerges at a higher level of "content." But the events recorded, around which the story line develops, are to a great extent not the *kind* of events which occur in real life.

The story line is this: David and Jennifer, two typically cool, contemporary high school students, have a fight in their home over the TV remote control. A station is broadcasting a *"Pleasantville* marathon"—reruns of a black-and-white 1950s sitcom *Pleasantville,* which presents us with a perfect suburb of perfect people. David knows the Pleasantville scenes and events forward and backward, and he is set to watch it for hours. Jennifer, however, wants him out of the house so she can enjoy a tryst with her boyfriend while their mother is away. Brother and sister struggle for the remote. It flies from their hands and shatters against the furniture. What to do now? The doorbell rings and a TV repairman (Don Knotts) appears, asking if they need repairs. (They hadn't called!) He gives them a new remote, and when they use it, David and Jennifer are transported *into Pleasantville.* They become a part of the story, as "Bud" and "Mary Sue," children of George and Betty. They are *stranded* there, and the TV repairman won't let them come back—for now. Life there is all so dreadfully perfect and boring, especially for Mary Sue. The high school basketball team always wins. Nothing burns: the firemen, who only rescue stranded cats, have never seen a fire. It never rains. The pages in all the books are blank. No one knows there is anywhere else but Pleasantville. Nothing ever changes but just repeats over and over, day after day, as might well appear in a fifties sitcom.

After a while Mary Sue breaks away from the routine and takes her clueless boyfriend to lover's lane, where, to his surprise (about everything), they have sex. He comes back in a daze and tells all the basketball team members what it's like. They then take their girls there and do that, and pretty soon things start to take on color. Here a bubblegum bubble is pink. There some girl's tongue and mouth is pink. (She consults a puzzled doctor.) Color begins to show up in odd places. The basketball team begins to lose.

Mr. Johnson, who operates the soda and hamburger place where Bud works, just keeps wiping the counter when Bud is late to fit into the routine as seen on TV. He doesn't know he can break the routine of what he is shown doing in the TV series. Bud tells Mr. Johnson what to do next time, and, later, he finds he *can* break it. He rushes to Bud's house to tell him. There he sees Bud's mom, Betty, and is captivated, while she in turn gazes back at him. An emotional connection sparks into existence.

Mary Sue wants to liberate the people of Pleasantville. Bud cautions her not to do it. They are happy as they are. But Mary Sue says they aren't happy.

(How could anyone be happy wearing tight sweaters and poodle skirts?) They just don't know any better. (She and Bud, by the way, remain in black-and-white all this time.) Anyway, something has been started. A double bed, where a man and a woman can sleep together, shows up in a furniture store window and a crowd comes to stare at it. (There were only twin beds in old films and TV.) Rock music floods in and the young people jive. Kissing in public begins. Mr. Johnson tells Bud he wants to stop making hamburgers. "It never changes," he says, "never gets any better or worse." He wants to paint. Bud brings from the library an art book with nudes and colors to show Mr. Johnson. He starts to paint his whole shop in daring colors and images, including nudes—and, later, a nude Betty!

During a card game, Betty's cards and fingernails become red. She later asks Mary Sue what goes on at lover's lane. The answer is sex, described in detail! Shocked, Betty says, "Father would never do anything like that." Mary Sue replies, "Well, you know, Mom, there are other ways to enjoy yourself . . . without Dad." Betty discovers what Mary Sue means that night in the bathtub. The bathroom wallpaper takes on color, to celestial music, and a tree outside bursts into flame! Bud has to yell "Cat!" to get the firemen moving and then has to show them how to use the hoses to douse the flame.

The mayor and town council are now alarmed. Someone has quit his job at the grocery store just because he didn't want to do work there any more. And now Bud takes his girl to lover's lane. But Mary Sue has discovered the novels of D. H. Lawrence and, pondering the transformations into color, thinks, "Maybe it's not just the sex." (She and Bud are *still* in black-and-white.) Significantly, Bud's girl brings him a red apple and he bites into it. Meanwhile, George comes home from work to no Betty, no supper. Betty has gone to be with Mr. Johnson. A storm breaks over lover's lane and the young lovers, over George, over the town council, and over Betty and Mr. Johnson. It pours rain.

Betty lies to George about where she's been and refuses to do what he asks any longer. Some boys on the street harass her because she is now in full color. Bud strikes one of the boys and blood flows. Then *he* becomes colored. Anger does it this time. It's *not* just sex, after all. It's what you feel deep inside that gives life its color. Mobs gather. They stone Mr. Johnson's shop and break up his window and wall paintings. They riot and burn books. The town council writes rules governing what can be done with color and music and writing. Bud and Mr. Johnson paint an exterior wall with all the forbidden colors and images. They are brought before the town council. "What went wrong?" George asks Bud, as Bud sits in jail. "Nothing went wrong," Bud replies. "People change." (Of course no one changes in the old sitcom—or in life that is *really* no more than a sitcom or in life that runs like one.)

The town gathers at the council meeting, and the mayor charges Mr. Johnson and Bud. Mr. Johnson pleads, but Bud stands up and says: "You don't have a right to do this!" He explains that what brings out color is what is inside you: silly, sexy, dangerous—but all better than merely *pleasant*. To demonstrate, he gets George to look at Betty and feel deeply his longing for her and love for her as she now is in color. George gets colored! The mayor then tells Bud to stop it. But Bud says, "You can't stop something that's inside of you." He will prove it is in the mayor, too. He asks him what he would like to do to Bud right now. He taunts the mayor by telling him that if this keeps up *everything* will change. Men may even start staying home to take care of the house while women go to work. The mayor explodes in exasperation and disgust and *color!*

The whole town is now in permanent color. Bud takes the magical remote and travels back to his real life. He finds his mom weeping over the mess of her life as she grows older. She's forty. She laments, "I had the right house. I had the right car." Bud says, "There is no right house. There is no right car." But she continues, "It's not supposed to be like this." More persuasively now, Bud says, "It's not supposed to be anything." In his newfound wisdom, *any* way is fine.

So what is the moral vision that forms the content of this film as a work of art? It is that following one's strong feelings makes life unpredictable and good. Rules, including moral rules, and regularity (especially for the sake of being pleasant) make life stale, dead, boring—in short, not worth living. If you need to break rules of morality, which here are depicted entirely as rules of propriety or niceness, then it is altogether worthwhile to have intense feelings and the joy and unpredictability that comes with them. To subvert the feelings— the implication being that everyone really does have deep and intense feelings but that many repress them—is to make life not worth living. For it is to wind up doing what you have no real interest in doing, to do things just because they are supposed to be done. The good life is a life lived for deep and strong feelings, and what one ought to do—what the good person does—is to live for feelings and to help others do the same. Some ideal of authentic human existence (nonhypocrisy) no doubt lies in the background, but the film is not a serious defense of anything. It simply presents a certain vision of good and evil.

American Beauty

With *American Beauty* we are back in the suburbs, but this time a very contemporary version, where Lester Burnham and his wife, Carolyn, live with their teenage daughter, Jane. They are a severely dysfunctional family: Carolyn is desperately trying to keep things looking nice, Lester is on the verge of disintegration, and Jane is totally disgusted with her father for his lascivious obsession with her sexy friend, Angela. The story is narrated by Lester, who is already dead when he begins to narrate. He starts by saying, "In less than a year I'll be dead. . . . And in a way, I'm dead already." He talks about Carolyn, who "used to be happy" but now just tries to make everything in the yard and house pretty (where everything matches) and who is (unsuccessfully) in the real-estate business. Jane thinks her dad is a gigantic loser. And he agrees: "I have lost something. I'm not exactly sure what it is, but I know I didn't always feel this . . . sedated."

Ricky Fitts, a schoolmate of Jane and Angela, lives next door. Ricky has had some sort mental episode that got him hospitalized, and Angela fears and dislikes him. Jane does, too, initially, because he is always videotaping things, including her and Lester, through the windows of their home next door. Ricky also smokes marijuana and makes a lot of money selling it. Soon Lester is one of his customers. Ricky's father, the "Colonel," is a retired officer who verbally and physically abuses Ricky; he is determined to teach him to follow rules of behavior and to be responsible, but he leaves Ricky with no real privacy. The Colonel is sure society is going to hell, and he despises the homosexual couple, Jim and Jim, who have moved in next door and who try to be friendly. Ricky's mom walks about in a quasicatatonic state, obsessively keeping things neat.

Lester's *reawakening to life* begins when he and Carolyn attend a basketball game where Jane and Angela are among the cheerleaders. Lester stares lasciviously and begins undressing Angela in his mind. As he opens her blouse a flood of lush, red rose petals spill out ("American Beauty" rose petals, of course). Later, when he kisses her (still in his imagination) a rose petal is on his tongue. Floods of rose petals show up in other (imaginary) settings with Angela. They symbolize the lush, sensual beauty that is associated with sexual enjoyment or desire and that pervades the entire film. Lester is inspired to get into better physical shape and to return to the rock music and cars that he loved as a youth. ("I feel like I've been in a coma for about twenty years, and I'm just now waking up.")

Lester writes for a monthly media magazine. Brad, the efficiency expert at Lester's work, is having Lester laid off from the company, but Lester manages to blackmail him into a severance package of one year's salary, with benefits. Lester is seen next flipping burgers at a fast-food place, something he did when he was young (in order to buy an eight-track tape player). He says he wants a job that involves "the least possible amount of responsibility." This leaves him free to work on his physique and other revitalizations—and to inch toward Angela, who is now (really) coming on to him. Angela talks to Jane as if she has had a lot of sex with a lot of people (although she has had none) and is really turned on by Lester. Jane is disgusted but still thinks Angela has really *got it* (whatever "it" is), while she herself is a nothing.

Usually Jane rides home from school in Angela's car. But one day Ricky asks for a ride and Angela scornfully rejects him. Jane, sympathetically, walks home with him and they become close. They go to his house and Ricky opens his father's locked cabinet of war memorabilia. He shows Jane a collector's item: a fine china platter with a swastika on the back. The two are filled with loathing. Ricky shows her some film of a plastic grocery bag lifting and swirling in the wind for fifteen minutes. It is, he says, "the most beautiful thing I've ever filmed." "Sometimes," he says, "there's so much beauty in the world I feel like I can't take it . . . and my heart is just going to cave in." Jane looks deeply at him, takes his hand and kisses him.

Meanwhile, Carolyn has hooked up with the most successful real-estate man in the area, Buddy "The King" Kane. She wants his secrets of success, and he tells her: "In order to be successful one must project an image of success at all times." They hit the motel for riotous sex.

Later, Carolyn and Buddy stop by the fast-food place where Lester is working—although Carolyn believes he is still at his previous job—and she orders over the drive-thru speakers. Lester recognizes her voice and moves to the window to serve them. Carolyn and Buddy realize they are found out. They drive back to the motel and he gets out of the car and leaves. They understand that to be involved in a divorce would be contrary to projecting an image of success at all times. Buddy leaves and Carolyn sobs, then screams with uncontrollable rage at Lester and at her situation.

Meanwhile, the Colonel has been looking at Ricky's videos of Lester exercising and watching Ricky and Lester do drug deals. He decides that they are homosexually engaged. (Lester has also been jogging with Jim and Jim on their daily runs.) The Colonel throws Ricky out of the house, and Ricky implores Jane to go with him to New York where they can live together and run a drug business. (He has saved up forty thousand dollars.) She agrees, and Angela, who is in Jane's room talking about having sex with Lester, ridicules them. Ricky tells her she is unattractive, boring and totally ordinary—the very worst thing to be, in Angela's mind. She leaves the room and sits on the stairs weeping.

Meanwhile, Lester has been in the garage exercising, and the Colonel has walked over, robotlike, in the rain. Lester lets him in and the Colonel, assuming Lester is homosexual, kisses him on the mouth. Lester says, "I'm sorry, you got the wrong idea." The Colonel turns and woodenly walks off into the rain. Lester goes into the house and finds Angela weeping. She says, "You don't think I'm ordinary?" Lester replies, "You couldn't be ordinary if you tried." "Thank you," she whispers, "I don't think there's anything worse than being ordinary." He begins to undress her on the couch when she, obviously experiencing some uncertainty, explains, "This is my first time." Lester stops. She urges him to go on with it, but now he won't. They talk for a while, and she goes to the bathroom. Lester is feeling great. He sits at the dining table and contemplates a happy picture of himself and Carolyn and Jane when Jane was small. A pistol appears at the back of Lester's head, the murderer fires, and his blood splatters on the kitchen wall.

The screen returns to the white plastic shopping bag floating about. Lester's voiceover is accompanied by an overhead view of the city. He says one just has to relax and stop trying to hold onto things. In his newfound wisdom, he says, "I can't feel anything but gratitude for every single moment of my stupid little life."

The moral vision (of what is good and what people ought to do) conveyed in *American Beauty* has some striking similarities to the vision communicated in *Pleasantville*. In both cases it is sex—*illicit* sex, of course—and sexual desire and imagination that start the emotional thaw or breakthrough to a "better life." Whether homosexual or heterosexual, sex is presented as a source, if not *the* source, of genuine goodness in life, and its repression by rules and a framework of propriety is wrong, even deadly. Its repression fills you full of pain and

meanness. The relationships in the film are pervaded with sex, though—
except for the relationship between Jim and Jim, whom we don't really get to
know—they are all bleak and hopeless.

The lush beauty of the American Beauty rose is a bitter illusion, one that
must be supplemented by the "beauty" of the aimless and bland plastic bag and
also of death, as seen by Ricky, and the goodness of the "stupid little life" seen
by Lester after his death. But a life of stifled desire or passion under the sup-
pression of rules that dictate "ordinary" life—a respectable life where people
play "Bali Hai" as background music for hellacious family dinners—is worse
than anything. Angela, the "American beauty," can't stand the thought of being ordinary and so makes up an imaginary life of riotous sexual action. Lester,
discussing his job description with Brad, the efficiency expert, says he just
wants "a life that doesn't so closely resemble hell." The two most rigidly
"moral" and "proper" people in the film wind up doing the worst things: Carolyn, who tries desperately to keep things nice for those around her even
though she is dead and starving inside, cheats on her husband. The Colonel,
the most wooden and repressively respectable of all, is a closet homosexual, totally brutal to his son and, very likely, his wife. Morality in any traditional
sense of rules and virtues for living well doesn't show up, for the most part—
and certainly does not present itself as something hopeful—in *American
Beauty*. Death is more beautiful than life.

The Cider House Rules

The Cider House Rules differs significantly from the two previous films. In the
first place, the location is not in suburbia, past or present, but in rural Maine in
the 1940s. The story is set first in an orphanage outside a little whistle-stop
town, St. Cloud, and then on an apple farm by the ocean. The family produces
cider there and hence have a "cider house." Second, the feelings that moral rules
confront in this story are, mainly, feelings of compassion and sympathy for suffering human beings. Of course sex is the background, implied by unwanted babies, who become orphans by rejection, and by abortions, as are violated relationships, including violence and murder. But sex itself is not really glorified in
this story. Homer, the central figure, is ceaselessly taunted for his idealism by the
doctor who directs the orphanage, and he has been thoroughly compromised by
the end. Moral rules, virtues and ideals are seen as unsustainable or irrelevant in
the face of the crying needs of human beings. Circumstances force people to

act—in efforts to help others—in ways that simply cannot conform to moral rules and abstract moral ideals. These rules and ideals cannot stand in the face of *the feeling of compassion*. A higher sensuality must rule.

Dr. Wilbur Larch has come to the orphanage to be a hero and now is trapped there. He soon finds there are no heroes in the world of lost children, only people struggling to do the best they can for women and children ensnared in their circumstances of life. He helps women have unwanted babies, to be left at the orphanage for possible adoption, or to have abortions, which are illegal and, arguably, immoral. But he must act to help; he cannot stand back and let things take their course, merely hoping for the best. He loves the babies left at the orphanage, and he and the two nurses who live and work there treat the children like their own. Many of the children are never adopted, so they grow up there. Together they all make a beautiful but sad setting for life.

Homer is one who grows up there. As he grows up, Larch makes him his assistant and trains him in all the medical procedures. He becomes as good a doctor as Larch himself. But he will not perform abortions. It is wrong, he thinks, and he will not compromise. He cites himself and the other living orphans as reasons against it. Larch keeps after him about it, especially after a young woman comes to them after a botched abortion attempt and dies. Homer is unrelenting, however—to this point.

Dr. Larch leads a hard life but cares faithfully and sympathetically for the orphans. At night, a nurse puts the girls to bed with a touching prayer. Larch reads to the boys. And every night he says, "Good night, you princes of Maine, you kings of New England." He does not sleep well, using drops of ether on an open mask to get himself to sleep.

One day, Candy and Wally drive up to the orphanage seeking an abortion. They're not married. Wally is in the air force, flying the B24 Liberator. He expects to be called to overseas duty soon and asks Homer whether he is going into the services. Homer replies that he has a heart defect (discovered by an x-ray) and can't enlist. He asks Wally if he can ride out with them when they leave. But Larch doesn't want Homer to leave. Homer is "still a boy," and "there's no taking care of anybody, not out there." Homer leaves anyway, taking a job working in the orchard on the farm belonging to Wally's parents. Candy's father is a lobsterman in the same area. Wally is off to war, and soon Candy and Homer are romantically and sexually involved. This is Homer's first moral lapse or departure from "the rules."

Several black migrant workers live on the farm during the summer and bunk in the cider house, where Homer also lives. Mr. Rose bosses the operation. His daughter, Rose Rose, is one of the workers. Posted on the wall is a set of rules—the cider house rules, of course. The workers can't read, don't know what they say and totally disregard them. Here's the complete list of profundities:

1. Please don't smoke in bed.
2. Please don't operate the grinder or press if you've been drinking.
3. Please don't go up to the roof to eat your lunch.
4. Please, even if you are very hot, do not go up to the roof to sleep.
5. There should be no going up on the roof at night.

With Wally off to the war, the summer progresses. Candy and Homer carry on happily, oblivious to where their relationship is headed. At summer's end, the migrant workers leave.

Meanwhile, Dr. Larch continues to implore Homer to return to practice medicine at the orphanage. He even works up a convincing set of medical credentials that qualify Homer as a doctor. Then, by clever lies and manipulations, Larch arranges for the board of the orphanage to give Homer a job there. Larch dances with the nurses in celebration, but Homer still won't come back. The sad but beautiful life at the orphanage goes on. Larch sends Homer a gift package containing a fully equipped medical bag, but Homer won't open it—at least for a time. Larch writes to Homer about playing God: "Do I interfere when absolutely helpless women tell me they simply can't have an abortion? That they simply must go through with having another orphan?" Larch wants Homer to replace him at the orphanage, but Homer writes back, "I can't replace you. I'm sorry." Larch responds, "Sorry? . . . I'm not even sorry that I love you."

In due course, Candy and Homer begin fighting, not knowing what to do about their situation and Wally. They seem suspended in time and space. They can't *act* to resolve the situation, so they wind up just waiting for something to happen.

Eventually, it's apple harvest time again and the migrant crew returns. But Rose is in trouble. Morning sickness indicates pregnancy. Candy presses Rose to identify the father, and Rose finally indicates that it's her own father, Mr. Rose. Homer confronts the man, but Mr. Rose denies everything. Rose says she will take care of it, and Homer pleads with her not to perform an abortion on herself. But will he do it instead? Now he *must* act; he can't just stand by and hope for the best.

News comes that Wally has contracted encephalitis and is paralyzed from the waist down. Candy wants him to return home so she can care for him. Sitting on the beach, Candy and Homer realize now that someone is going to get hurt. Homer acknowledges what he's been thinking: "Maybe if I just 'wait and see' long enough, then I won't have to do anything." Now Candy has made a choice and has acted. Life will go on.

Homer approaches the cider house and sees Mr. Rose restraining his daughter. Homer says he can help. He retrieves the medical bag he had received from Larch and sets Rose up for the abortion procedure. Mr. Rose won't leave, so Homer tells him to make himself useful by administering the ether. Mr. Rose agrees to this, but ultimately he can't take it and staggers in a crying fit out into the rain. A little later, Candy is caring for Rose, and Mr. Rose is lying in his bunk in deep misery. Homer has broken the rules.

While lying in recovery on her bunk, Rose asks Homer to read the rules posted on the wall. He does, and the workers are all astonished at their irrelevance and stupidity. Mr. Rose comments, "Somebody who don't live here made those rules. These rules ain't for us. We the ones supposed to make our own rules. And we do, every day. Ain't that right, Homer?" Homer now agrees. The orchardmen tell Homer to remove the rules and burn them in the stove. Homer does. He now accepts the wisdom of Dr. Larch. Rose muses about the rules: "That don't mean nothin' at all. And all this time I been wonderin' about 'em."

Alone with Candy, Homer acknowledges that in life one can't just do nothing. "Nothing is nothing, right?" he says. "You needed me, and now Wally's gonna need you. . . . At least there's no more waiting and seeing." Compassion made Homer take Candy (though this may be hard to believe) and compassion makes Candy take the now-invalid Wally.

Returning to the cider house, Homer finds Mr. Rose bleeding from a knife wound. Rose had been leaving and he "just wanna touch her hand," but she stabbed him. She's gone. To protect her from criminal charges, Mr. Rose has stabbed himself in the same place. He convinces Homer and the others to tell the police he committed suicide in grief over Rose's departure. Mr. Rose says, "I just tryin' to put things straight. Sometimes you got to break some rules to put things straight. Ain't that right Homer?" Homer agrees. Mr. Rose dies. Larch and compassion win again. Moral idealism and its rules are too much to bear in life. Compassion for others will not allow it.

Later, as Homer is loading apple boxes on a truck, Candy hands him a letter from one of the nurses at the orphanage, informing him that Dr. Larch has accidentally overdosed on the ether he used for sleeping and is dead. Homer heads back to the orphanage, and the kids and nurses lovingly mob him as he approaches. The nurse shows Homer an x-ray that is supposed to show his heart defect. She tells him it wasn't an x-ray of *his* heart after all, but of another child's. His own heart is just fine. She explains that Dr. Larch's heart could not handle Homer's enlistment in military service, so he replaced Homer's x-ray with that of another child. The defective heart no doubt symbolizes Larch's life of compassion.

Homer becomes the orphanage doctor under false credentials and carries on Larch's compassionate work with women and children. He reads to the boys at night and says at the end, "Good night, you princes of Maine, you kings of New England." And so the cycle of compassion continues.

* * * * *

Now there are obvious differences between the three films discussed above. *Pleasantville* is light, bright and frivolous. *American Beauty* is brutal and sardonic. *The Cider House Rules* is compassionate and profoundly moving in its portrayal of life at the orphanage. But these and many other contemporary films—*Chocolat* is an especially silly version of this type—have in common the view that *sensuality or feeling is foundational to goodness* in life. Goodness certainly does not consist in conformity to well-known moral rules that really matter. Standing on principle in neglect of your own feelings makes you less good as a person and your life less worth living.

Of course, not every noteworthy contemporary film takes that position. A different perspective—an alternative vision of goodness in life—is here and there represented by excellent films such as *Driving Miss Daisy, Places in the Heart* and *Changing Lanes*. And not very long ago people still generally assumed that traditional moral rules and order were a good thing: that the Pleasantville type of life—where people did not routinely do what they felt like doing but did what they were supposed to do—was the moral ideal. That the shift of moral mood has been relatively recent is indicated by the fact that some fifty years ago the Pleasantville type of sitcoms were taken to be realistic portrayals of life in suburbia, which itself was thought to be a good place to be and life there a good way to live. Exposing the presumably dirty underside of such an "ideal" suburban existence as a major and constantly reiterated theme is only quite recent in filmmaking. It almost seems that we today are compelled to defend ourselves against a past we can no longer sustain and to which we are now morally superior.

There is, of course, an important point to be made, and films of the type in question do make it. *Mere* outward conformity to moral rules and propriety does not make a good life, a good person or outstanding moral character. This has been understood by thinkers since ancient times. Moreover, if that is indeed *all* one has to make of a life, it is a crushing burden to bear and will lead to hypocrisy in one's self and to the manipulation or brutalization of others. The rigid, implacable and mean moralizer (nearly always fanatically religious, though not so in the films discussed here) is a long-standing figure in Western literature (Molière, Charles Dickens, Theodore Dreiser, etc.) and now has a justifiable, standard place in TV and cinema. There's no disputing this. It is the alternative vision of goodness presented by so much recent filmmaking that must be questioned.

And what is that alternative? It is precisely the one presented by the three films and here discussed in some detail. It is an alternative where life is dominated by feeling or sentiment as the ultimate basis of choice and action. Even in perhaps the most worthy case—Dr. Larch's service to distraught pregnant women and their babies ("I just give them what they want")—what someone *wants* is the ultimate criterion of the good life. There is no good, no issue of responsibility or character, above that. No distinction is made between wants and needs, or between needs in a moment of crisis and needs in the larger contexts of life. Thus, Homer's concerns about the rightness of abortion are never addressed, and the voice of the unborn child is never heard. It is no wonder, then, that in the end Homer is so morally compromised by his own feeling-dominated choices and by pressures to act that he is willing to live and practice under false credentials as a doctor simply doing whatever needy women want. Today that is known as supporting women's "choice," and choice is presented as an unqualifiedly good, if sometimes sad, thing. But what really is in view here is choice and life ruled simply by individual desire. Candy's decision to care for Wally, an invalid, is simply her choice, based on nothing more than what she (for the moment, at least) *wants* to do, her feelings. Not a word is said about duty, honor or obligation. That would have spoiled the aesthetic framework of the film. There is no question of character and objective values underlying her choice. And the same goes for Homer's return in acquiescence to a life of falsehood and service at the orphanage.

We have, then, one vision of life as outward conformity governed by rules that make no sense: cider house rules. That vision, of course, is not at all adequate to human needs. It is not a vision of courage, nobility, compassion or, in general, admirable human character. It is Pleasantville before color, Lester before his reawakening, Homer paralyzed by his idealism. The great moralists from antiquity have understood all this. Such conformity is what Jesus of Nazareth called the righteousness of the scribes and the Pharisees (Matthew 5:20) and marked as disastrously harmful and wrong. The alternative vision artistically championed in the films we have considered is of a life liberated from the oppression of moral rules and conformity by following and indulging feelings of various kinds, usually sexual. Can this alternative vision be an accurate portrayal of life and of what it is good to be and do?

Let us acknowledge, again, that *Pleasantville* is simply a fantasy. It does not try to confront what feelings, left unchecked by what is truly good, actually do to human life. Viewed with any pretense of realism, its ending is simply goofy. The other two films, by contrast, present us very directly with the ravages of unchecked human desires and feelings. After viewing *The Cider House Rules* when it was first released, I could not help but wonder whether it was not ironic in intent. Wasn't it actually depicting the horrors of life *without* conformity to rules—rules that would prevent people from committing the stupid and disastrous actions they routinely carry out in life? These tragic consequences are, after all, faithfully brought out in that film. Perhaps. But that surely is not what the ordinary viewer will conclude after seeing either it or *American Beauty*. Instead, the viewer will find the vision of liberated feelings as the basis of whatever goodness is achievable in life, even if life as a whole is admittedly tragic.

There may be good reason to think that, for most human beings, life within the boundaries of individual human abilities *is* tragic or at least quite disappointing. But life need not be anywhere nearly as tragic as it in fact is precisely *because* of unchecked feelings and desires, together with their consequences. Most of the actual tragedies one sees in real life, as in these pictures, are precisely the result of feelings ungoverned by good—from drug addiction to un-wanted pregnancies, ethnic cleansing, and on and on. The tragedy of living a Pleasantville life or even a Lester Burnham life (before his reawakening) is very small indeed compared to the tragic lives of multitudes ravaged by unbri-dled feelings and desires, whether their own or those of others. For real life re-quires a point of reference as to what is good for people, and a firm under-standing that what we want or how we feel is not the same as what is good for us and for those whose lives we affect—even though what we want and what we feel has some importance. *This crucial point of reference is altogether absent from the vision of life communicated by cinematic productions that represent sensu-ality as the path to moral liberation.*

A certain false "moral" rigidity is rightly condemned in the films considered here. But this rigidity is not *moral* at all. It is, rather, immoral, as most people rightly see. Its platitudes include in *no* case should an abortion be performed, in *no* case should life be taken, in *no* case should one intentionally deceive an-other, in *no* case should there be a divorce, and so on. Moralists who obsess about rules are, in their own odd way, enslaved by *their* feelings rather than by genuine moral insight and character. They *feel* these rules to be unqualifiedly right (and their opposites wrong). Their claims are not based on moral under-standing and moral character. Such morally rigid individuals stand under a certain moral fanaticism, usually involving a misplaced sense of moral purity. But persons of good moral character do not stand back and hope for some-thing to happen to avoid soiling their hands. Rather, they act for the greater good in whatever situation—often, to be sure, with fear and trembling; but they do act. They act with genuine love, as a matter of the will and of character and not just of feeling—whether feelings of legalistic reprisal or feelings of un-relenting self-indulgence. This is what it means to be *responsible*.

But how, today, can one find the confidence to go forward with responsible moral judgments and perhaps to express them in works of art? I have spoken above of the need to have, as a point of reference in action, a conception of what is *good* for people, as distinct from what is desired or felt. But here, at present, we have a major problem. Ours is a sensual culture not only in its tastes and practices, but also in its theory of what counts as knowledge. As a result, it is generally assumed that *there is no knowledge of what is good as distinct from what is desired and felt.* Feeling is everything. In life it is just one feeling against another. Philosopher David Hume (d. 1776) taught us that. Reason, he said, could never oppose *or* support the feelings ("sentiments") that, on his view, totally govern action. Reason is the slave of the passions. For a long while this theory didn't catch on in the general culture, but now it passes for street smarts. We have no *knowledge,* the current "wisdom" holds, of what is right and wrong, good and bad. In practice, then, we are caught between the unsustainable alternatives of a dead outward conformity to moral rules and of "liberation" from dead conformity by the indulgence of sensuality, whether in crude or refined forms. We have nowhere else to stand. This is the grand vision brought to aesthetic expression in the films we have considered.

The broader and more basic problem underlying this tendency in contemporary films is the problem of establishing a certifiable knowledge of human goodness that gives us a third way between the two alternatives noted. Since the dominance of a refined version of Judeo-Christian ethics vanished at the end of the nineteenth century, we have had nothing that could pass as moral *knowledge* in Western culture. Friedrich Nietzsche saw clearly the cataclysmic nature of the historical passage beyond that ethics into nihilism, but neither he nor anyone else has been able to find a suitable replacement for it in human life. In the vacuum that remains, there is little we can do but vacillate between outward conformity to rules (our political correctness being a kind of secular pharisaism) and the indulgence of feelings. Neither comes to realistic terms with the human heart and personality. This explains many things about our culture, such as how easily addicted we are, how our essential individual and communal covenants cannot be maintained, the abysmal failure of education, and the high percentage of our population that is ensnared in the legal and penal system. Cinema and TV can, of course, only reflect this sad situation. They cannot correct it. But we should at least understand what they offer to us and not mistake the vision of liberation through sensuality for a vision of reality.

From a Society of Fear to a Community of Trust

Moving Beyond *Bowling for Columbine*

SARA L. H. SHADY

* *

In 2002, filmmaker Michael Moore released the documentary *Bowling for Columbine*. In spite of the controversy surrounding the film, it won an Oscar for best documentary in 2003. As Moore explains, "I made [the film] in hopes of generating a national debate and discussion not only about the nature of guns and violence in America, but about who we really are as Americans. What is it about us that makes us seemingly a more violent people than other peoples around the world?"[1] The film explores myriad answers to this question and challenges common assumptions about the root of violence in society, such as the prevalence of guns, violence in the media, the breakdown of traditional family relationships, the alienation of youth and the lack of prayer in schools. Admittedly surprised by his own conclusion, in *Bowling for Columbine* Moore suggests that the problem of violence in America is really rooted in the American people. He claims, "This isn't a film about guns. This isn't a film about gun control. It's a film about the American psyche such as it is."[2] According to Moore, even if we rid American society of guns, the problem of violence would remain. Why? Moore's provocative answer is that we are afraid of each other.

The purpose of this essay is to explore and assess Moore's view that fear is at the root of American violence. Using the philosophical work of John Macmurray, I will support Moore's claim by demonstrating that fear is linked to problems of social injustice and the breakdown of community in American society. Macmurray's philosophy provides a framework for understanding

Moore's documentary by explaining how the tension between the motives of love and fear affect our personal relationships and the possibility of creating and sustaining genuine communities. I will also argue that while Moore's film begs the important question of what should be done, it suggests that the beginning of an answer lies in the critique of social justice in America that is a pervasive theme in all of Moore's works. It is here that I find Macmurray's work again very helpful, and I will explore his view of the role of justice in building communities as a partial solution to the problem of fear in our society. Finally, reflecting on the religious themes in the work of both Moore and Macmurray, I will argue that to move beyond our culture of fear we must put faith into action.

Moore's Argument for Fear as the Root of Violence

What began, for Moore, as an attempt to tell the story of what happened at Columbine High School on April 20, 1999, soon became a much larger project of telling a story spanning over three hundred years of American history. Moore acknowledges that the question of why the Columbine massacre happened has been on the minds of many. And many answers have been proposed. Everything from violent video games to the music of controversial singer Marilyn Manson has been a potential object of blame.

It is in this attempt to place blame that the message behind the title of the film becomes clear. After explaining that the Columbine shooters, Eric Harris and Dylan Klebold, went bowling the morning of the massacre, Moore asks a cynically rhetorical question: "Why isn't anyone blaming bowling for warping the minds of Eric and Dylan to commit their evil deeds? Was it not just as plausible to blame bowling as Marilyn Manson?" Moore's point is that Americans too easily identify and latch onto a scapegoat as the cause of our social ills. The plausibility of these scapegoats is called into question, however, when we look at the question of violence from a global perspective. Moore asks us to consider that Germany is the home of goth rock, that most violent video games are made in Japan, that the United Kingdom's divorce rate is much higher than the United States' divorce rate and that unemployment is twice as high in Canada than in the United States. If violent entertainment, nontraditional family systems and poverty are causing violence, one would assume that the rates of violence would be just as high in these countries as they are in the United States. Moore dismantles this myth, however, by comparing the numbers of people killed by guns each year in various countries: in Germany, the number is 381; in France, 255; in Canada, 165; in the U.K., 68; in Australia, 65; in Japan, 39; and in the U.S., 11,127.[3]

Moore also questions the thesis that the sheer number of guns in America and the ease with which they can be obtained are to blame for the violence in society. In one of the first scenes in the film, Moore investigates a promotional ad offering a free gun to anyone opening a certain type of bank account. After opening the account and being provided with his firearm, Moore wryly asks, "Don't you think it's a little dangerous handing out guns in a bank?" In contrast, Moore notes that Canada's 30 million people comprise 10 million families and own 7 million guns. If the ratio of guns to people corresponds to the amount of gun violence in a society, one would assume that Canada has a high rate of gun violence. This, however, is not the case, calling into question the idea that the presence of guns, in and of itself, precipitates violence. Certainly this does not contradict the fact that if Harris and Klebold had not been able to obtain the weapons they used at Columbine High School, the massacre might not have occurred. In fact, in a poignant moment in the film, Moore and two survivors from the Columbine massacre succeed in persuading the Kmart Corporation to stop selling bullets; Harris and Klebold had purchased their ammunition at a Kmart store. But guns alone are neither a necessary nor sufficient condition for violence. Here it seems that Moore is agreeing with the adage often cited by members of the National Rifle Association: Guns don't kill people. People kill people.

So the questions remain: why is American society so much more violent than other societies? And why do so many Americans kill others? For the answer to this question, Moore turns to American history. He does not, however, accept the theory that the violence in our history is to blame. He argues that if a history of violence is to blame, then other historical instances of violence— such as what took place during the reign of Nazism, the Japanese occupation of China, the French massacre in Algiers and the British occupation of India—should also be causing violence today. He maintains, however, that this is not the case. Instead, Moore suggests that the proper target of blame in American history is fear.

In a short satirical cartoon inserted into the middle of the film, Moore offers "a brief history of the United States."[4] Beginning with pilgrims fleeing to America to avoid religious persecution, Moore paints American history as a transition from one reason to be afraid to another. He claims that the following are all rooted in fear of the other: the American Revolution, the Salem witchcraft trials, the wars between settlers and Native Americans, slavery, the Civil War, the Jim Crow laws, the civil rights movement, the creation of both the National Rifle Association and Ku Klux Klan, and the development of gated suburban communities.

To defend this thesis further, Moore offers several examples suggesting that fear resides deep in the American psyche. On the level of personal relationships, he cites the increasing number of home security systems being installed across America and the increased level of security that these systems can provide. Moore takes the viewer on a tour of a home in Littleton, Colorado, that has its own "safe room," where a family can hide securely in the knowledge that it would take a large ax to break down the heavy door to the inner room. He also shows how schools have changed across America in the years since Columbine. They have installed metal detectors, developed strict dress codes and implemented strict no-tolerance policies that have resulted in seemingly absurd decisions to suspend or expel children who play cops and robbers with paper guns, who bring a nail clipper to school, who use a chicken strip as a pretend gun, and who wear a pro-anarchy T-shirt to class. According to Moore, this fuels the idea that any child, anywhere, is a potential "little time bomb waiting to go off."

In a speech given at the University of Denver six months after the release of *Bowling for Columbine*, Moore recounts raising a difficult question to the police officers who responded to the shooting in order to highlight the problem of fear in personal relationships: "Why didn't you go in [Columbine High School for two hours after the shooting stopped]? [There were] people dying, bleeding to death."[5] He cites the Jefferson County Police Department as saying they were afraid they were going to be shot. Moore, however, does not place the blame solely on the police department. He pushes the question further, asking, "What is that about us as human beings? Why wouldn't hundreds, thousands, rush the police line [outside of the school]? . . . If it won't happen then, when will it happen?"[6] In this narrative, Moore expands his argument by suggesting that fear not only inspires people to commit violence against each other, but also prevents us from helping others when we see genuine needs.

Why are we so afraid? Where do we get the idea that the other is a potential threat? Moore extends his theory about the relationship between fear and violence to the level of social relationships by suggesting that the media is responsible for fueling our fear. Moore uses an interview on the infamous streets of south central Los Angeles with Barry Glassner, author of *The Culture of Fear*, to give the audience the statistic that while the murder rate has gone down 20 percent in the last few years, the number of murders covered on the evening news has actually gone up 600 percent. It is as though the media would have us believe that violence is an inescapable part of living in American society. Here Moore's central claim is developed further. The problem is not merely that the American public is generally afraid, but that the object of fear is, specifically, other human beings. In particular, we fear those who are different, whether the difference is one of race, gender, religion or sexual orientation. Moore's interviews with news reporters and media executives confirm that the American public is shown many stories involving gun violence, particularly when persons of color are the suspected criminals, because that is what sells. He maintains that this prevents us from caring about things that *should* frighten us because they are more likely to harm us, such as environmental destruction and pollution.

Moore continues to provide evidence in support of his thesis that fear is at the heart of the American public by exploring the connection between fear and violence at the national level. Moore draws a controversial parallel between the violence perpetrated at Columbine High School and the violence perpetrated by the United States government. Several times throughout the film, Moore mentions that April 20, 1999, the day of the Columbine massacre, was the largest single day of bombing in the war in Kosovo. Although not openly discussed in the American media, several international news agencies reported that on this day American missiles destroyed residential areas, including a hospital and a primary school.

Throughout the film, Moore also suggests that there is a connection between the Columbine massacre and the fact that the largest employer in Littleton, Colorado, is Lockheed Martin, the "world's largest weapons maker." In the University of Denver speech, Moore explains that there is not a direct correlation between Lockheed Martin and Columbine, but he maintains that this points to "the fabric of our society and all the threads that weave into the fabric of what a violent, violent nation we are. Toward each other and the rest of the world."[7] Based on this statement, it does not seem accurate to portray Moore as placing blame on the employees of Lockheed Martin for the Columbine tragedy. Rather, he is extending his thesis to the national level to argue that the violence called for by the political leaders of the United States sends a message to children growing up in the United States that violence is an acceptable, and at times preferable, way to solve problems.

In *Bowling for Columbine,* a group of Canadian teens recognize this message. Describing the difference between Americans and Canadians, a Canadian adolescent remarks about her friends, "We don't go to the point of shooting someone just to get revenge, it just stops at teasing." She then extends this mode of behavior to the level of foreign policy by adding, "Americans resolve everything through fighting. Canada wants to negotiate and work something out." Moore believes this is an accurate portrayal of American foreign policy, at least over the last fifty years. Toward the beginning of the film, a public relations representative from Lockheed Martin suggests that there is no connection between the weapons that his company builds for the United States government and the massacre at Columbine, saying, "I guess I don't see the connection, because the missiles that you are talking about were built and designed to defend us from somebody else who would be aggressors against us. Societies, countries, governments do things that annoy each other, but we have to learn to deal with that annoyance, frustration, and anger in appropriate ways. We don't get irritated with someone and just because we're mad at them drop a bomb on them or shoot them."

Moore responds by showing footage of the death and destruction caused by American military and economic involvement around the globe, beginning in 1953 with the removal of Prime Minister Mohammad Mossadeq from Iran. He concludes by informing the viewer that in the year preceding the al-Qaeda attack on the U.S. on September 11, 2001, for which Osama bin Laden has taken responsibility, the United States government gave over $245 million dollars in aid to Taliban-ruled Afghanistan. According to Moore's statistics, the fifteen examples of American foreign policy he cites resulted in over 4,808,000 deaths.[8]

In assessing Moore's thesis, the essential question is whether it is plausible that fear could be the primary cause of violence in American society. Can fear really be at the root of the violent crimes that take place between neighbors and fellow citizens? Can fear really make us suspicious of others to the degree that everyone becomes a potential perpetrator of a violent crime? The ideas of

John Macmurray are useful for understanding and evaluating these claims.

Macmurray and the Relationship Between Love and Fear in Social Relationships

John Macmurray (1891-1976) was a Scottish philosopher who emphasized the importance of integrating the theoretical and the practical in one's scholarly work. The son of a Presbyterian minister, Macmurray initially wanted to become a missionary. He was, however, sent to fight in the trenches during World War I. Deeply impacted by the inhumanity of the war and by the church's openly supporting and even celebrating the killing of the enemy, Macmurray abandoned all participation in organized religion. He became very active in political affairs, giving public lectures on topics such as reconstructing Europe after decades of war and finding unity between eastern and western European worldviews. Toward the end of his life, he returned to Christianity and joined the Society of Friends, which he believed shared his concern for issues of peace and justice.

Macmurray is arguably most famous for his 1953-1954 Gifford Lectures, entitled "The Form of the Personal," in which he describes the cultural and intellectual situation of the early twentieth century as a "crisis of the personal." The personal refers to those aspects of human life that bring persons into meaningful interaction with other persons, so that the wholeness of their being is revealed.[9] Macmurray maintains that only personalism, a school of philosophy that considers the person to be the primary component of reality, recognizes and defends a mode of authentic being-with-others in community.[10] "Now we understand," he writes, "what the personal life is in distinction both from the individual and the social life. It is the life which we live as persons, and we can live it only by entering into relationships with other people on a fully personal basis, in which we give ourselves to one another; or, to put the same thing the other way round, in which we accept one another freely for what we are, and in which therefore there is and can be no purpose other than the sharing of our lives in fellowship."[11] Macmurray's project in the Gifford Lectures—as in his philosophical work generally—is, therefore, an attempt to provide a philosophical foundation for the necessity of creating and sustaining meaningful relationships between persons.

According to Macmurray, the solution to the crisis of the personal in its social form is ultimately to be sought by overcoming the crisis on the philosoph-

ical level. He locates the root of the philosophical crisis in the modern characterization of the self as primarily a thinking thing, isolated as a subject who
stands over and against a world of objects.[12] Macmurray maintains that this
philosophical tradition has erased the personal aspects of the self in two ways.
First, it has neglected those activities in addition to thought that constitute the
self as a whole, such as the emotional, social and active dimensions of being
human. Second, it has posited the self as an ego, rather than as a person who
is constituted in and through relationships with other persons.

Macmurray argues that the crisis of the personal can be overcome, at a theoretical level, by replacing the modern conception of the self with a view of the
self as primarily an acting person in relation to other persons. The self is both
a thinker and an agent, but emphasizing thought excludes all other activities
and limits our understanding of the self to that of a subject. Thought is a necessary but insufficient condition for personhood. Giving priority to action, on
the other hand, includes all other aspects of being human. As Macmurray
writes, "The unity of experience as a whole is not a unity of knowledge, but a
unity of personal activities of which knowledge is only one. It considers the
fact that the same person may be at once scientist, artist, moral agent and sin-
ner."[13] Once we accept a more holistic view of the person, it becomes evident
that "the self is constituted by its relation to the Other; it has its being in its
relationship and this relationship is necessarily personal."[14] In fact, Macmurray describes the "ideal of the personal" as "a universal community of persons
in which each cares for all the others and no one for himself."[15] This unified
view of the person also demonstrates Macmurray's belief in the fundamental
connection between the theoretical and practical aspects of his philosophy, apparent in this famous statement: "All meaningful knowledge is for the sake of
action, and all meaningful action is for the sake of friendship."[16]

In Macmurray's view, the possibility of friendship between persons depends
on whether those persons are primarily motivated by love or by fear.[17] When
the self approaches the other with love, the possibility for genuine fellowship
arises. When the self acts out of fear, however, fraternity is lost, because the
self cares more about protecting her own interests than about caring for the
interests of the other. It is interesting to note that by juxtaposing love and fear,
Macmurray is departing from the traditional opposition of love and hate. He
recognizes the reality of hatred as a motive for human action but maintains
that it results either from the feeling of rejection and resentment when love is

not reciprocated or from the continual perception of the other as one to be feared. Hatred is, therefore, secondary to the primary motives of love and fear. It is here that I believe Macmurray's work can be used to support Moore's thesis in *Bowling for Columbine*. Following Macmurray's argument that unchecked fear can all too easily harden into hatred, one can see how a society fueled by fear could easily become a violent society.

To make the argument clearer, it is helpful to understand Macmurray's ideas about how love and fear affect human relationships on both personal and societal levels of interaction. Macmurray maintains that community is actualized when individuals are in direct and personal relation.[18] In this case, individuals actually interact and acknowledge each other as more than mere objects. There is mutuality between them, and they are motivated by love to be open toward each other as potential or actual friends. This form of relationship stands in contrast to relationships that are direct and impersonal, where individuals who interact with each other fail to recognize each other as persons who encompass more than their objective usefulness. As Macmurray explains, "The impersonal attitude is the one in which we do not treat other people as persons in personal relation with ourselves, but as *men*, that is as members of a determinate class of objects in our environment . . . of whom we must take account, since their presence conditions our own actions."[19] In this case, the self may be forced to interact with others, but there is no meaningful relationship established to create a foundation for trust between persons. An additional problem results when relationships are indirect, because a mere theoretical awareness of personhood is insufficient for the actualization of personal relationships.[20]

In addition to distinguishing between forms of relation on the level of interpersonal interaction, it is also important to apply these distinctions to the social level. This will help to illuminate the role of fear and love in destroying or promoting communal relationships on both the personal and social levels of interaction. Macmurray maintains that any relationship between individuals, whether direct or indirect, constitutes society. He argues, however, that community can only be actualized in and through direct and personal relationships. Consistent with his style of argument, Macmurray maintains that the realization of community is dependent on the cooperative activities of society. "The reality of community implies society . . . as necessary to it, in due subordination within it," he says. "Community which does not express itself in cooperative activity for common purposes is illusory—a mere sentimentality."[21] Macmurray, however, does not want to reduce community to a merely cooperative system, because cooperation does not require that relationships be personal in nature. This leads him to conclude that "every community is . . . a society; but not every society is a community."[22]

To illustrate these distinctions, consider the following. When neighbors form a neighborhood association for the purpose of ensuring a peaceful and secure environment in which to reside personally, their relationship is merely instrumental. On the other hand, when neighbors socialize together on a regular basis and willingly care for the specific needs of each other, they form a communal relationship that extends beyond their cooperative relationship. The former relationship is an impersonal social relationship, while the latter is personal.

By looking at each of these forms of relationship in terms of the tension between love and fear, we can identify the negative effects of fear on interpersonal interaction. At the level of direct interaction, fear prevents relationships from becoming personal. There is no intentional fellowship between persons and no potential for building mutual understanding between them. According to Macmurray, fear also has negative social consequences.[23] These negative consequences are clearly portrayed in *Bowling for Columbine*.

First, Macmurray observes that fear prevents positive action. Rather than being concerned with her action for and toward the other, an individual who is afraid is concerned with whether or not the other will respond. She is paralyzed by the fear and does not act unless the other acts first. Thus, fear promotes the stagnancy of remaining in a form of organization that is social but not communal. The second negative consequence is that fear isolates the self from others. The absence of interaction between the self and the other that results from the self's failure to act breaks the relation between them. In this sense, fear promotes either a form of individualism, where all persons are out for themselves, or a collective, where selves are anonymously linked together for security. Both of these limited forms of relation require external constraint to preserve the relation, and neither form of relation unites whole persons who are free to act responsibly for the sake of preserving the relation. Third, when an individual is motivated by fear, she is egocentric—on the defensive to protect herself from being rejected by the other. It follows that fear results in a view of the world as hostile, rather than friendly, which in turn influences the choice of future action.

In *Bowling for Columbine,* Moore gives us clear images of a society where persons view the world as hostile and are isolated from each other, disinterested in pursuing meaningful relationships with each other. This is a world where citizens form militias to protect themselves from what is perceived to be imminent danger. It is a world where children must pass through metal detectors, as they are regarded as potential agents of violence. It is a world where Wal-Mart's gun sales surge 70 percent immediately following the attacks on September 11. This is a world of "blanket alerts" and "general threats." It is a world where military funding takes top priority. It is a world where neighbors are perceived to be potential foes rather than potential friends. And it is a world, according to both Moore and Macmurray, where the failure to see the humanity of the other person easily turns fear into violence.

The Role of Justice in Building Inclusive Communities of Trust

So is there an alternative to our culture of fear? Is there a solution to the problem of violence in America? If fear is at the root of the violence, how can we overcome our fear? Moore does not provide any direct answers. His project shows what is wrong with American society, but it does not give a clear prescription for the future. However, by looking at one of the prominent themes of Moore's work as a whole, his proposal becomes clear: we must actively work toward social justice for the poor and oppressed.

Moore first gained national recognition for the 1989 documentary *Roger & Me,* which gives image to the economic devastation brought on by the closure of the General Motors plant in Flint, Michigan, leaving more than 30,000 workers unemployed. In his unsuccessful attempts to gain an interview with Roger Smith, the head of General Motors at the time of the plant closure, Moore depicts a society where wealthy corporate America cares little about the plight of the working class.[24] Using narrative accounts of various citizens of Flint and their attempts to overcome the challenges of being unemployed, Moore builds an argument for a causal connection between the economic status of a community and the health of the communal bonds within that community. The closure of the GM plant creates a domino effect of economic depression in Flint, which leads to higher eviction rates, higher rates of crime and an eventual decline in the population, as people are forced to move elsewhere.[25]

In *Bowling for Columbine,* the idea that there is a causal relationship between the economic health and the social health of a community is once again emphasized. This can be seen initially as Moore searches for an answer to the question of why American society is so much more violent than Canadian society. The question is puzzling since Canadians entertain themselves with just as many violent movies, video games and music; have a much higher unemployment rate; have a high rate of gun ownership; and are racially diverse. Moore believes that Canadians are not nearly as afraid of each other as Americans are, but he does not stop here. He emphasizes that a primary focus of the Canadian government is social welfare. In Canada there is a universal healthcare system and affordable housing is provided for poor families, which, according to Moore, suggests an underlying belief that the way to build a good society comprising good citizens is to take good care of your citizens. Moore contrasts this with the American system, which he believes all too often hurts the people who cannot defend themselves and benefits the people who don't need the assistance. In an interview given at the opening of *Bowling for Columbine* at the Toronto Film Festival, Moore contrasts Canadians and Americans by suggesting that the former believe they "are all in the same boat . . . all Canadians." He believes that the mentality of the Americans, however, is one where it is "every man for himself and to hell with you. . . . Me, Me, Me, Me. . . . I, I, I."[26]

The lack of concern for the welfare of others so prevalent in American society is also poignantly shown in *Bowling for Columbine*. Moore tells the story of a tragedy at Buell Elementary School, where a six-year-old student shot and killed another six-year-old classmate. Moore's visit to Buell Elementary signifies a return to Flint, Michigan, but this time the emphasis is on the effects of poverty on children. According to Moore, 87 percent of children in Flint live below the national poverty line. This was true of the child who killed his classmate. His mother, Tamarla Owens, was enrolled in Michigan's Welfare to Work program. Each day she traveled eighty miles to a wealthy Detroit suburb, where she worked two jobs and made $8.50 per hour. Her wages were not enough money to pay the bills, so she was eventually evicted from her home. She sent her children to stay with her brother for a few weeks until she could find new housing. It was at his uncle's house that the little boy found the loaded gun that he brought to school. Moore's position on the issue is made clear through the statements of the sheriff of Genesee County, where the shooting at Buell took place. Questioning how sending a single mother to work hours away from home can possibly help a community raise healthy children, the sheriff asks, "What's the point? How does the state benefit? We drove the one parent [in that household] out. How can that serve the community?"

Similar to Moore, Macmurray maintains that communities must be economically just. Macmurray also argues, however, that while economic justice is a necessary condition for the actualization of healthy interpersonal and social relationships, it is not a sufficient condition:

> The spiritual life—the culture of the individual or the community—can be distinguished from the material life, but in actual fact they cannot be separated. Without material resources we cannot live. Without adequate material resources, the personal life must remain stunted and undeveloped. The economic activities of a community are the indispensable basis for its cultural life. . . . Now, if the economic life of the community is excluded from the control and direction of a democratic government, then there is no way by which the community can secure for all its members the means of realizing the cultural freedom which it is the purpose of democracy to make possible.[27]

Justice is limited in its ability to produce community, Macmurray believes, because it cannot necessitate friendship.[28] If justice is merely maintained in indirect relationships by the rule of law, individuals will likely defer to an authority rather than accept personal responsibility to care for one another. Additionally, Macmurray claims that bolstering justice with social norms to act for the sake of social harmony is still insufficient. Macmurray describes this limitation of justice:

> If you must serve, or use the word service, then I will not object to your serving the people you know—your friends and acquaintances. But serving people in general usually means serving nobody in particular. You can't be human if you live by statistics. That is why I insist that morality means friendship. If you are anxious to do your duty by the unemployed, then you have got to do something for the family you know about in the next street. If you mean by social service, doing good to definite, living, suffering people, that is all right. I have only this to say, that you will find that the only way you can really serve people in a way that really matters is to enter into friendship with them.[29]

For Macmurray, justice may require that the self meet another's needs, but it does not require the self to care for another person as a person. Genuine care is required to move from fear to love and trust.

It is clear that for both Moore and Macmurray, the keys to building a more

peaceful America are to alleviate fear by encouraging persons to seek meaningful relationships with each other and to alleviate the oppression of the poor
with a more just distribution of resources. But this does not seem to be a complete solution. While it is impossible to be moral without justice, justice alone
does not constitute morality. The problem with relying solely on justice to alleviate social ills is that justice does not entail a necessary obligation to befriend others. As Macmurray notes, "I can demand justice for myself from
others, and even enforce it, but [I can not demand] benevolence or generosity
or affection."[30] Arguably, benevolence, generosity and perhaps even affection
are just as essential as justice to fostering a healthy community. This begs an
important question that reveals a limitation of Moore's film: how does one
motivate persons to care about others in meaningful ways? Macmurray maintains—and I concur—it is here that religion provides an important part of the
answer.

Faith in Action

Macmurray believes that the development of genuine community requires
that the role of religion have priority over the role of politics. A political solution to the problem of the lack of community is inadequate for turning fear
into trust, because while the law can require justice, it cannot require love.
Macmurray maintains that only religion can provide the motivation for persons to form genuine relationships of their own accord. "The task of religion,"
he writes, "is to produce and to sustain in us that structure of emotional motive, and therefore that system of habitual action in the daily round of the
common life, that alone can make social life possible and can keep it unified
and harmonious. Only religion can create and maintain the community of the
personal life of mankind; for religion alone speaks direct to the emotions of
the common man in the common life."[31] According to Macmurray, emphasizing the religious aspect of life fosters the fraternity that constitutes community. This is made possible by the fact that there is an infinite Personal Other
who stands in mutual relation to every member of the community.

It is important to note that when Macmurray speaks of religion, he is not
referring to a specific organizational structure. Rather, he is describing a mode
of being in the world that sees the world as a unity of the material and the spiritual. He says, "We relate ourselves rightly to the world by entering into communion with God, and seeking to understand and to fulfill his intention [i.e.,

communion with others]."[32] So in Macmurray's theory of community, religion functions as a transforming and motivating force that brings persons into meaningful relation with God, other persons and the natural world. While Macmurray does not believe that Christianity is the only religion capable of fostering genuine community, he does believe that Christianity can play a central role in the process.

One might initially assume that Moore rules out the role of religion in solving American social ills. In *Bowling for Columbine*, he does not make reference to the role of faith in combating fear and violence, for example; he does, however, show Christians blaming everything from Marilyn Manson to lack of prayer in schools for our social problems. For Moore, the problems of violence and economic injustice require changes in the political sphere as well as a more personal initiative toward building healthy communities. I do not believe, however, that this means Moore's films are void of Christian themes. In fact, Moore argues that his work captures Christ's mandates more authentically than the work of some self-described Christians. In his speech at the University of Denver, he says,

> I was raised in an Irish Catholic family, and I wonder sometimes who this God is that Mr. Bush, Mr. Ashcroft, and Mr. Cheney invoke as they attempt to lead us to war, as they attempt to convince the American people that the American dream is still for them. Who is this God that they invoke? Because the one that I was taught about says that we will be judged by how we treat the least among us. Right? What happened to that story? Was that not taught in their Sunday School? You know, I was taught that a rich man will have a harder time getting into heaven than a camel will have passing through the eye of a needle. . . . Isn't that story in there somewhere?[33]

It seems as though Moore is challenging Christians to ask whether these passages really motivate us to action or whether they merely illustrate principles we would cognitively acknowledge but fail to act on.[34] Macmurray believes Christians have detrimentally shifted the emphasis in faith from the notion that "by their fruits ye shall know them" to the idea that "by their opinions ye shall know them."[35] It is not enough to say we want to live in a different America with less violence and less poverty and then to retreat to what is safe and familiar. Moore and Macmurray are challenging us to act on our beliefs. So what is to be done?

Perhaps a solution can be found in returning to the tension between fear and trust that is central to the work of both Moore and Macmurray. If it is true that positive relationships cannot be based on fear and that a society of fearful persons is a violent, hostile and alienated society, then we must figure out how to move beyond fear. If we only critique the existing institutions, however, it is hard to picture the avenues for change. We become afraid of ourselves and afraid that we will never become other than what we are. Moving beyond this fear requires that we trust other human beings—and God—enough to desire to enter into community. Trust, however, is a difficult task, because we *fear* that the trust will not be reciprocated. To really trust others, we need hope that our care will be reciprocated. Christianity provides such a hope and a vision in the form of Christ, whose perfect love casts out fear (1 John 4:18).

The example of Christ's love as a factor motivating us toward healthy social relationships is consistent with the arguments put forward by Moore and Macmurray that community building is dependent on social justice and real interaction with other persons. Christ's love demands that we befriend the Eric Harrises and Dylan Klebolds in our sphere of influence. It demands that we help to meet the concrete needs of persons like Tamarla Owens. It insists that we challenge the media's depiction of the stereotypical criminal. It requires that we confront political regimes that increase the gap between rich and poor and choose violence as a primary means of conflict resolution. Christ's love is a love that condemns hoarding wealth for selfish gain, a love that requires more from those who have been given much, a love that establishes giving away all of one's possessions to the poor as the standard of perfection.[36] When the disciples ask, with exasperation and trepidation, how anyone could possibly be saved by this standard, Christ responds by telling them to *trust*. He says, "With man this is impossible, but with God all things are possible" (Matthew 19:26).

A clue to Moore's vision for moving beyond the Columbine massacre is found in the musical anthem of the film, which suggests that we "take the Skinheads bowling."[37] Being motivated by love to put fear aside and seek genuine and meaningful relationships with "the other," whoever that may be, is not a new idea. Christ challenged and transformed society by doing just this. We are called to do the same.

10

Vengeance, Forgiveness and Redemption in *Mystic River*

CAROLINE J. SIMON

• •

"We bury our sins; we wash them clean." So goes the tag line publicists chose
for Clint Eastwood's *Mystic River*. Rivers function within the Christian tradition as symbols of grace—of hope for cleansing and redemption. Yet in *Mystic
River* the promise that buried sin can be cleansed meets bitter irony. The film
emphasizes the difficulty of acting wisely in light of our fragmentary understanding and tumultuous desires, vividly illustrating what philosopher Sissela
Bok asserts is the dual aspect of our human condition. On the one hand, says
Bok, human life is of highest worth; on the other hand, we are "caught up in
a joint existence beset with unpredictable and at times incomprehensible difficulties." We inhabit a world where loyalties conflict, where virtually all of us
injure one another inadvertently and where some among us operate with active
malice.[1] Wounds, whether inadvertently or intentionally inflicted, too often
fester. How should we conduct ourselves in light of our human predicament?
When the answer to the question, what can I know? appears to be "not nearly
enough," acting as one ought seems impossible, with suffering and evil too often the dire consequences of our ignorance. *Mystic River* offers an ambiguous
and thought-provoking meditation on whether hope of redemption is futile.

Eastwood's film, based on an adaptation of a novel of the same name by
Dennis Lehane, depicts the scarred lives of three friends in a late-twentieth-
century Boston Catholic neighborhood.[2] The claim of *Slant* magazine re-
viewer Ed Gonzales that *Mystic River* is "one of the most spiritually profound
works ever to come out of Hollywood" is not just hype.[3] Its rich, human tex-

ture weaves together more themes that merit philosophical exploration than can be treated within one essay. One huge issue in *Mystic River* that I will largely leave aside is the ongoing effect of childhood sexual abuse. I will concentrate on three other questions raised by the film that have special significance for the Christian tradition: What kind of justice can be found in a world where the sins and wounds of the fathers are visited—through vengeance, mischance and ignorance—on their children? What is the function of forgiveness and truthful confession in short-circuiting the cycle of vengeance? And, given the limitations of organized religion and institutional justice as sources of hope, can Christianity be lived out in a way that provides alternative transcendent sources of healing?

Sins of the Fathers

At the most straightforward level, *Mystic River* is a police procedural, tracking the official investigation carried out by the official authorities of the brutal murder of a nineteen-year-old and the parallel quest for justice of her family. Yet viewers soon discover that the film has the complex texture of a Shakespearian or Greek tragedy.

Past suffering and evil enter the film from the outset. In the opening scene, three grade-school aged children—Sean Devine, Jimmy Markum and Dave Boyle—are playing in the street of their working-class neighborhood. As their play turns toward minor vandalism, a car containing two men drives up. The boys take them for policemen, since one has a badge on his belt. Dave, who complies with the men's order to get in the car, is abducted and sexually abused for four days before he escapes. Most of the action of *Mystic River* takes place twenty-five years later, when Sean, Jimmy and Dave—who have maintained only loose ties into adulthood—reconnect around the brutal murder of Jimmy's daughter, Katie. Sean, who has become a police detective, is assigned to the investigation. Though Dave and Jimmy are no longer close, Dave has become Jimmy's relative through his marriage to Celeste, the cousin of Jimmy's wife, Annabeth. As the film unfolds, Dave, who still bears psychological scars from his abduction, becomes a prime suspect in Katie's murder. He is opaque and scary, yet he is also a devoted father. Moreover, he arrives home in the middle of the night of Katie's death covered in blood—his own, gushing from a knife wound, mingled with someone else's. His explains to his wife that he has struggled with a mugger, whom he may have killed in self-defense. The next day, when no wounded or dead mugger is found but Katie's body is discovered, Celeste begins to wonder who or what to believe.

Yet Dave is neither the only damaged individual in the film nor the only suspect in the case, and his abduction is not the only past crime haunting the present. Brendan Harris is a young man who was planning secretly to elope with Katie, even though Jimmy has forbidden their relationship. As the film unfolds we learn that Jimmy's hatred of Brendan is rooted in anger at Brendan's father, "Just Ray" Harris. Just Ray, Jimmy's former partner in crime, informed against Jimmy, sending him to prison. As we learn much later in the film, Jimmy's attitude toward Brendan is also colored by guilt stemming from Jimmy's vengeful murder of Just Ray. Brendan seems to love Katie deeply and also to be well adjusted, especially compared to his younger brother, "Silent Ray." Silent Ray, whether as a response to his fatherlessness or to his verbally abusive mother, is voluntarily but relentlessly mute.

At one point Jimmy, in a soliloquy addressed to his dead daughter, says, "I know in my soul I contributed to your death, but I don't know how." Could Jimmy's murder of Brendan's father have something to do with his daughter's murder? Jimmy asserts that "the apple never falls far from the tree." Could Brendan have murdered Katie? Could Brendan be the knowing or unknowing avenger of his father's death? Jimmy is desperate for revenge but uncertain whom to hold responsible.

The tragic twists and ironies are deeper and more complex than either those who suspect Brendan or those who suspect Dave can fathom. The truth concerning exactly how the sins of the fathers have impinged on the present, resulting in Katie's death, comes to light too late to prevent more killing and betrayal.

Virtuous Vengeance?

A considerable part of the dramatic tension within *Mystic River* is the race between Sean and Jimmy to solve Katie's murder and bring her murderer to justice. Jimmy's boyhood friend Sean, the detective assigned to the investigation, represents legal justice, but Jimmy's aspirations to be a self-styled righteous avenger convince him that he is in a better position to get to the truth and do something about it. The race is fueled not only by Jimmy's doubts that the police and the courts will succeed in doing justice, but also by his personal need to exact vengeance on Katie's behalf. He vows, "I'm going to find him before the police do and I'm going to kill him."

Questions of virtue's relation to vengeance lie close to the surface in the film. *Mystic River* bears comparison with tragedy in other narrative forms. Contemporary philosopher Peter A. French's closely argued book *The Virtues of Vengeance* looks to both Greek tragedy and classic Western movies for narrative illumination on issues of vengeance and justice.[4] Is vengefulness ever a virtue? Has legal justice completely displaced a morally legitimate role for personal avengers? For French, the *Oresteia* by Aeschylus is the seminal treatment of these issues.[5] The first two plays of the *Oresteia* show how personal vengeance breeds ongoing retaliation. Agamemnon, the son of Atreus, is cursed by his father's crime against his uncle. On returning from the Trojan War, Agamemnon is killed by his wife who, as it happens, is avenging his sacrifice of their daughter. Agamemnon's son Orestes then kills his mother to avenge his father's death. Only in the final play, when the gods intervene to set up the first court of law, can the cycle of vengeance be broken by a trial.

Mystic River is no generic tragedy. It is, in fact, steeped in the theme of the *Oresteia*. As in the *Oresteia*, the present of *Mystic River* is rank with the stench of past crimes. Moreover, the film raises many of the issues explored by Aeschylus and tackled philosophically in French's *The Virtues of Vengeance*. As French observes about the psychology of revenge, "There is little satisfaction in the villain's death for the would-be avenger who has not been the direct or proximate cause of his or her demise. A feeling of personal failure to achieve an important moral task is likely to grip the would-be avenger" if the perpetrator is "brought low" by other means.[6] This aptly describes what drives Jimmy. We must ask, is he, indeed, a righteous avenger?

French, who sees himself as indebted to Aristotle and Thomas Aquinas, among others, argues that there is such a thing as moral anger.[7] Moral anger is anger over injustice. Acts of personal revenge can be legitimated by moral anger, as long as the avenger fulfills certain conditions, including striving to verify appropriate targets for retributive harm and wisely attending to "fit" between the violation and the punishment.

Solomon Schimmel, in contrast, doubts that personal vengeance is ever virtuous. Schimmel points out that "although the desire for revenge is natural and at times moral, it is also very dangerous. If allowed to run its course without social control or judicial due process, it can result in injustice. The retribution exacted by an avenger will often be disproportionate to the original injury being avenged."[8]

French does not ignore these concerns. He acknowledges that anger can distort judgment and can be excessive or misdirected. At the same time, he also argues that an appropriate amount of anger toward those who harm others, both for the sake of victims and out of respect for morality itself, is not only permissible, but required. "To teach morality . . . is to teach when and how and at whom to be angry, who and when to retributively hate, and when and how to act because of one's moral anger and retributive hatred."[9] Moreover, French argues that institutional justice should not completely supplant personal vengeance, even within civilized societies with effective legal systems. Leaving all vengeance to legal systems will, French thinks, risk inculcating moral insensitivity, cowardice and passivity and also provide too little scope for courage, fortitude, loyalty, friendship and familial love—"virtues identified in the earliest literature in our culture and intimately intertwined with vengeance."[10]

Vengeance is commended by French for giving moral agents scope for exercising personal psychic strength in a way that institutional justice never can. Moral avengers "may be emotionally anchored in home, family or friends, but their moral sense and confidence are drawn from an inner strength, a physical and moral self-sufficiency. They are self-reliant and motivationally independent. Their sense of honor is personal, not public."[11] Viewers of *Mystic River* cannot fail to see that this passage expresses the sentiment of Jimmy's wife in her speech to Jimmy after he kills Dave. Jimmy is a "king" with a "big heart" who will stop at nothing to keep those in his family safe; nothing, says Annabeth, that Jimmy does for such reasons can be wrong. Others are weak, but she and Jimmy are strong enough to rule the neighborhood together, thus ensuring that their two remaining daughters will be safe.

This is one of the most chilling scenes in *Mystic River,* for by this point both Jimmy and Annabeth know that Dave is not their daughter's killer. Katie's actual killers are teenagers—Silent Ray and his friend—who start out "just wanting to scare her" for a lark, but they end up accidentally shooting her and then clubbing her to death with hockey sticks to keep her from accusing them. This is revealed when Sean's detective work uncovers their guilt and precipitates their confession. Jimmy misinterprets Dave's odd behavior, suspecting him in Katie's death, and brutally extracts a false confession. Dave's strange actions and attitudes are actually rooted in fears that the sexual abuse he endured as a child has made him into a homosexual pedophile. He has also lied and is guilty of a cold-blooded act: the blood on his hands the night of Katie's death is not that of a mugger, but of a man who was having sex with a child prostitute in his car. Dave beats the man to death in rage, which pours forth from his dread of becoming that man. Jimmy's rush to identify (and kill) Katie's killer before Sean does results in the death of a pitiful, confused and deeply wounded man—a man who was Jimmy's childhood friend and who has become a cousin through marriage. Jimmy, whose deepest loyalties are to his family, his friends, and his own sense of inner strength and personal honor, must now live in the light of the violation of his core values.

It appears, however, that Jimmy meets the requirements that French sets out for the virtuous enactment of vengeance. Jimmy performs the private avenger's equivalent of "due diligence." He relies on trusted investigators—his aptly named brothers-in-law, the Savage brothers. He carefully cross-examines Celeste, who tells him her suspicions concerning Dave's role in Katie's death. He even exacts a confession from Dave before executing him, though Jimmy's interrogation methods resemble trial by torture. And surely the punishment— a death for a death—seems to fit the crime. French's stipulations about proportionality seem to be met, for though Jimmy's execution of Dave is far from painless, it falls short of the brutal beating that Katie receives as she lays dying of her gunshot wounds. Jimmy is mistaken in his verdict, but police and law courts also sometimes err. Is Jimmy's mistake a merely tragic accident befalling a virtuous avenger, or is it the result of a tragic flaw—either in him or in the whole idea of virtuous vengeance?[12]

We will be in a better position to examine these questions after exploring another important theme of *Mystic River*: forgiveness. Whether and when vengeance's surgical strikes are virtuous depends on the scope of forgiveness's often subtle—but perhaps more efficacious—healing power.

Let Mercy Flow

"I'm sorry." These words introduce the first ray of hope into *Mystic River*'s dark meditations on the opacity of the human heart. Throughout the film Sean gets calls from his estranged wife, Lauren. Repeatedly she calls, but she says nothing. Sean tries to engage her in a way that will make her speak, but he fails. He does all the talking, trying to find out where she is and to get her to explain herself, until each time he plunges into exhaustion or despair or anger by her silence and hangs up. Because director Clint Eastwood and scriptwriter Brian

Helgeland choose to leave these exchanges underexplained and enigmatic, a casual viewer might see them as an intrusive and distracting subplot. Yet the fruitless phone calls are key to the theme of reconciliation that functions as a foil to the more frontally explored theme of vengeance. Eventually, during one call, Sean says, "I'm sorry," and, to his amazement, Lauren speaks, saying, "I'm sorry, too." In a film full of shattered relationships, the reconciliation of Sean with his wife is the one positive element.

In *Mystic River,* silence is the symbol for human disconnection. Both Lauren's silence and Silent Ray's self-imposed muteness are manifestations of their respective wounds and their capacities to wound. Throughout the film, wounds are also manifested and inflicted through loquacious secrecy—the empty talk and distorted speech that obscures more than it reveals. Dave tells many stories but has remained silent too long about his boyhood crisis—his physical escape from the "wolves" who kidnapped and abused him and his fears that his abductors are "in him" like vampires, waiting to turn him into the very predator he loathes. The hollowness of his narratives and his brooding secretiveness are the sources of his wife's mistaken conclusion that he killed Jimmy's daughter. Brendan's secrecy about the gun left in the family apartment by his absent father is the indirect cause of his beloved Katie's death. If he had not kept the hidden gun, Silent Ray would not have found it and used it in the gunplay that results in Katie's death.

At the same time, *Mystic River* makes it clear that confession is not in itself an antidote to destructive silence and secrecy. Celeste confesses to Jimmy her real but misgrounded fears about Dave. "What kind of wife does that?" asks Annabeth as she seeks to shift responsibility for Dave's death off Jimmy's shoulders. In a grisly parody of the sacrament of confession, Jimmy makes Dave kneel; Dave, lured by a false promise of clemency, makes a false confession to killing Katie in preparation for "washing" these sins away and "burying" them in Mystic River. Brendan, for years his brother's patient interpreter and mediator to the world of speech, repeatedly and futilely hits the boy, screaming, "Speak or I will f***ing kill you," in an attempt to get him to explain what motivated Katie's murder.

What is the difference between these ineffectual or destructive "confessions" and Sean's simple "I'm sorry"? From their fragmentary exchanges we deduce that Sean and Lauren are estranged because an extramarital affair has resulted in a daughter of uncertain parentage—is her daughter Sean's daughter or the daughter of her lover?[13] Barring a paternity test, no one knows. Surely she is the one in the wrong; surely she should be the one who first says "I'm sorry." But, for whatever reason, she cannot. And somehow, Sean is able to own his own portion of responsibility.

In his philosophical analysis of the concept of forgiveness, Joram Graf Haber argues that "in the absence of repentance, forgiveness amounts to little more than condonation of wrongdoing."[14] Haber asserts that repentance comprises two elements: remorse and the promise to refrain from repeating the misdeed in question. In the absence of these two conditions, forgiving is inappropriate—perhaps even impermissible—for giving up justifiable resentment displays lack of self-respect.

Is Lauren repentant? She seems to care about reconciliation. After all, she phones time and time again. But she is mired in silence and the revelation of her remorse remains ambiguous. Her silence has also precluded promises not to repeat the past. Sean can stand on his rights (as Haber would think he should). He can wait for reconciliation until she appeals to him for forgiveness. But he may very well wait in vain. Haber would take such waiting to be a matter of taking the moral high ground.

Miroslav Volf disagrees, for the view that forgiveness should be offered only after the demands of justice have been satisfied makes forgiveness into nothing more than "the refusal to allow an adequately redressed wrongdoing to continue to qualify negatively one's relationship with the wrongdoer."[15] Volf offers a Christian alternative to the "first justice, then reconciliation" model that he rejects. Christian faith is faith in "the God of indiscriminate love who died for the ungodly to bring them into the divine communion (cf. Rom. 5:8) . . . the God who offers grace—not cheap grace, but grace nonetheless—to the vilest evildoer."[16] Christian reconciliation is grounded in the primacy of the will to embrace even the offender, and it wills embrace even when reconciliation is not based on a clear answer to the question, what's in it for me? "Without the will to embrace, each party will insist on the justness of his or her own cause, and strife will continue," Volf explains. "The will to embrace—love—sheds the light of knowledge by the fire it carries with it. Our eyes need the light of that fire to perceive any justice in the causes and actions of our enemies. . . . If there is any justice in their causes and actions, only the will to embrace will make us capable of perceiving it, because it will let us see both them and ourselves with their eyes."[17]

Sean's willingness to say "I'm sorry"—before Lauren explicitly repents—allows him to see that he also needs to admit, "I pushed you away." Tellingly, this turning point comes after Sean explains to his old friend Jimmy that if, as Sean suspects, Jimmy has killed Dave, this act is a miscarriage of vigilante justice. Sean sees the devastating consequences of enmity in Jimmy's case. As Volf observes, both the willingness to embrace and its alternative stance of continuing resentment are "epistemic stances"—the former allowing us to see that we inhabit a world in which justice and injustice, innocence and guilt crisscross and intersect, and the latter blinding us to our own need for grace. If Sean had said, "I forgive you," rather than, "I'm sorry," would Lauren have hung up on him and stopped calling altogether?

Haber would have us believe that it would have been inappropriately generous of Sean to be willing to forgive Lauren before she has expressed appropriate contrition. Sean goes beyond what Haber would see as premature forgiveness and chooses to see the beam in his own eye (cf. Matthew 7:3-5). In doing so, he exemplifies an important point that Hannah Arendt makes about the contrast between revenge and forgiveness. Revenge, she says, is a natural automatic response that in re-acting against the original trespass permits a predictable, ongoing chain of reaction. In contrast, "forgiving can never be predicted; it is the only reaction that acts in an unexpected way and thus retains, though being a reaction, something of the original character of action. Forgiving, in other words, is the only reaction which does not merely re-act but acts anew and unexpectedly, unconditioned by the act which provoked it and therefore freeing from its consequences both the one who forgives and the one who is forgiven."[18] By choosing the primacy of embrace, Sean takes the steps that open the way for welcoming home his wife and the daughter whom he can choose to embrace as his child. Without the illumination granted by his willingness to forgive, Sean might have remained blind to his own responsibility in what has gone wrong with their marriage. Instead, in his decision, Sean Devine lives up to his surname.

Redemption: Vain Hope or Reality?

Volf anchors his account of forgiveness and reconciliation in the narrative of the cross of Christ. Crosses and Christian rituals are ubiquitous in *Mystic River*. A crucifix hangs in the home of Dave and Celeste. Jimmy and Annabeth proudly watch their youngest daughter's first communion. Yet in *Mystic*

River the cross points to more questions than the film itself unambiguously answers.

Whatever stance the film as a whole takes toward Christianity, it clearly is not neutral. The religious depictions are much more than sociological color, adding texture to the portrait of the film's setting in a Catholic section of Boston. Chillingly, the first cross we are shown in the film is on the signet ring worn by one of Dave's abductors as he drapes his hand across the seatback of the departing car. Is this man a priest, or is this "badge of office" as bogus as the badge on the belt of the man who ordered Dave into the car? Whatever the case, young Dave is deceived by false or treacherous symbols of authority—symbols that appear to represent the law and religion, traditional guardians of the good.

The most conspicuous cross in *Mystic River* is tattooed on Jimmy's back. Scattered scenes early in the film expose the top of this cross, visible just above his shirt collar. The view is too fragmentary, however, for us to know what it is. The cross is fully revealed only after Jimmy learns that he has killed the wrong person in the attempt to avenge his daughter. The tattoo is huge, reaching from Jimmy's neck to the small of his back, its crossbeam spanning his shoulders. Its thematic importance for the movie is signaled by the fact that it is not featured in the novel on which the film is based. So what is the significance of this cross?

The film supports multiple interpretations. At the level of a metaphor so crude as to amount to cliché, it is a heavy-handed reference to the "cross that must be borne" by someone with Jimmy's vast responsibilities as "king" and protector of his family. More subtle options are also available. For example, his tattoo is an invitation to understand the great and grave responsibilities that Jimmy feels he must shoulder and thus an invitation to empathic understanding.

More profoundly, Jimmy's cross may represent his own dual burden of unconfessed sin and self-appointed messianic mission. As the film concludes, Jimmy seems convinced by his wife that he can and must be not only his own savior, but the suffering servant of his extended clan also. Is Jimmy's tattoo a symbol of the perversion of religion—as is, perhaps more clearly, the signet ring worn by the abductor-priest in the film's opening scene? Where can self-appointed messiahs go to have their sins washed away?

Clint Eastwood has given us far more than a compelling portrait of what urban life in contemporary America can become when vigilante justice, rooted in clan loyalties, leads a parallel existence alongside officially sanctioned authorities for keeping the peace and ensuring justice. Viewing *Mystic River*, we are pushed to ask, in whom can I put my trust? This question has a personal dimension and individual aspect: Can Celeste trust Dave? Can Jimmy trust Sean? Can Sean trust Lauren? Can any of them trust themselves? Can any of *us*?

As we have seen, the question of trust in *Mystic River* has not just a personal but a religious dimension: How do we know whether we can rely on a person cloaked in religious authority? What rituals are living embodiments of grace and holiness, and which are perverted simulacra? Are all crosses linked only to betrayal, or is there a way of the cross that does lead to redemption?

Although *Mystic River* is complex enough to support multiple interpretations, numerous hints point in a profoundly Christian direction, away from an endorsement of French's "virtuous vengeance" and Haber's parsimonious, tit-for-tat view of forgiveness. Philosopher Marilyn McCord Adams argues that while the concept of forgiveness can survive transplantation into secular moral theories, it is particularly "at home" within a Christian framework. Her account of forgiveness helps us see that the alternative "epistemic stances" that Volf attributes to forgiveness and continued enmity are rooted in alternative worldviews. Forgiveness makes particular sense when seen within a robustly theological framework where the interpersonal context for forgiveness includes not just the person injured and the offender, but God who created and loves each and both. Forgiveness—especially generous, preemptive forgiveness—coheres less naturally with a world lacking an eschatological hope of ultimate justice. In a world where God will see to it that, in the words of the psalmist, "Steadfast love and faithfulness will meet; /righteousness and peace will kiss each other" (Psalm 85:10 NRSV) forgiveness is not acquiescence to evil but rather patient and hopeful participation in God's redemptive restoration project. In contrast, in a godless world, where human beings must rely on their own resources to bring about whatever measure of justice will ever ultimately exist, forgiveness can look not only risky but, as Haber avers, morally irresponsible.

Adams observes that the natural human response to injury is to feel that "victimhood uniquely qualifies one for the role of *judge, jury* and *executioner*."[19] Christian forgiveness, in contrast, requires the victim to relinquish these roles to God. Adams maintains that Christian forgiveness involves "a *process* of letting go of one's own point of view . . . and entering into God's point of view."[20] Christians refrain from being judge and jury because they know that no human can see deeply enough into another human heart to render an ultimate verdict. Moreover, their relinquishment of vengeance and their prayerful quest to transcend hatred, resentment, anger and indignation are rooted in a profound trust in God's commitment to truth, ultimate justice, and their own and others' ultimate personal well-being. As Christians strive to see those who have injured them as God does, they will desire what God desires—not revenge but reform and redemption.

Adams's acknowledgment that forgiveness is a process provides her with the conceptual equipment to respond to concerns similar to those raised by Haber. Forgiving wrongdoers before they have displayed remorse does not condone wrongdoing and undermine self-respect. This is because the Christian process of forgiveness does not hide or suppress vindictive emotions; it lays them before God. "All of the pain and humiliation, all of the retributive and vindictive feelings and attitudes, will be put out on the table between the victim and God in prayer."[21] As the victim enters more and more into God's view of the situation, the victim does not trade self-respect for an acceptance of the degradation embodied in the offense. Rather, the forgiving victim sees the implications of the offense "contradicted and compensated by the healing power of Divine love, whose omnipresent care builds a foundation" for forgiveness.[22]

Adams emphasizes not only that Christian forgiveness is a process, but also that it does not passively condone or acquiesce to evil. Recall French's fear that providing no room for personal vengeance risks inculcating moral insensitivity, cowardice and passivity and providing too little scope for courage, fortitude, loyalty, friendship and familial love. But Christians, as they come to see the world and all those in it through God's eyes, will become *more* morally sensitive, *more* loyal and *more* loving. Even as they place vengeance in God's hands, Christians are called to exercise courage and fortitude while fulfilling various active roles in the public and private identification of and opposition to wrongdoing. As Adams asserts, "What is pernicious from a Christian point of view is not active opposition to evil and the promotion of reform, but the notion that 'everything depends on us' with its correlative zeal for success that outruns human wisdom and power to insure it."[23] French's "virtuous" vengeance is all too prone to the pernicious notion that "everything depends on" the human avenger.

The perniciousness of this notion is aptly displayed in *Mystic River.* Jimmy is the avenger of betrayals—real betrayal in the case of Just Ray (a name with ironic double-entendre) and supposed betrayal in the case of Dave. Jimmy acts as though the cross he bears is indeed *his* rather than Christ's. Consequently, he must try to wrest the world into a sphere he can control. How else will he do "whatever it takes" to protect his family? Annabeth—perhaps a conflation of Lady Macbeth and Eve—tempts Jimmy to see this role as a burden that must be borne. That burden, thus constructed, precludes the willingness to admit that he is not only betrayed but a betrayer and to acknowledge that the world he inhabits is not one he can control.[24]

Jimmy seems to have moments of lucidity when he dimly intuits that this is a destructive distortion. At one point, when remembering his killing of Just Ray, he recalls a sense that God was watching him—"Not angry," he says, "like you do when a puppy s**** on the rug." In such moments Jimmy seems, however briefly, to forego what Adams calls "a one-dimensional picture of the offender qua offender" and adopt "a more complex characterization, which recognizes him/her (i) as a person with problems, (ii) in response to which s/he has deployed inefficient adaptational strategies, (iii) resulting in behavior harmful to his/herself, sometimes (but not always) as a person with similar problems and comparable faults."[25] Unfortunately, while Jimmy believes, imagines or hopes that this is how God sees *him*, he is unwilling to extend the scope of this leap of spiritual imagination to God's view of *others* or enter into the process that would conform his view to God's view. Like the cross on his back, Jimmy's theology is no more than skin deep. In contrast, Sean, who sports no religious trappings, enacts a reconciliation with Lauren apparently undergirded by a process of re-imaging similar to Adams's characterization of Christian forgiveness.[26]

Throughout the film, Eastwood uses a panning camera that climbs from a particular focal point to the wide view and then tilts toward the sky. Coupled with *Mystic River*'s studied ambiguity concerning religion, this cinematic device seems to invite viewers to choose between two fundamentally divergent "big pictures." Is the world a place where "everything depends on us," or is it not? Each viewer's answer to that question will make an enormous difference in how he or she evaluates, or even makes sense of, the actions of the film's various protagonists. And more importantly, our answer to that question will make all the difference in how we view crosses and where we place our trust and hope. In the final analysis, our answer to that question will make all the difference in how we live.

Ending the Cycle of Vengeance: Can the Personal Become Political?

As if such questions were not already overwhelming, the final scene of *Mystic River* alludes to corporate and communal—and, arguably, political—dimensions of trust, justice, vengeance and reconciliation. As the movie draws to a close, the community gathers to watch a parade—traditionally a celebration of collective identity and collective power. As parade participants dressed as colonial troops shoulder their weapons, the parade furnishes a context for bringing out the surviving cast members for final encounters, some enigmatic, some painfully ironic. As poor Celeste runs along trying to get the attention of her now fatherless son riding on a float, we are reminded that the cycle of vengeance may go on and on. What tragedy will *this* child's wounds lead to in the future? Sean, contentedly reunited with his family, makes eye contact across the throng with Jimmy, who is viewing the parade from the other side of the street with Annabeth. Sean forms an imaginary gun with his pointed figures, sighting down its barrel at Jimmy. Jimmy gives a mock salute. "I've got you in my cross hairs," one gesture implies; "bring it on," implies the other—yet another allusion to the probable continuation of conflict.

The patriotic music of the parade's marching bands can remind us that our global village bares all too many similarities to this Boston neighborhood. Such reminders raise pressing questions about whether forgiveness is relevant only in the personal arena. Can the personal become political?[27] Thomas Hobbes famously maintains that a "state of nature" without a political authority to settle disputes will become a war of all against all. The local solution to this, according to Hobbes, is that private individuals hand over their right of personal vengeance to the sovereign at the head of a political state. Where the sovereign is weak or mistrusted, as the civil authorities are in Jimmy's neighborhood, the war of all against all continues, episodically erupting into violence. Annabeth declares that Jimmy is a king—she crowns him the sovereign with the right to use whatever means necessary to protect kith and kin.

It is possible to view the cross on Jimmy's back as at least an indirect reference to what many political commentators, following the September 11 attacks on the Pentagon and World Trade Center, described as the burden borne by the United States as the "only remaining superpower." Is the United States the only force capable of vindicating freedom in the world and seeking justice against international terror? Yes, this is arguably the case. Yet in political conflict, each side tells "a story that justifies its own violence and delegitimates the other's." Moreover, attempts "to do justice in one side's terms will be seen by the other side as the continuation or resumption of war" by other means.[28]

Contemporary philosopher Jeffrie G. Murphy observes that the danger in doing battle with monsters is that we may, in the process, all too easily become monsters ourselves. How can we face the evil in ourselves and others—how can we grapple with it without plunging into evil rather than being delivered from it? Murphy's answer, like Sean Devine's, is through forgiveness. In its closing scene, *Mystic River* can call us to ask whether Murphy's answer applies at not just the personal but also the international level. Seeking justice through retaliation will all too easily turn us into monsters, but

> forgiveness can be seen as a healing virtue that brings with it great blessings— chief among them being its capacity to free us from being consumed by our angers, its capacity to check our tendencies toward cruelty, and its capacity (in some cases) to open the door to the restoration of those relationships in our lives that are worthy of restoration. This last blessing can be seen in the fact that, since all of us will sometimes wrong the people who mean the most to us, there will be times when we will want to be forgiven by those whom we have wronged. Seeing this, no rational person would desire to live in a world where forgiveness was not seen as a virtue.[29]

The political realist might say that although this is a fine sentiment for Boston neighborhoods, it cannot be applied to acts of aggression by nations or by politically or religiously motivated international terrorist organizations. Political philosopher Jean Bethke Elshtain espouses application of the just-war tradition to counterterrorism, advocating a Christian realism that she contrasts with both a realpolitik that severs the political from the ethical and a pseudo- or crypto-pacifism emanating from many mainline Christian pulpits in the wake of September 11.[30] Seeing herself as a contemporary follower of Augustine, Elshtain says, "It is better to suffer harm than to inflict it. But the obligation of charity obliges one to move in another direction: To save the lives of others, it may be necessary to imperil and even take the lives of their tormenters. The latter response is the appropriate way, suggests the just war tradition, to meet the challenges of systematic violence. As theologian Joseph E. Capizzi writes: 'According to Augustine, nonviolence is required at the individual level and just-war is mandated at the societal level.' "[31] Maintaining that "when a wound as grievous as that of September 11 has been inflicted on a body politic, it would be the height of irresponsibility and a dereliction of duty for public officials to fail to respond," she also acknowledges that " 'responsible action' involves contamination—one cannot altogether avoid getting 'dirty hands' when acting in the political world in a responsible way."[32] As "king" of his neighborhood, Jimmy Markum knows this well.

But if the political realist, whether Christian or not, is right, then does not Aeschylus's refrain in the *Oresteia*— "Ancient violence breeds / more violence comes"—have more practical purchase on humanity (for the time being) than Jesus's words "Love your enemies, do good to those who hate you" (Luke 6:27 NRSV)? Between Aeschylus's time and ours, Jesus hung on a cross. Volf maintains that there *are* political—and not just personal—implications of the cross and that these implications throw doubt on the compatibility of Christianity and the just-war tradition:

> It may be that in a world suffused with violence the issue is not simply "violence versus peace" but rather "what forms of violence could be tolerated to overcome a social 'peace' that coercively maintained itself through the condoned violence of injustice." . . . But if one decides to put on soldier's gear instead of carrying one's cross, one should not seek legitimation in the religion that worships the crucified Messiah. For there, the blessing is given not to the violent but to the meek (Matthew 5:5).
>
> There are Christians who have a hard time resisting the temptation to seek religious legitimation for their (understandable) need to take up the sword. If they give in to this temptation, they should forego all attempts to exonerate their version of Christian faith from complicity in fomenting violence. Of course, they can specify that religious symbols should be used to legitimate and inspire only *just* wars. But show me one warring party that does not think its war is just![33]

Can the way of the cross be applied to international politics, even in a post-9/11 world? *Mystic River* cannot answer that question for us. Films like *Mystic River* provide elegantly crafted narratives that push us to ask perennial philosophical questions. They enrich our humanity, not by providing neat answers, but by pointing beyond themselves to our need for wisdom. For Christians, such films point us to God, whose self-revelation in the cross is our hope for forgiveness and the wellspring of our capacity to forgive—most clearly at the personal level but, given that with God all things are possible, perhaps within the political realm as well.

Moral Monsters

Horror's Indispensable Need for Good and Evil

RONALD K. TACELLI, S.J.

. . . .

A new century is upon us, with all its attendant uncertainty. Where are we going? What kind of world will those about to be born inherit from those who helped draw the last century to a close? What will the world look like in the year 3000? Will there even exist beings recognizably human to ring in *that* new millennium?

Those able to remember the last half of the twentieth century know well the awesome rapidity of technological progress, and they know from bitter experience that technology can be used for evil ends as well as good. Think of the chaos and destruction that a few men armed with nothing more than box cutters (and deadly purpose) were able to effect. What could some with similar purpose do using weapons just as small but far more sophisticated? In this time of the so-called war on terror, where no clear demarcation of victory is possible, where the terror alert is perpetually elevated, the threat of devastation can weigh on our psyches like a chronic fatigue—sometimes barely noticed, but always there, and at some level always felt.

And even apart from intentional acts, the unintended effects of progress (e.g., the superbugs to which powerful antibiotics give rise) can occasion a hitherto undreamed-of sense of danger. So the very same forces that bring solace and comfort can also be a cause for abiding unrest and uncertainty.

Horror as Therapy

A recent news item made the claim that horror films were flourishing in these troubled times—were flourishing, in fact, precisely *because* these times are so parlous.[1] It may seem strange: we sit alone in the dark, viewing misshapen monsters, shuddering before images that pose no genuine threat to ourselves. But this experience, so the theory goes, gives shape and usually name to a constant burden of shapeless, nameless anxieties; and in doing so, it gives us a certain measure of distance from them. The current popularity of cinematic horror, then, can be seen as testimony to the therapeutic effect of controlled dread. For a few hours our ambient anxieties are projected outside us, reduced to various twisted contours, controlled by genre conventions; and in this rule-governed reduction and control we find comfort.

And so it may be. I'd like, however, in this essay, to suggest another reason why horror (in fiction and cinema, though here we focus on cinema) contains—and necessarily contains—a component that, if not profoundly comforting, is at least in a sense reassuring.

The Good in the Bad and the Ugly

It was a commonplace of scholasticism that any intentional act, however painful, burdensome, physically ruinous or morally depraved, is done *sub specie boni:* under the aspect of some *good*.[2] Those firefighters who ran into the burning skyscraper on 9/11 were trying to save lives; those student-athletes taking steroids know about the harm they're doing to their bodies, but they want strength, bulk and speed *now*.

So here we sit in this theater. The vampire has risen from his grave. He has crept up the castle wall, entered the young woman's chamber and is about to sink his teeth into her throat, drain her blood, make her his slave. If we find ourselves frightened by this, if we find ourselves tempted to turn away as the monster bares his fangs, it's not improper to ask, why are we here at all watching something we're tempted to turn away from?

Or perhaps we're watching another sort of horror film. Perhaps the silent killer with the strange mask is somewhere in the house, ready to emerge from the shadows as the heroine fumbles for a light switch. We feel a wrenching tightness in our stomachs. We feel tempted to close our eyes or at least avert them. But again, if this is so, then why are we watching? What is the *bonum*, the good, that is worth all this tension and sinking dread?

More than one good may of course inflect our enjoyment of horror. It may well be that in particularly troubled times the depicted horrors of cinematic art can in their way be a comfort. But horror, like the poor, we have always with us—in good times and in bad.[3] Is there a more universal cause for horror's perennial appeal? I believe there is.

Let's enter that darkened theater once again. Why do we react in horror when the vampire is about to claim his next victim or when the silent masked killer is about to strike? We do so partly, as least, because the vampire and the killer are *evil;* more precisely, they *embody* evil in an intensely focused and concentrated form. If we didn't see them that way, they could never inspire the kind of sinking dread that is the very hallmark of successful horror, the thing its black heart unceasingly aspires to achieve.

Also, if the evil that these creatures embody were not aimed, and necessarily aimed, at something *good* (or something at least containing elements of good), then we wouldn't perceive it as posing an identifiable threat—the peculiar kind of threat that ignites the internal engines of fear. If, for example, the vampire were attacking a ghoul, this might excite interest, amusement or—if the special effects were realistic enough—disgust. But *horror?* Again, suppose the silent fiend hidden in the house were stalking a gleefully vicious serial killer. We might be morbidly interested in what was going to happen, in who would be able to do what to whom. But since no element of moral good attaches to either character, the peculiar element of horror disappears from the scene of their conflict.

Moral Monsters

The important word here is *moral.* Horror requires the notion of a moral good that is able to be violated, overcome and destroyed as well as the notion of an evil that aims to destroy it. This is one of the ways in which horror can be a source of existential reassurance. The universe in which it exists *must* be a moral one, containing genuine goods and real evils—goods that can and *ought* to be morally valued, evils that *ought* to be reviled.

I do not mean that successful horror requires saints to be the object of evil's threat; successful horror requires merely that the object of evil's threat possess *some* good, something that truly *ought not* be destroyed—something beyond mere existence. Nor does successful horror require a peculiarly Christian understanding of good and evil. In some ways the moral universe of horror is pre-Christian or, perhaps better, proto-Christian. It may be that nature is the product of an all-good God, capable of mercy and forgiveness. But nature itself is not capable of these things. It possesses an order whose violation brings with it terrible consequences. This is the order that is horror's *conditio sine qua non.* Other genres may have their anti-heroes, their moral chaos, their nihilism. But to the extent that horror abandons a moral world and tries to occupy the empty spaces beyond "mere" good and evil, it chokes and dies for lack of the one thing necessary to sustain it.

Bad Examples

I would like now to examine three films that have variously attempted to traduce this simple rule. Each is acknowledged to be a failure—commercial or artistic or sometimes both. I want to suggest here that all of them fail as horror films for precisely the same reason: they seek to expunge the moral element necessary for the horror they aspire—and must aspire—to evoke.[4] These films span the two principle subgenres of the horror film: the one in which the source of fear is more than human, and the other in which it is only and all too human. The first film is Richard Blackburn's *Lemora: A Child's Tale of the Supernatural;* the other two are Ridley Scott's film of Thomas Harris's novel *Hannibal,* and Stuart Gordon's film of Charles Higson's *King of the Ants.*

Lemora: The Corruption of Innocence

Lemora is what some people are now calling a "lost classic," an expression that usually denotes a bad film retrieved from well-deserved oblivion by those whose nature compels them to defend aesthetically hopeless causes. The DVD's liner notes tell us that the film had "a disastrous first screening and difficulties with securing a distributor." This comes as no surprise to anyone who's seen the finished product.

But to be fair, the film—especially in Synapse Films' new digital restoration—does have some impressive features: Robert Caramico's sometimes stunning cinematography, with its eerie lighting and expressionistic use of color design; first-time director Richard Blackburn's staging of a few memorable set pieces; and the late Cheryl Smith's haunting portrayal of Lila Lee, the "child" whose tale the movie tells. But none of this can change the movie into something other than a cheaply produced and for the most part abysmally acted catastrophe, whose central conceit ensures its failure as the one main thing it seeks to be: a successful horror film.

Lemora begins with a murder. A gangster, Alvin Lee, guns down his cheating wife and her lover. We then cut to thirteen-year-old Lila Lee, dressed in immaculate white, a gold cross around her neck, standing before an all-female Baptist congregation. She sings "Just a Closer Walk with Thee." From his pulpit, the young reverend addresses the faithful with these words:

> Today, as every day, I'm going to speak about good and evil. But this time . . . it's not going to be no story from the Holy Book, about folk who lived thousands of years ago. For today we have an example of the influence that God can have over evil right here within our own very midst. . . . I'm speaking about our own singin' angel, Miss Lila Lee. Newspaper men, vultures who live off the weak, have printed the fact that our little princess is the daughter of Alvin Lee, an evil gangster who just now murdered his own wife. . . . [But] our own Lila Lee is the most innocent creature on God's earth. Removed from her monstrous parents for more than three years, she has been washed clean of their evil counsel and has been truly reborn, finding Christ's parental guidance as the ward of this our Church.

Sometime later, Lila receives a mysterious letter; it reads: "Dear Lila, I am writing you this at your Father's request. He is on his deathbed and in his fever constantly asks for you to come and forgive him for any harm he has done to you. Come alone. [If you do not,] you will not be taken to him and he will die without salvation. Because of your good works and intense devotion to God I know you will not fail him. Your fellow Christian, Lemora."

Immediately, Lila packs a small suitcase and sets out on her mission of forgiveness. She leaves a note for her guardian, the Reverend: "I am going to see father and forgive him. I'm still afraid but I want more than anything to be a good Christian and make you proud of me." To get to the bus station, some distance away in town, Lila hides in the back of a sedan. She overhears the couple in the front seat talking with undisguised scorn about her and the Reverend, imputing less than Christian motives to her beloved guardian: "I bet that old Reverend can't *wait* to teach her! He's ripe and ready to go!" These words call to Lila's mind episodes clearly indicating—to the viewer, though not apparently to her—that the Reverend finds her sexually tempting.

Once in town, Lila sees that she has ventured into a moral sewer. A man, urinating against a wall, turns to leer at her. A prostitute bathed in red light grins at her from a window and seems to beckon. Everything and everyone in the town appears to be fueled by violence or lust or both. Even the ticket agent at the bus station speaks to her in ways that are perversely suggestive.

Lila does at last find her way to Lemora—a strange, stately woman clothed from head to foot in black. Naturally, Lila is eager to see her father, but Lemora says she'll have to wait: her father has a disease to which Lila must become immune. But from outside her father's room, Lila overhears some deeply disquieting words between him and Lemora. He says in a weak though resolute voice, "I don't want to turn against my own kin." To which Lemora answers, "It's not like that at all; you'd be setting her free."

The film reveals soon enough the nature of this intended liberation. Lemora coerces Lila into consuming a strange red-colored drink (LILA: I'm so hot and dizzy! LEMORA: The drink has done that to you. Isn't it nice?), forces her to dance (LEMORA: Is fun evil?), and bathes her (LEMORA: What an exciting figure you have!). By this time, Lemora's interest in the girl has become unmistakably erotic. But Lemora, unlike the Reverend, does not view any part of her interest with shame or guilt. She tells Lila, "If someone has it in them to love me, they love me from the minute that they see me. Sometimes they don't even know it." The clear implication is that Lila is one of these people.

In quick succession Lila makes two harrowing discoveries: her father has been transformed into a ghoulishly deformed and violent monster, and Lemora herself is revealed to be a vampire who sucks the blood of children (though the word *vampire* is never spoken during the film). Lila tries desperately to escape, but to no avail. She runs finally into the very clutches of the woman she has tried in vain to elude.

Lemora gloats, "You never had a chance. Each one of your moves has been directed from the very beginning," and again, "I know you, Lila, better than you know yourself. We are one and the same, and until you realize that you will never be happy." Lila screams out, "I hate you!" and Lemora replies, "You think so. But I fascinate you too much, and you can't help yourself. Do you think this has been all my doing? You've been drawn to me from the very beginning." But Lila still resists changing into what Lemora is. She screams, "It's evil! It wouldn't be me any more!" to which Lemora responds, "Oh yes you would. The *real* you!"

In an effort to escape, Lila pushes though a curtain and—lo and behold!—she is back in church, dressed in her immaculate white robe, the same female congregation seated before her, with the Reverend standing at the pulpit. The Reverend turns to Lila, saying, "Let us show her our love! Are you with me?"

The congregation shouts, "Amen!" "Let us show this angel that we love her for the love she bears us. Do you feel love?" "Amen!" "Do you know she is as distinct and blameless from her father as Christ is from Satan?" "Amen!" "As good is from evil?" "Amen!" "As light is from darkness?" "Amen!"

Then suddenly we are back in the blue-lit darkness, Lemora's minions holding the struggling Lila , mocking her with one voice, "You're not so good. You're a hypocrite, a liar. The Reverend—you know he wants you. You know why. You encourage him, don't you? You see everyone trying to seduce you, drain you, devour you. But it's *you! You* want to seduce! *You* want to drain! *You* want to devour!" Finally Lemora tells Lila, "Come into my arms and free yourself from all guilt!" She breaks the chain of the cross round Lila's neck. The cross falls in emphatic slow motion to the floor.

The film then cuts to the Reverend, who has been hunting feverishly for Lila. It is night; he calls her name loudly and repeatedly. Finally, he sinks down, exhausted. When he opens his eyes, there is Lila just above him. She kisses him—and then kisses him again and again, with ever-increasing passion. He protests and struggles at first. Finally, he gives in to his lust. It is then that Lila reveals her fangs and kills him.

Cut back to the church. Lila, in her white gown, sings "Rock of Ages."

Roll credits.

Blackburn, who also plays the Reverend, says in his director's commentary that the "whole film's about repression"—that, in fact, the real theme of all horror movies is "repressed sexuality." This means, of course, given the structure of the plot, that Lemora represents liberation from repression. And since repression is bad, then Lemora represents something good. But Lemora is a vampire who sucks the blood of children. So, on the one hand, she represents liberation from unhealthy sexual guilt and hypocrisy (a good thing); but she is a literal monster. And this makes any audience sympathy impossible to direct.

Lemora fails as a horror movie because it dramatizes no real good endangered by evil, no innocence threatened with corruption. In its little universe, there is no genuine and properly valued good or innocence at all. The Reverend is a hypocrite, full of repressed lust, which makes his personality brittle and remote. And Lila? Her innocence, or what we believe to be her innocence, is the thing that at first compels us to identify with her and hope for her safety, even though the world around her (not just Lemora and her minions but even the church, as represented by the Reverend, and the town surrounding it) seems utterly corrupt—so corrupt, in fact, that very early on it becomes clear that nothing innocent can survive there, not even Lila. So early on, the hope of the audience, which after all generates suspense and thus interest, is all but sucked dry. The sense of impending doom—of hopelessness and helplessness—becomes overwhelming. Then the script sunders the one single thread tying us to the story.

We realize that Lila herself is not really innocent, that she is no angel after all, that the depravity of the town was the town as seen through *her* eyes—eyes drawn to the things her religion held as forbidden: things that therefore took on an exaggerated air of threat and danger. Lila loves Lemora, who represents freedom from sexual guilt, even though she doesn't at first know it. That is why Lemora can say, "I know you, Lila, better than you know yourself," and why she can say that by joining her Lila would still be herself, but "the *real* you." "I only show people who they are," says Lemora. Well, who can complain about self-discovery? And if that's all Lemora shows us, can she really be so bad? By portraying her in this way, the film drains her character of any real threat; and by portraying the world around Lila, and finally Lila herself, as devoid of genuine moral goodness, the filmmakers leave us without an object of genuine horror. Just a weird therapist, a self-help guru with a "thing" for blood.

Hannibal: One Man's Meat, Another Man's Person

Any mention of weird therapists is almost sure to evoke some thought of the world's most famous psychiatrist-cannibal, Hannibal Lecter. Lecter is the brainchild of crime-reporter-turned-novelist Thomas Harris, author of *Red Dragon, Silence of the Lambs* and *Hannibal.* All three novels were turned into movies: the first into a moderately bad film and a more recent (unintentionally) humorous remake; the second into a moderately good film; and the third into something so cosmically awful that its degree of failure—as Harris himself put it regarding Lecter's "intelligence quota"—"is not measurable by conventional means." The movie, however, is at least better than its source material.

The apotheosizing of Hannibal Lecter began in *Silence of the Lambs.* Still, the novel was a decent enough page-turner, and Clarice Starling was an attractive, sympathetic heroine. But with *Hannibal,* all critical distance between author and anti-hero has been erased. The reader can't help but get the impression that Harris identifies utterly with Lecter—with his stratospheric "intelligence quota," his impeccable taste, his ascent beyond mere good and evil, and his unashamed enthusiasm for ridding the world of the rude, the crass, the untalented. (Or at least Harris seems to *wish* he could identify with these qualities. Any reader with the stamina to slough through his sticky, graceless prose would be forced to conclude that if Hannibal Lecter were real, he'd have eaten Harris's liver by now.)

How to summarize a plotless story? *Hannibal* chronicles two unsuccessful attempts to bring Lecter to some kind of justice. One of the parties in this doomed contest is the FBI (and that means, of course, Clarice Starling); the other is Mason Verger, Lecter's only surviving victim. Verger molested children at a (surprise!) Christian camp his father ran. Lecter was assigned as his therapist. Verger invited Lecter to his home one evening and attempted to demonstrate the sexual pleasures of near asphyxiation. While Verger was swinging from his noose, Lecter offered him uppers and then convinced him to cut off his own face. This Verger did with a shard of broken glass (because, as he puts it, it seemed like a good idea at the time). Never one to waste protein, Lecter fed Verger's face to the pet dog.

Now, many operations and skin grafts later, a crippled, scarred, wheezing Verger is consumed by thoughts of revenge. He plans to feed Lecter to specially trained wild boars. He knows, however, that the FBI are after the same prey and naturally wants to prevent them from getting to Lecter first. He realizes that Lecter's peculiar attraction to Clarice might be used to lure him into a trap. Verger is wealthy enough to buy off a corrupt agent, Paul Krendler, who uses his influence to put Clarice in a very bad professional light. Verger's plan is foiled (of course). He dies horribly. Lecter then lobotomizes Krendler, trepans his skull, cuts away bits of his forebrain, cooks them up with a delicate sauce and serves them for dinner. Krendler himself is made to join in the meal.

That's pretty much it. The movie version differs from the novel in several important respects, but most especially in this: at the novel's end, Clarice *joins* Lecter and feasts on Krendler's brain. She even asks for seconds. This scene of cannibalism and murder is presented as something positive, as part of Clarice's psychological liberation. In other words, in the world of Thomas Harris, the only evils are poor taste and cultural illiteracy (and *maybe* child molestation). Only if this is true could Lecter be presented as a genuine hero, someone for whom we're supposed to root; only thus could Clarice's capitulation be seen as something positive and she herself as someone with whom any readers this side of maximum security could conceivably identify.

The screenwriters knew that Harris's vision could not be successfully translated to the screen. And so in the film, Clarice looks on in revulsion as Lecter feeds Krendler bits of his own brain and feeds on them himself. This at least attempts to preserve some focal point of good to which an audience might direct its sympathies; and it testifies to the truth of our thesis, that without a real good that evil attacks or endangers there can be no genuine horror.

Unfortunately, Clarice is a minor character in the film. For the most part we have to choose between an ugly child molester and a brilliant, sophisticated cannibal. And clearly we're supposed to side with the cannibal. But since this is impossible for most of us, our sympathies go nowhere, and we watch the lushly photographed carnage with a kind of dull detachment. The movie cannot chill us because it does not interest us: it does not engage the part of us attuned to good-threatened-by-evil that evokes the response peculiar to horror. By the time Clarice does enter the picture, her moral scruples seem pallid and weak. It's as if she lacks the psychological strength to join Lecter on the other side of good and evil. Since no one wants to identify with psychological weakness, Clarice is not an effective prism through which horror can be successfully refracted. And so *Hannibal*, though markedly different from, and significantly better than, the novel at its source, is still a failure. It wants us to identify with a man who is "beyond good and evil," even though good and evil are the prerequisites for the horror it seeks to evoke.

Myopic *Ants*

The locution *beyond good and evil* naturally recalls Friedrich Nietzsche. Our final example of failed horror, *King of the Ants*, makes clever use of themes found in (and perhaps consciously taken from) Nietzsche—among them that mere conventions of morality cannot prevent the overman from doing the deeds that express who he is.

Stuart Gordon's film tells the story of Sean Crawley, a young man who drifts from one odd job to another, well on his way to becoming a loser. Duke Wayne, a fellow he happens to meet while painting someone's house, introduces him to Ray Mathews, a contractor. Mathews asks Crawley, "So . . . what would your feeling be on . . . things that are immoral . . . ?" Crawley answers, "Well, I suppose it's up to us to sort it out for ourselves, I guess." Mathews seems satisfied with Crawley's answer and attitude and makes a tantalizing offer: Crawley is to tail someone named Eric Gatley. He is to report on Gatley's comings and goings—especially those that seem significant in some way. Crawley jumps at the opportunity to play detective.

Since Crawley doesn't have a car, he'll have to tail Gatley on his bicycle. He parks himself outside Gatley's home and pretends to be fixing the bicycle chain when Gatley emerges with his wife and daughter. Gatley's wife Susan is strikingly beautiful. Crawley is transfixed and stares intently at her. She looks up, meets his gaze, and then turns away to her daughter and husband. But Crawley feels a powerful attraction to her. He even takes time off from tailing Gatley to follow Susan to the place where she works, the Midnight Mission, a shelter for the poor and homeless.

One day, Crawley's detective work seems to pay off. He spies Gatley speaking to a television reporter. He tells Mathews. That same evening, an inebriated Mathews confronts Crawley and asks, "How far are you willing to go?" Crawley isn't sure what Mathews means. Mathews explains that he wants Gatley dead and wants Crawley to kill him.

CRAWLEY. I'd need a reason why I was gonna do it.

MATHEWS. Such as?

CRAWLEY. Such as . . . uh . . . reward.

They settle on $13,000. "That's my lucky number," says Crawley, forcing a grin.

The next day Crawley goes to Gatley's home and brutally murders him. He also takes incriminating papers from Gatley's briefcase. That night, scenes of the murder keep playing in his head, preventing him from sleeping. The next evening, when Crawley is at a bar with his friend George, who works in a dog kennel, the story of Gatley's murder is reported on the television news. Crawley is horrified to see that Gatley is pictured wearing the same gardener's hat he was wearing at the time of the murder. George, with cynical humor, comments, "A guy who wears a hat like that deserves to die."

But Crawley has more than the murder on his mind. He can't seem to make contact with those who hired him. And he wants his money. Finally he hears from Wayne, who tells him they'll meet at the zoo. When they do meet and Crawley asks for his money, Wayne puts him off and suggests they play a game of finding the animals in the zoo that most resemble them. Crawley begins to get angry; he repeats his demand. Wayne heaps abuse on him: "You're a clueless little turd." Wayne tells Crawley that Gatley was never supposed to die. In fact they had hired Crawley in the first place figuring he'd be so incompetent that Gatley would certainly notice the tail and become spooked and then make a false move. But Gatley was more oblivious than Crawley was incompetent. Mathews was just drunk and ranting when he'd made Crawley the offer. Now, says Wayne in disgust, they've got a murder on their hands.

By this time Wayne and Crawley have moved into the tunnel housing the zoo's insect exhibits. Crawley is adamant. He says he doesn't care whether or not Mathews was drunk, whether or not Gatley was supposed to die. He killed Gatley and he wants his money. "I did a job and I want to be paid." Wayne becomes livid, grabs Crawley from behind, and squeezes his neck with his forearm. "You're nothing," he tells Crawley. "You're a worthless piece of s***. I don't want to ever see you again. And if I do, I can kill you. I could kill you and I wouldn't even break into a sweat."

Wayne lets go and Crawley falls to the floor, gasping for breath, tears streaming from his eyes. Then Wayne's gaze fixes on one of the exhibits. "O look!" he says in a brutally mocking voice. "I think I've found you. Yeah, there you are. O look, Sean, look. I found you right there. You're an insect, a f***ing ant!" It dawns on Crawley that his situation is desperate. He bundles up the file and gives it for safe keeping to George.

Almost immediately after this Wayne tracks Crawley down and stuffs a bus ticket to Chicago in his pocket. Crawley then tells Wayne that he has Gatley's file. He refuses to leave Los Angeles and adds that if he does not get his money he'll turn the file over to the police. Wayne throws Crawley into the back of his van. In the front seat are two construction workers, Carl and Beckett. Wayne calls Mathews, who instructs him to bring Crawley to his place in the desert.

Mathews devises a plan. They will bash Crawley's head with golf clubs until his brains are so addled he'll never be able to find the file or corroborate it—if there even is a file. Crawley is stuck in a shed, tied to a chair and beaten repeatedly. These beatings take a terrible toll. Crawley begins to suffer from nightmarish hallucinations involving Susan Gatley. She approaches him with apparent desire; he steps forward eagerly and then notices a monstrous phallus where her vagina should be. As he shrinks back in horror, she begins to curse at him in a deep male voice. Later, he sees Susan as a huge insectlike creature eating its own excrement. The creature says, "Feed me, Sean!" and pulls him toward itself as he screams, "I'm sorry! I'm so sorry!"

At some point during this torture Crawley seems to become oblivious to the pain, almost addicted to it. One night, while Carl and Beckett are away getting beer, Crawley viciously kills Wayne. Carl and Beckett return to find Crawley running free. Mathews drives up seconds later, sees the chaos and orders Crawley killed on the spot. Then suddenly, as if out of nowhere, George arrives in his van and, in all the ensuing confusion, is able to whisk Crawley away.

As they're driving off, George explains how he found where Crawley was being kept. He's also read the file. He thrusts it furiously into Crawley's arms, demanding an explanation. "They're just ants," Crawley explains. "They don't matter. Back there I realized what my part is. I finally know now what I was always meant to be. . . . I'm an exterminator." This is not what George had hoped to hear. "You killed a guy!" he screams. Crawley corrects him, "Two guys."

GEORGE. Why? Help me understand why!

CRAWLEY. Why? It just happened. It was his hat. You said it yourself, man; he just looked so f***in' dumb in that hat.

GEORGE. You killed him because of a *hat?*

CRAWLEY. I killed him 'cause I wanted to. . . . I'm not the same guy I always was.

George throws Crawley out of his van. Crawley, clutching his file, limps— swollen, bruised and bloody—to the Midnight Mission shelter and, of course, to Susan Gatley. Susan finds herself strangely drawn to this badly beaten stranger. She feels that he somehow knows her, that he understands things about her he couldn't be expected to know. So when, after some weeks, Crawley is well enough to leave the mission, Susan makes the impetuous decision, over the objections of a colleague, to take him home till he can get fully back on his feet.

It doesn't take long for Susan and Crawley to become sexually intimate. But one day, after Susan has given Crawley her husband's bicycle and he bends to adjust the chain, she remembers that she's seen him before—right there in front of her house, staring at her and her husband. Once Crawley leaves on the bicycle, Susan rushes into his room and finds the file. Minutes later, when Crawley returns, Susan furiously confronts him. She tells him the police are on their way. But so great is her rage that she physically attacks him. Without really wanting to, Crawley kills her. He then avenges himself on Mathews, Carl and Beckett. He traps and kills them at Mathews's place in the desert. He burns Mathews to death. He's preparing to finish off Carl and Beckett when Beckett asks, "Why?"

> CRAWLEY. There needs to be a reason? . . . I'll tell you what this is all about. You ever watch ants? . . . I saw some at the zoo once. Thousands of 'em, just eating, s***ing, f***ing, dying, just like they always have for millions of years. . . . What I'm trying to say is that it doesn't matter what any of us do. It's a sh***y world or it's the best of all possible worlds. Just depends on how you look at it. But there's nothing anyone can do about it. The ants'll just keep on doing what they do and we'll just keep on doing what we do.

Beckett pleads, "I never did anything wrong." And in fact Beckett never has participated in the beatings, has in fact treated Crawley with some measure of kindness. But Crawley is unmoved.

CRAWLEY. It doesn't work like that.

BECKETT. You're going to kill us then?

CRAWLEY. That's what I do.

And that is the last sentence spoken in the film.

Perhaps the deepest insight into the failure of *King of the Ants* as a horror film was articulated by its director. In the DVD's commentary track, Gordon states, "This movie is about a guy finding himself and finding out what it is that he does well. . . . There's something positive about that. No matter—even if it's about a guy becoming a killer—the idea of someone finding out their vocation, their calling, is always positive." And that is precisely why *King of the Ants* fails to generate real horror. We're supposed to root for a man who achieves the insights, through torture, that the world is not a moral place, that we human beings are the excrescence of a nonbenevolent nature that consumes what it excretes, and that he has a taste and talent for killing. This insight undermines even the point of rooting for his act of vengeance. For since the universe doesn't work according to norms of right and wrong, there is no real moral point, no real justice, in the killing of his tormentors. He's just fulfilling his desires (including the desire for immunity from implication in Gatley's murder).

The film is in many ways more sleek and linear than the source novel by Charles Higson, who also wrote the screenplay. But the novel spells out things the screenplay as filmed leaves completely unthematized. For example, the novel contains an explicit "revelation" of atheism. Crawley asks himself through his throbbing pain whether he's being punished, whether there is some "external justice" behind what is happening to him, whether God himself might be swinging the implements of torture. "Am I guilty?" he asks himself. Then suddenly a "light" cuts through his pain.

> Of course he wasn't being punished. Of course this wasn't hell. Of course he wasn't guilty. God had no hand in this. How could he? He didn't exist. It was as simple as that. This wasn't punishment, it was just revenge. Mathews was caught like a rat in a hole, and he was desperate, striking out at the nearest thing at hand, and that was Sean.
>
> Not guilty. Never guilty.
>
> Gatley and Duke were dead. So what? People died every day.

This is followed by a reference to Nietzsche: "They hadn't made him weaker; they'd made him stronger."[5]

Later Crawley muses that "the only thing stopping you from doing whatever you wanted was yourself. Once you could kill the policeman inside you, you were free."[6] But this plunges Higson's audience into a world where the engines of horror are deprived of any possible fuel. If there is no right or wrong, no real good or evil, then what exactly in *King of the Ants* ought not to be but is? On Higson's own terms, the answer is nothing.

One more thing—in the novel, Higson presents his "hero" as pretty much soulless right from the start. One of Crawley's most vivid early memories is of deliberately letting a young boy named Gordon drown.

> Sean could easily have rescued him, but he hadn't wanted to. He'd hated the boy, hated him for falling in, hated him for being called Gordon, hated him for having a talking Action Man. In fact, he'd hated the whole family. What sort of people went on boating holiday when none of them could swim?
>
> But there had been something else, a tremendous feeling of power. By simply standing there, watching, doing nothing, he'd felt he'd had the power of life and death over these people.[7]

In light of this, Crawley's transformation into an active killer does not come as much of a surprise. And it greatly reduces our ability to sympathize with him during his time of torture (especially since, by that time, he has already murdered Gatley). But in the film, Chris McKenna plays Crawley with great charm and humanity. His fear, hesitation and disbelief when he agrees to kill

Gatley, as well as his greed and jealousy for Gatley's wife—somehow McKenna manages to convey all these emotions, and this keeps the audience aligned, however tentatively, with his character. The later, tender scenes with Susan undercut Crawley's claim that he's become an exterminator. But these very human moments are themselves undercut by the nihilistic philosophy Crawley spouts during the last minutes of the film. By the end, we feel merely confused and empty—not exactly what a successful horror movie should evoke.

Sympathy for the Devils

Through all of this I have tried to emphasize a single, simple point: without a moral human good, there is no possibility of horror. And films that dispense with any such good, as so many contemporary horror films have sought to do, end up at best as exercises in induced nausea. But nausea, while it may be horrible, is not horror.

If the great characters from the great horror films of the past could collectively address this trend toward morally empty "horror," what would they say? Picture them standing together. Vampires. Werewolves. Ghouls. Depraved killers, masked and unmasked. They might, I think, say something like this: "Stop! We cannot exist without the good; in eliminating it from your films you are also eliminating *us!* For then the very point of our being, to destroy and corrupt the good, is lost to us. And then *we* are lost as well!"

To this, the closest these evil creatures will ever come to a prayer, I can only add, "Amen."

PART FOUR

FAITH AND RELIGION

Religion and Science in *Contact* and *2001: A Space Odyssey*

BRENDAN SWEETMAN

● ●

From the point of view of the relationship between religion and science, a hot topic these days, both *Contact* (1997) and *2001: A Space Odyssey* (1968) are fascinating films. Both are rich in suggestions and possibilities for the viewer interested in exploring what philosophers call *ultimate* questions—questions dealing with the origin and nature of the universe, and with the purpose and destiny of human beings. Along the way, other questions are also raised that are an integral part of that larger conversation, for example, about the rationality of religious belief versus the rationality of atheism, about the nature of consciousness and free will, about the role of science in the quest for human knowledge and, of course, about whether there might be intelligent life on other planets. Even the most casual viewer of these films cannot fail to be provoked by them, will not be able to resist being seduced by the wonder of life in our universe, cannot but be engaged by the ultimate questions. It helps that the films explore these themes in a fairly evenhanded way, with the main viewpoints (religious and atheistic) well represented, leaving most viewers satisfied that their own concerns have been raised and acknowledged as the stories unfold.

The plot line in both films is deceptively simple. Stanley Kubrick's *2001* is an early, serious film that begins with the story of the evolution of man. This is conveyed by focusing on evolving apelike species out in the wild, as it were, with no dialogue or human characters. During the course of their evolution, the apes come across a black monolith, a large upright slab. The implication is that somehow, through the power of the monolith, they make the "break-through" to tool making. The film then switches to a future, advanced age of human development whose emergence has been suggested by the evolutionary story. An apparent communication from some other life form has been found on the moon in the form of another black monolith. While the monolith is being examined, it suddenly starts emitting signals aimed at Jupiter. So the plan is for astronauts Dave Bowman and Frank Poole, along with three others who are in a state of hibernation, to travel to Jupiter to investigate the origin of the monolith and its purpose. What makes the journey to Jupiter interesting is that the spaceship is largely operated and controlled by an intelligent, talking machine, called Hal. Hal (the HAL 9000 computer) is supposed to be much more intelligent than human beings. Eventually he kills all but one of the crew and takes over the ship. But the remaining astronaut, Dave, ingeniously manages to outwit Hal and succeeds in disconnecting him! Dave then proceeds with the mission. The film ends with some cryptic and perhaps ultimately unsatisfying suggestions about the origin and nature of life.

The lead character in *Contact* is Dr. Ellie Arroway, a clever scientist and astronomer, who is also an atheist and supporter of the view that science can explain all of reality. (This view is now known in philosophical and theological circles as *naturalism*, and I will say more about it presently.) Her ideological foil is Palmer Joss, a former seminarian. He is a religious scholar, well-known for his book warning against the dangers of deifying science and technology in modern society because they cannot tell the whole truth about human life. For her part, Ellie is mostly interested in discovering whether intelligent life exists on other planets. Despite being shunned by her colleagues for pursuing what they regard as a far-fetched project, she persists and eventually receives a message from Vega (a star in the midst of our galaxy). The message appears to contain information about how to build some kind of space machine. After the usual political wrangling, and after the sabotage of the first machine, a second machine is built, with Ellie slated to travel out into the unknown. As the machine is powered up to take off, Ellie has an experience of traveling through a space tunnel (perhaps to Vega, twenty-five light-years away?) and meeting her dead father, who tells her that the message she received is genuine but that he does not know who sent it. While this is going on, the staff at the launch pad see only the machine powering up, suffering a malfunction and falling into the sea. The film then ends with a debate about whether she really had the experience—whether it might have been a delusion—and what it might all mean for the human race.

Both films are visually stunning, with masterly use of special effects, to convey fabulous vistas of space travel—sometimes at high speed—and sequences of planets, stars and worm holes; these are all accompanied by evocative soundtracks, which cannot fail to convey to most viewers the enormity and majesty, as well as the beauty and mystery, of the universe. Indeed, it is important not to forget what we are dealing with here. The universe consists of galaxies (ours is called the Milky Way, and a near neighbor is Andromeda); each galaxy is thousands of light-years in length; and there are estimated to be a hundred billion galaxies with a billion trillion stars! In short, this place we live in is indeed awe-inspiring, even mind-boggling, and calls out to us the questions, how did it all get here? and what is *our* purpose here? Both films present us with these questions in an engaging way that is quite rare in any art form.

The relationship between religion and science is a hot topic these days, generating much interest and discussion not just in academic circles but also in popular culture. This explains the success of *Contact* and the enduring relevance of and interest in *2001*. In this essay I wish to explore, through these films, four issues related to the religion-science debate, focusing especially on the more recent *Contact:*

- the debate between religious belief and naturalism
- the nature of the human person, particularly in relation to consciousness and free will
- the nature of religious experience
- the question of intelligent life on other planets and its possible significance for religion

Naturalism Versus Religious Belief as Background Theme

As noted above, the main character in *Contact*, Ellie Arroway, is an atheist. She is also what is known in contemporary thought as a naturalist. A naturalist is somebody who believes that all of reality is physical in nature, consisting of some configuration of matter and energy. The way to understand reality, therefore, according to the naturalist, is by means of science. Science is a discipline that studies the nature of the physical realm by means of the scientific method, which involves gathering data, performing experiments, making em-

pirical observations, and forming and testing hypotheses. So if one believes
that all of reality is physical, then one normally has a correspondingly strong
commitment to the scientific endeavor, since science is the way to study the
physical.

Ellie's view entails that God does not exist and that there is no soul and no
afterlife (at least as traditionally understood). These beliefs are a consequence
of her naturalistic views, rather than a reason for them. In this sense, it is more
accurate today to regard naturalism as a kind of positive atheism. This means
that naturalists like Ellie try to look on the positive side of what they believe—
unlike atheists in the past, who tended to be more negative, both in stating
their view and in defending it. In the past, an atheist would almost always define herself as someone who did *not* believe certain things (e.g., in God, in religious morality, in the authority of the clergy), rather than as someone who
did believe certain things (e.g., that all of reality is physical, that human beings
are completely physical beings, that we need a secular account of morality).
The denial of other (religious) views would then follow from these positive
claims. In addition, atheism was almost always defended in a negative way,
usually by attacking religious belief, perhaps by attacking the specific arguments often offered for theism, such as the first cause and design arguments
for the existence of God (which I will come back to later). But today all of that
has changed. Indeed, even as a young girl in the film, the scientific view is beginning to emerge as the only way Ellie thinks about life.

Ellie's worldview is becoming more influential and is found in the work of
many well-known scientists, such as evolutionary biologists Stephen J. Gould
and Richard Dawkins, Francis Crick (of DNA fame), physicist Steven Weinberg, and, perhaps most famously of all, astronomer Carl Sagan, the author of
the original novel *Contact,* which inspired the film.[1] Naturalists like these are
interested in certain scientific theories, especially those that might have a bearing on the ultimate origins of the universe and the nature of the human person. So they often turn to the theories of evolution, genetics, quantum me-
chanics, relativity and so on as theories that would be most fruitful for their
task of providing positive evidence for their positive claims. But because of the
link between these well-known theories and the attempt to defend naturalism,
there is confusion—not just in popular culture (e.g., in the media, such as PBS
science programs), but even in the universities—about the distinction between
science and naturalism. Perhaps this is understandable, since naturalists so

often turn to science to make their case. Nevertheless, it is crucial to appreciate that science and naturalism are not the same thing. Many, perhaps most, scientists are not naturalists, and this is significant in any comparison of the rationality of religious belief, such as theism, with the rationality of naturalism (i.e., atheism).

Ellie differs from many scientists in that she gives a lot of credence to the view that there is intelligent life on other planets. Although the belief that there may be intelligent life on other planets is compatible with either theism or naturalism, it is perhaps most closely associated with an atheistic interpretation of the theory of evolution. Evolution is the theory that all life forms have evolved from simpler life forms through common ancestry. This occurred through a process known as natural selection, which means that all life forms compete with each other in their environments and nature favors or selects those life forms best able to cope with, or which are the best "fit" for, their particular environment. According to the theory, all life forms (including plants and animals) are, therefore, *genetically* related to each other on the tree of life. (This is *the key* claim of the theory of evolution from a philosophical and religious point of view.) If the theory stopped there it would not perhaps be quite as controversial as it is, and many hold that officially it does stop there.

But among large parts of the philosophical and scientific community, the theory does not stop there, and it is not possible to understand the deeper points of *Contact* without appreciating in what ways the theory is then extended. Evolution still leaves us with some momentous questions:

- How did the whole process begin? And where did the first life form come from?

- Is the process designed, or is it entirely random?

It is essential to point out that the theory of evolution itself does not answer these questions. This is not because we don't have enough evidence yet, but because *logically* it cannot answer them. The theory is supposed to be an explanation of how species change over time; it is not an explanation of how the first one got here. It tells you what happened after the first one got here. And the question of whether the process is designed is generally regarded as being *outside* the domain of science proper, belonging instead to the domains of philosophy and religion. It is a question that science as a discipline cannot and should not address.

This means that a scientist, or a strong supporter of science (like most of us), who takes a position on whether evolution is designed or directed is making a *philosophical* claim, not a scientific claim. It is easy to see that this is true when the scientist is also a religious believer. But it is equally true when the claim is made by Ellie Arroway. When she claims that the universe is all that exists—or, in the words of Carl Sagan, "The cosmos is all that is, or ever was, or ever will be"—this is a philosophical statement, not a scientific statement.[2] And it is a philosophical statement that in Ellie's and Carl Sagan's case is on the side of atheism (naturalism). So Ellie's answer to the question of where life came from is the same answer that naturalists like Carl Sagan would give: living things originated out of *nonliving* things (out of the primordial soup, as it is sometimes metaphorically put) when the conditions were right at a certain time in the history and development of our planet. In addition, she holds that this was a chance, random occurrence, not a designed event. And so her answer to the second question is already given: there is no overall design to human life or to the universe itself. Both of these beliefs, which Ellie holds fairly strongly, will be challenged by her "trip" into space.

The other main character in *Contact*, Palmer Joss, represents the theistic view in the film. His worldview is the complete opposite to Ellie's; the adventure into space and the questions it raises bring out the contrasts and the debate between the two worldviews most sharply. As a theist, Palmer is an opponent of naturalism. At several points in the film, he says that he is interested in the pursuit of truth and is prepared to follow it wherever it leads. He does not believe that naturalism is the truth about the universe and the human condition. He believes that the physical universe must have had a creator and that there must be an overall design plan. He also holds that there are other ways of knowing, in addition to the scientific approach, though he does not denigrate science and is a strong supporter of the scientific method. He does, however, warn against making a mistake that naturalists are prone to make, which is to almost deify science, to regard science as the *only* way to knowledge. As he tells some of the leading scientists in the film, "I am against the men who deify [science and technology] at the expense of human truth." The danger is that any knowledge or experience that seems to be outside of science, such as human relationships, love, honor, trust and sacrifice—indeed many of those profound experiences that often evoke or inspire a religious response—will be diminished or downplayed.

Ellie is supposed to be the hard-nosed scientist who does not need religion and who pursues science in a practical way to seek knowledge and benefit mankind. To the filmmaker's credit, her views are challenged at several points. For instance, at a party with Palmer, where they've gathered with presidential advisors to discuss their response to the message from outer space, Ellie tells Palmer that there is no proof that God exists, that a scientific explanation is the best explanation for the universe. She would need proof to believe in God. Palmer responds by asking her if she loved her father. Ellie says she did, very much. But Palmer asks her to prove it! This gives her pause, since she can't prove it in the scientific sense, and the point is made that not all forms of knowledge are open to a scientific proof, because of the nature of the subject matter. Human love is one of those experiences. It points to something greater than ourselves. Ellie could reply, perhaps, that based on various types of external evidence it is reasonable to believe that she loved her father. But the same approach can be used to argue for the existence of God—that based on an examination of the existence, complexity and beauty of creation, it is reasonable to believe in a creator. This reasoning could be extended further to argue that the evidence taken as a whole supports theism better than naturalism, since theism can explain in a better way than naturalism so much that a questing human mind wants to explain in a fascinating universe.

Arguing for the existence of God in this way—by examining the overall cumulative evidence from a variety of sources throughout the physical universe (including human experience), along with seeking the most reasonable account of the nature of life and of the human person—is called *natural theology* by philosophers. The two best known arguments of natural theology, best known to the layperson at least, are the cosmological argument (the first cause argument, from the Greek word *cosmos,* meaning "world") and the teleological argument (the argument from design, from the Greek word *telos,* meaning "purpose" or "end"). Both arguments are clearly present in both films. Viewers can hardly fail to wonder how the universe got here (the first cause question) and whether it is the product of chance (the design question) while watching these films.

Both of these arguments are an important part of the overall argument that theism is more rational than naturalism, a position I believe both films easily support. Despite the fact that *Contact* was based on a novel written by a naturalist, the film does convey sweepingly, as does *2001,* the universe in all its majesty, and a Christian may claim that this evidence speaks for itself! The cosmological argument revolves around the fundamental question of the ultimate cause of the universe, a question raised in both films in a very evocative way by the visual experience of space travel and its mysteries, which also gives us a moving sense of the sheer size of the universe. Where did this vast universe, with its huge number of galaxies (including our own Milky Way) come from? The answers a viewer might consider are that the universe is eternal and so does not need a cause; that it came into existence *with no cause;* and that it was caused by something other than itself, something outside the physical order. Many Christian philosophers hold that the first two possible answers are unreasonable. William Lane Craig is well known for arguing, on both philosophical and scientific grounds—reviving an old argument of Saint Bonaventure's—that an eternal universe makes no sense, by showing that an actual infinite series of physical events is impossible in the real world. In addition, medieval philosopher Thomas Aquinas argues that even if the universe is eternal, it still needs a cause, because a contingent series of events (which the universe would be) cannot cause itself, *no matter how many members are in the series.* This cosmological argument leaves us with a supernatural cause for the universe, a cause *outside* or beyond the physical order. It is also reasonable to conclude that this cause is personal, intelligent, rational and powerful.

The modern version of the argument from design is based on the claim that the universe in which we live shows clear evidence of *design* or *order* and that this order suggests a *designer* or a *orderer* behind it. The order referred to here is not the overt order that we often think we can detect in nature in our own ordinary experience (such as the order in the seasons or the opposites in nature) but the *underlying order* in the whole universe: the laws of physics—laws that are progressively discovered, not invented, by science.[3] The argument from design is inspired by the evidence that we live in a lawful universe, not a lawless or chaotic one, such as one might expect to find if the universe really were a product of chance. The analogy of spilling a can of alphabet soup is useful here as a metaphor for how naturalism thinks our particular universe came about. If the can is toppled by accident, what are the chances that the letters would spell out *Rockhurst University is number one!* or *Go Irish?* They are not very high, I suggest! Yet of all the possible universes we could have ended up with, if it truly was an accidental occurrence, we ended up with a lawlike one, an ordered one, one that follows laws consistently, laws that make life itself possible. One could perhaps reply that there is no order in the universe at all, or that even if there is order, there is a natural cause for this order, and so we do not need an orderer. But it is hard to deny that there is order in the universe (especially understood as the underlying laws of physics); and the excellent visualization of the majesty of the universe in both films forces on viewers these questions: Is there—could there be—a natural explanation for this order? What is the probability that the order came about this way? Could it all have come about by chance? Chance, however, seems a very unreasonable explanation.

I should also briefly mention another version of the argument from design that has gotten significant attention in recent years—the argument from the fine-tuning of the universe (sometimes called the *anthropic argument*). The idea behind this argument is that various sciences have shown in the last few decades that the existence of intelligent life on Earth depends on a complex and precise balance of initial conditions that were a part of the big bang (which is the main theory today to explain the beginning of the universe). The upshot of this discovery is that the emergence of life depends on a fine-tuning that is almost mind-boggling and the probability of which is so low that it is difficult to calculate. Again, the conclusion of the fine-tuning argument is reasonable: that our universe very likely did not happen by chance and is instead the product of a designer. This is the only conclusion the evidence supports. As astronomer Fred Hoyle succinctly expressed it: science shows that the universe looks like a "put up" job![4]

The appeal by naturalists like Ellie in some vague way to the theory of evolution to explain the order and design in the universe does not succeed because the theory of evolution obviously cannot explain the origin of the universe or the laws of physics. It cannot explain the origin of matter and energy, since the theory must *presuppose* these properties, and an environment, in order for evolution to take place. It is not possible after all for *A* to evolve into *B* if *A* does not yet exist! Evolution also *presupposes* the laws of physics, just as all scientific theories do.

Both films raise the theism-naturalism debate in a quite overt way, and they call on the viewer to engage with the questions and work out their own responses. Neither film, sensibly, takes a clear position on the ultimate questions. Indeed, there is a crucial moment in *Contact* when Ellie has the experience of traveling through space (a worm hole, she thinks) and of meeting her father. She asks him who is responsible for making this possible, how did it begin, what is the aim of it all? His reply is, "Nobody knows." The film refuses to answer the ultimate question, leaving it up to viewers to answer it for themselves.

What Kind of Beings Are Humans?

One of the other momentous questions raised by both films concerns the nature of the human person. What kind of beings are human beings? This is a cutting-edge question from the point of view of the theism-versus-naturalism discussion. These two related questions are especially prominent: Are human beings completely physical beings? Do human beings have free will? Let us look at each question in turn.

The first question comes up in a consideration of Ellie's naturalist worldview. Since she believes that everything that exists is physical, she must believe that all life forms, including human beings, are physical too. This means that human beings are made up of matter and energy only, operating in some very sophisticated way, no doubt, but still just matter and energy. There is therefore no soul, no nonphysical or spiritual substance distinct from the body that gives life to the body and that might have an independent existence of its own. Ellie is not necessarily committing herself to a cold-hearted, mathematical, functional view of human life (though it might come down to this ultimately). She still believes that human beings have consciousness and are capable of love and other profound experiences; perhaps she even believes in a type of spirituality. Ellie's view is that science can, at least in principle, give a full and complete account of what it means to be a human person, with all our ideas, beliefs, joys, fears, loves, moral concerns and such.

Ellie is in full agreement with Francis Crick's astonishing hypothesis about human consciousness: "The Astonishing Hypothesis is that 'You', your joys and your sorrows, your memories and your ambitions, your sense of personal identity and free will, are in fact no more than the behavior of a vast assembly of nerve cells and their associated molecules."[5] So we get the intriguing naturalistic interpretation Ellie offers for her experiences after she makes the trip through space, when she meets her father walking along a beach (which appears to be modeled on her childhood drawings of Pensacola, Florida). She does not interpret this to mean that her father really exists in this strange place (and he himself may not understand how or why he is there). Because she is committed to naturalism, she interprets this to mean that the alien intelligence was able to read her mind (in some unknown way, involving computer scanning perhaps) and, as she puts it, "You downloaded my thoughts, even my memories," and re-created them in a program. This perhaps would be Sagan's view! One can see how far-fetched this is, but it is the only explanation a naturalist could give for these kinds of phenomena. She puts this interpretation to her father, who simply says, "We thought this might make it easier for you"—a deliberately ambiguous answer, though the film does seem to exclude a religious interpretation because it suggests that her father has not survived death or that if he has, he knows neither why he has survived nor who is responsible for his survival. Or does it suggest something else? Ellie's father also says that the one thing that makes the loneliness bearable is that we have each other, a religious message perhaps, an optimism that opens up the possibility of a religious response. (And let us not forget that the aliens, too, are faced with the ultimate question of how everything came into being.)

This brings us to the second question, which is raised more directly in *2001*. The presence of the machine, Hal, inevitably gets us thinking about human free will and also about the question of artificial intelligence. Free will, a major theme of *2001*, is sometimes overshadowed by the movie's focus on extraterrestrial life. Hal is portrayed as a machine capable of performing "most of the functions of the human intellect, and at a speed vastly superior to man." He is often referred to as a sixth member of the crew and is interviewed from Earth, along with his fellow astronauts, by a TV station. All of this sets the stage nicely for the question of whether Hal can truly think and whether he is truly free. The traditional answer to this question, which supports the religious worldview, is that since thinking requires a nonphysical mind and since Hal is simply a physical computer, however sophisticated the program is, he cannot think. Yet this point brings out a contradiction in *2001*. The film clearly suggests that Hal is free, and so he freely decides to take over the ship. Yet because Hal's intelligence is completely physical and programmed, he cannot be free! (The freedom of the astronauts faces the same problem!) This contradiction most likely escaped the filmmakers, but it is nevertheless there, bringing to light the dilemma that faces naturalism with regard to the body-mind relationship. There is no explicit discussion of free will in *Contact*, which is fitting because free will is a topic that many naturalists often downplay or ignore. Nevertheless, Ellie is portrayed as somebody who clearly believes in free will and in moral behavior, but she does not seem to realize that there is no place for free will in her universe.

Free will may be defined as the unusual capacity of human beings to make a genuine choice between two or more alternatives. Although there may be reasons for the choice, we are not *compelled* to choose one option over the other. We always have a real choice. This is the root of morality, democracy, responsibility, and theories of reward and punishment. The major problem for the naturalist worldview in general is that it does not seem to have any room for free will. If everything is simply a matter of physics, and all can be explained by science (in terms of cause and effect, let us not forget), then this would apply to the human mind as well. All human actions would have to be explained as a sophisticated, complex causal chain of physical events that involves a combination of our environmental influences and the physical states of our brains. Like Hal, we would be just sophisticated machines. This is why many naturalists reluctantly conclude that—although they know it has serious, undesirable consequences—they can't see any place for free will in a totally physical universe. This is one of the most obvious, strongest arguments against naturalism for the layperson. It is almost impossible to believe that human beings don't have free will and also impossible to recommend how we should live and organize society if we really came to believe that there is no free will.

The existence of free will and the nature of consciousness are powerful arguments in favor of a theistic worldview. These features of human experience can be included in the overall argument for the rationality of religious belief. The naturalist account of these features of human experience is very implausible and, in the case of free will, very difficult to believe without some kind of evidence. The existence of consciousness, the difficulties of reducing it to just a function of brain states (reductionism) or of explaining mental life in physical terms, with its strangeness and remarkable properties, including free will, seem to point to the conclusion that consciousness is nonphysical. This increases the probability that some kind of supernaturalism is true. The most reasonable understanding of reality is that it contains features that are not reducible to physics and that are, therefore, outside the scientific domain.

The Power of Religious Experience

A topic we have not yet touched on in *Contact* concerns the nature of religious experience. Perhaps this matter is raised in a more subtle way in the film, at least in the sense that many viewers do not seem to notice it, but I am convinced that it is an important theme. The first point to note is that when Ellie asks Palmer early on in the film why he believes in God, he does not refer to the traditional arguments in his answer; instead, he tells her that his belief is based on a religious experience. He describes this experience as being very powerful, as prompted by wonder at the size and beauty of the universe, his feeling that he is not alone and that he is not scared of anything, even death. "It was God," he concludes. The filmmakers employ this particular argument to support Palmer's belief in God, I believe, because many Americans would identify with his description of this experience and would claim that this is why they believe in God as well. The problem, from a philosophical point of view, with such experiences is precisely in the fact that they are private and so can't be publicly verified. While they are profound and emotionally moving to the person who has the experience, they can always be second-guessed by doubters.

What is fascinating about this film, though, is that Ellie has a similar type of experience on the spaceship! It is not a religious experience as such, since it does not overtly have religious content. Yet, significantly, Ellie describes this experience in much the same way that religious believers (like Palmer) describe their experiences. She is frustrated when she later appears before the doubting members of the congressional committee because, she says, while her experience is hard to understand and explain, she is convinced it was real and says that it changed her forever. It was an experience of the universe that tells us we are not alone, that we are precious. It involved awe, humility and hope. But because nobody saw the spaceship leave the launch pad, they doubt she had the experience at all, and some believe that it was probably some kind of psychotic episode (or perhaps even that the whole thing was an elaborate hoax). All of these doubts will sound familiar to religious believers, of course.

At the congressional hearings set up to investigate her account of her experiences onboard the spaceship, her scientific way of looking at the world is challenged. When a hard, clinical, scientific approach is brought to bear on her experience, the kind of approach she herself has championed, she is forced, however reluctantly, to admit that as a scientist, she must acknowledge that the experience might not have been of actual events, even though she is sure it was genuine. Ellie appears to have revised her view of science here and is now moving close to allowing that science may not be the appropriate domain for investigating and thinking about these types of experiences. She is on the verge, perhaps, of admitting that because of its limited application to the realm of the physical, science may end up dismissing something that is real and powerful. This view is in sharp contrast to her attitude, expressed earlier in an appearance before the same committee, when the subject concerned who should travel in the machine and represent mankind. At that time, she insisted that *as a scientist,* she relies *only* on empirical evidence and proof!

Once again, the film does not come to any definitive conclusion on these matters but simply plants these ideas in the mind of the viewer. The universe calls forth experiences that demand an answer, and it is suggested that a scientific, naturalist answer may not be reasonable or even possible. In addition, we can see that science itself can lead people to have profound experiences of the universe, experiences that point *beyond* science and especially beyond naturalism. In this way, Ellie's "trip" into space contains the seeds of a challenge to her whole worldview.

Life on Other Planets?

No discussion of these films can be complete without considering the question of whether intelligent life exists on other planets. This is perhaps the least interesting and least engaging question raised by both films, which is ironic, given that both at first sight appear to be mainly about the subject of intelligent life on other planets! But this assessment is probably an indication that most people agree with Ellie's initial critics in *Contact*—that commitment to the search for extraterrestrial intelligence (SETI) project is a waste of time and talent! Yet Ellie's reasoning certainly gives us pause: given that there are four hundred billion stars in our galaxy alone, if only one out of a million stars in the universe had planets, and if just one of those had life, and if just one in a million of those had intelligent life, there would be millions of civilizations out there in the universe.

What would be the implications for humanity if we did discover life forms, especially intelligent life forms, on other planets? This would be determined in part by the type of alien species encountered. One of the most challenging features of making a science fiction film is how to portray the alien species. This explains why in many of these films there is often a feeling of disappointment when the alien species is actually encountered onscreen. The filmmakers seem to run out of ideas in this admittedly difficult area; sometimes they appear to lack imagination. This is the case with both of these films. *Contact* basically avoids the question of the nature of the alien intelligence altogether, and *2001* is not much better, portraying the astronaut going through various stages of aging (presumably caused by an alien intelligence), a sequence that can be interpreted in a number of ways. But would the existence of intelligent life on other planets support theism or naturalism (or neither)? Many naturalists seem to think that it would support their view, but the picture is not so clear when we probe a little deeper.

The discovery of alien species would, in my view, make the existence of God more likely. If one takes the anthropic argument, in particular, seriously and appreciates the extremely small probability of our universe being suitable just by chance to support intelligent life, then this, as we have noted, is an argument that life on Earth was designed. But surely if life on earth is that improbable, the existence of life on more than one planet in the universe is just as improbable. And so, if it turns out that there is life on some other planet, this may be even more support for the argument from design. Naturalists like Sagan believe that if we discover life on other planets, this would confirm the hypothesis that life originated out of nonliving things here on earth and be further confirming evidence for an atheistic or naturalistic interpretation of evolution. However, it would not necessarily show this, because we would have no direct evidence of life originating from nonlife. (This would still remain a hypothesis.) But based on the evidence from the big bang, the possibility of life occurring on several planets in our universe is so incredibly low in terms of probability that its discovery would better support the conclusion that a designer is responsible.

A lot may also depend on what alien life turns out to be like. If we discover human beings on another planet, and they are the highest, most advanced form of life there, as they are on Earth, this would surely be an argument in favor of theism. The hypothesis that it just so happened that the kind of life that developed by chance on both planets turned out to be exactly the same is so improbable as to be not worth taking seriously! On the other hand, suppose that the alien species had a different biological structure, body structure and so on than ours but still had the same logical and reasoning ability as we have, along with free will and moral agency. (This is how most science fiction films portray alien species.) This may be an argument again in favor of theism because it would show the centrality of reason and morality in intelligent life, bespeaking a creator. Only if the alien species were radically different from us in almost every respect—biology, reason and morality (though it is hard to con-

ceive of intelligent life without a system of reason at least similar to ours)—
might one see it as an argument in favor of naturalism. But even here it would
not show this, because of the possibility that God's creation may be vastly
more spectacular than we had hitherto thought. It would certainly diminish
the centrality of human life but not the view that life is created according to a
particular plan for a particular reason. Let us not forget that the alien species
would share our ultimate question, what is the cause of the universe? They
may even, indeed most likely would, believe in God.

In conclusion, all of these fascinating, and often literally mind-boggling,
ideas are raised by *Contact* and *2001: A Space Odyssey*. They are well worth our
time and reflection as we probe the most ultimate questions of all. These are
rare films that leave us face to face with the questions that the universe calls
out to every human being who takes only a few moments to think about its
nature and about our own valuable and unique place in it.

Bottled Water from the Fragrant Harbor

The Diluted Spiritual Elements of Hong Kong Films

WINFRIED CORDUAN

"My kung fu is good. I will kill you," proclaims the evil enemy.

"You are nothing. Prepare to die," replies the good protagonist.

With this less-than-subtle dialogue, a battle commences between two men, each one using his martial arts to their full extent. They may fight with their bare hands and feet; they may use swords; they may pick up objects conveniently within their reach and turn them into weapons. They may remain on the ground; they may be on the furniture, roofs, tree tops, ladders or burning poles; they may even fly as they seek to annihilate each other. In the end, after perhaps ten minutes of uninterrupted fighting, the protagonist will win out. The enemy is defeated, and good triumphs one more time.

Such a scene may be the climax of a two-hour film, in which there are numerous similar battles, not only between the main protagonist and the chief enemy but between supporting characters as well. How can one even begin to look for philosophical or religious meaning in this kind of a production? My contention in this chapter is that even though it is fruitless to see most martial arts films as vehicles for reflective thought, these films do give evidence of their roots in serious East Asian thought. These philosophically interesting worldview features, then, do contribute to the development of the plot and the characters.

The genre I will discuss in this essay is frequently called "Hong Kong films."[1] Obviously, the primary reason for this name is that these films were made in Hong Kong, the City of the Fragrant Harbor. However, even though naming the location alone does not imply a particular approach, Hong Kong films follow a general style and formula.

The main language of these films is Cantonese, the prevalent language of Hong Kong, with Mandarin dubbing or subtitles usually a standard feature. However, since Hong Kong has become a part of the People's Republic of China, this practice may slowly be reversed. As a British colony until 1997, with a free harbor, Hong Kong provided an environment whose films appealed to a consumer-driven market without the encumbrance of extraneous nationalist or Marxist ideologies. Thus, rather than being a vehicle for education or indoctrination, the goal of these films has been to please an audience and, in proper capitalist fashion, to leave viewers wanting more.[2] And, given the subject matter, what the audience wants is action—plenty of martial arts combat.

The particular Hong Kong films in which we are interested, namely those featuring martial arts, can be roughly divided into two groups, which are somewhat sequential but largely overlapping.[3] The 1960s were the golden era of the *wuxia* films, which emphasized swordplay, romantic plots and greater freedom from the natural laws governing bodily movement, so that characters could even fly through the air. Contemporary readers will immediately recognize *Crouching Tiger, Hidden Dragon [Wo hu cang long]* (2000) as a recent attempt to reclaim the genre. *Wuxia* films began losing popularity to kung fu films, though they had been around for a long time. They eventually began to dominate the scene under the banner of Bruce Lee and his successors. Kung fu refers to barehanded fighting (often translated as *boxing*, hence the Boxer Rebellion of 1901). It portrays the fighters with highly developed skills but with purely human limitations, as was graphically portrayed in Bruce Lee's *The Chinese Connection [Jing wu men]* (1972), even ending with the death of the hero.[4] Today many films will combine *wuxia* and kung fu, as seen for example in *Iron Monkey [Siunin Wong Fei-hung tsi titmalau]* (1993), where the local doctor (the "Iron Monkey") demonstrates more of the *wuxia* style, while the traveling herbalist, Wong Kei-ying, is a master of kung fu.

Historical Echoes in Hong Kong Films

Given the contemporary appeal of Hong Kong films, it may seem paradoxical that much of their formulaic nature is an outgrowth of historical roots. Traditional Chinese performance arts come with strict rules. The presentation must follow standards of costume and makeup, include familiar plot elements, provide comic relief and contain certain forms of spectacular display, such as acrobatics or martial arts. There is a ritualistic quality about Chinese theater, which is expected by the Chinese audience within any medium, whether it be stage or film. These elements may strike a Westerner as excessively stylized and possibly as unsophisticated.

Understanding traditional Chinese drama and the scope of its influence enables us to better appreciate Hong Kong films as a legitimate art form. First of all, and most likely surprising to a Western reader, the Daoist (Taoist) funeral sets important patterns for how any story is acted out in Chinese culture. A Daoist funeral is a drama performed by the priest and his assistants, who display the journey of the recently deceased soul to the underworld. The soul must carry a writ of pardon for sins committed in this life, leap over obstacles, brandish a sword and win arduous battles in order to overcome the demons that stand in its way. In a highly choreographed performance that usually lasts about an hour (though it could last much longer), the priests portray the adventures of the soul until it attains final peace and rest. I have witnessed bored priests going through the required formulas while the family of the deceased pays little or no attention. But I have also seen priests rising to the occasion and drawing the audience along with them as they give a spirited performance. The eyes of the audience were fastened on the priests' every move, reflecting anxiety, fervor or humor as the soul met its many challenges. With their complex choreography, martial arts films cannot help but remind a Chinese viewer of the funeral drama.

Another part of Chinese dramatic tradition is the Wayang, the Chinese theater. Particularly during the time of the Hungry Ghost festival each August, one sees roadside stages where acting companies and musicians give free performances. The primary audience is the gods and spirits, which are believed to be roaming freely during this time, while the visible audience consists of human beings who follow the well-worn plots with keen interest. Even though the play will begin with an invocation to the spirit world, its actual subject matter is usually this-worldly: boy meets girl; boy loses girl; boy gets girl back. The play will be filled with stock characters: the rigid father, the wise and clever mother, the sneaky but devoted servant, the evil and selfish enemy, and so forth. Although the stories are well known and formulaic, they continue to entertain. Similar observations can be made concerning the predictable story lines of Hong Kong martial arts films.

A third facet of Chinese drama that sheds light in this context is so-called Peking Opera. Although in strictly technical terms this art form is only a few centuries old, it embodies millennia of Chinese culture; and even despite being named after the Chinese capital, Beijing, its patterns have left their influence in many provinces of mainland China and beyond. A website defines Peking Opera as "a synthesis of stylized action, singing, dialogue and mime, acrobatic fighting and dancing to represent a story or depict different characters and their feelings."[5] The important terms in this definition are "stylized action," "mime" and "acrobatic fighting," which lend the performances their distinctive elements. Masks painted on the faces of the actors clarify to the audience whether a character is a hero, a spirit, a warrior and so forth. For Peking Opera to work, it must conform to these standards or it simply would not be intelligible. Without meeting these rigid requirements, the performance would not communicate and, consequently, would not entertain the audience, which relies on the established template to understand the plot. Since audiences have been conditioned by this ancient art form, we can expect to see some transfer of expectations to the martial arts films under consideration.

In summary, we begin our look at Hong Kong films by recognizing their roots in the performance arts of ancient Chinese lineage. To be sure, there are significant differences as well, but the similarities help us understand that predictable plots and stereotypical characters are, from a traditional vantage point, assets rather than flaws.

Cultural and Spiritual Elements

We will now look at particular aspects of Chinese culture and how they are exemplified in a number of Hong Kong films. Before going any further, we must accept that the Western disjunction between a spiritual realm and a secular realm simply does not apply to Chinese thought. Not only is spiritual life thoroughly integrated into all of Chinese culture (as might also be an accurate description of, say, Islamic or Hindu societies), but the distinction itself simply does not apply. For any number of customs, what is secular is spiritual, and what is spiritual is secular, and there is no point in classifying these beliefs or practices as either one or the other. Thus, for example, filial piety—the unconditional submission to one's parents—is one of the central Confucian virtues. To call it either exclusively secular or exclusively spiritual would not do it justice. Nonetheless, given our specific interest, I will emphasize from time to time the more spiritual understanding of the cultural elements in question. But I will do so knowing that this can be an artificial perspective. In the rest of this chapter, I will discuss five specific examples of these elements: filial piety, social groups as inextricably religious and political, martial arts as integrated into spiritual orders, balance as the highest ideal, and portrayal of Western values as incompatible with Chinese ideals.

Filial piety. Think of Chinese culture and the idea of filial piety should spring to mind before anything else. Virtually all cultures teach children to obey their parents, but Confucianism has elevated this duty to a supreme precept overshadowing all others. Although Confucianism tends to be short on supernatural elements, there is no question that heaven (Tian, T'ien) has decreed this virtue to be the highest obligation. Filial piety trumps truth, respect for life and property, and even observance of religious rituals. One might say, by way of contrast, that in a biblical context the commandment to honor one's mother and father implies that parents be honorable; filial piety makes the honor of one's parents sacrosanct in its own right. In Hong Kong films, filial piety is generally assumed as a pervasive theme, though from time to time it becomes a crucial plot element.

A subtle but poignant example can be found in a very small addition to the plot of *Once Upon a Time in China [Wong Fei-hung]* (1991), starring Jet Li.[6] A Westerner almost certainly would miss it, but a Chinese person might catch its significance. In a comic relief segment, Lang, the rather heavyset pork butcher, replaces one of the actors in a Wayang theater, taking on the role of a rather corpulent Madam White Snake, a stock character from Chinese mythology. The moment is brief and ludicrous. Nevertheless, the allusion is clear because the story of Madam White Snake portrays filial piety as the highest virtue. According to Chinese legend, Madam White Snake was an evil sorceress, responsible for thousands of deaths that eventually lead to her imprisonment in an impenetrable tower. Still, her son prayed for her faithfully every day, and as a result of his unreserved filial piety, even this most evil of women was released from her prison. Including momentary allusion to this legend in a film about a young man, named Wong Fei-hung—who is struggling to maintain traditional Chinese virtues in the context of overpowering Western influences around the dawn of the twentieth century—this little slapstick moment reveals Madam White Snake, portrayed by a fat, bumbling butcher, to be an almost prophetic character, commenting on the fate of filial piety specifically and about all of traditional culture generally.

Filial piety takes on a more serious face in *The Legend of Drunken Master*

[Jui kuen II] (1994), starring Jackie Chan. Chan plays a young man, again named Wong Fei-hung, caught up in a struggle against international interests wishing to smuggle valuable artifacts out of China, thereby besmirching Chinese culture and impoverishing the local people. Fei-hung is skilled in all martial arts, but he has developed a particular aptitude in the style of "drunken boxing." The idea is that, as a fight commences, the combatant quickly guzzles one or two bottles of unspecified alcohol, putting him into a totally inebriated state. As he assumes the traditional stances associated with kung fu (imitating various animals), he looks droopy and silly but also enjoys a plasticity that makes it impossible for the opponent to land a clean blow, while he is able to surprise the opponent with unexpected successful hits. Fei-hung has mastered this skill and defeats his enemies with it.

However, his father, an herbalist doctor named Wong Kei-ying, is not only opposed to drunken boxing, he has forbidden his son to do any fighting whatsoever. Naturally, the plot of the film places Fei-hung into situations where fighting becomes unavoidable, but Fei-hung's father continues his unrelenting opposition. Fei-hung's first serious breach of his father's expectation results in severe corporal punishment, and after disobeying his father a second time, he is disowned and sent from the house. It is only a greater breach of family honor—Fei-hung is captured by his enemies and suspended naked from the village gate—that leads Kei-ying to permit the lad to return home. As you might expect, the film climaxes with Wong Fei-hung's having to decide once more between obeying his father or saving the whole community. Given the genre, it is not hard to predict which way he will choose. The point is that even with Wong Fei-hung's eventual defiance of his father, a Westerner might perceive this plot as arbitrary and contrived because a Westerner would expect to see the justice of the boy's cause fairly early on. However, understanding that filial piety overrides other obligations in Chinese culture makes the film far more realistic within its culture of origin. With this background understanding, a Westerner is in a better position to experience the film authentically.

Filial piety also plays a notable role in *Iron Monkey* (mentioned above), starring Yu Rong-gang and Donnie Yen. This film centers on the struggle of an impoverished community against a corrupt governor. Yen portrays Wong Kei-ying, an herbalist doctor, who comes to town and gets caught up in the fight. His approximately twelve-year-old son, Wong Fei-hung, has accompanied him. The youngster is learning all about the herbs and roots and winds up contributing to the fight significantly, though he is poisoned at one time and needs to make a slow recovery. Meanwhile the father is fighting for his life due to his misidentification as the notorious bandit, the "Iron Monkey."

Though a strong bond of love between father and son is clearly evident, Kei-ying will not permit any external display of affection. When father and son are first reunited, Fei-hung expects an embrace and some kind words, but instead Kei-ying immediately reprimands him for his supposedly sloppy dress. However, by the time the film is over and the evil governor has been ousted, the father is learning to express his love for his son. You see, in Confucianism a son is expected to relate to his father with filial piety, but the father is supposed to demonstrate kindness. Although no such explicit statement is made in *Iron Monkey*, presumably Wong Kei-ying has finally learned this fact.

Have you noticed that I have mentioned three films so far and that each one of them has a central character named Wong Fei-hung? Did you catch that two of them include his father, Wong Kei-ying, an herbalist doctor? In fact, there are many more films in which Wong Fei-hung is the name of an important protagonist, usually the central hero.[7] Here we get a glimpse of the trait to which I alluded earlier, that Hong Kong films, as all of Chinese dramas, use standard characters. In this case, the name is that of an actual martial arts expert, Wong Fei-hung, who lived from 1847 to 1924. In addition to having a reputation in kung fu, he was loved and revered as an herbal healer who never turned away anyone. The films endow him with many dimensions, including a reference to his fictional childhood in *Iron Monkey*, his adolescence in *The Legend of Drunken Master* and his young adulthood in *Once Upon a Time*.[8]

Social groups as inextricably religious and political. Let me set the stage for the second major point by referring to recent events in the People's Republic of China. A self-help meditation group, called the Falun dafa (or Falun gong), attracted a large number of adherents—perhaps millions. As the movement gained momentum, the Chinese government outlawed it as treasonous, sparking massive protests, which in turn brought further repression; for a time there were international condemnations of how the Chinese government treated the Falun dafa. What made the whole scenario so strange to Western eyes and ears was that it was extremely difficult, if not impossible, to construe the message of the Falun dafa as in any way political or subversive. Even if this group carried a political subtext (which would be a real strain to discern), its basic mes-

sage was that of finding health and happiness through the time-honored techniques of meditation and physical exercises.

However, without taking too strong a stance on the specific situation concerning the Falun dafa, let me return to my earlier comment that a strict distinction between secular and spiritual dimensions does not apply to Chinese
culture. This perception also applies to associations of people. An organization
cannot ever be just a group of people connected for a particular purpose; it is
religious as well as secular, and it is political. It is now conventional wisdom
that one cannot fully understand Chinese communism without seeing it as
continuous with the ancient religious and political groups, going back as far as
the Mohists and the Legalists that arose out of the turmoil of fifth century B.C.
in China. If just a few hundred people were to start a group in China for the
sole purpose of wearing pink carnations to decorate their clothing every day,
in Chinese thought they would be considered both religious and political—
and not just because the government might be intolerant. Western analytic
thought wants to find the specific elements that define a particular group as
cultural, religious or political, but to the Chinese mind, any organization includes all three.

We must be alert to this cultural distinctive when we consider the way organized groups are portrayed in Hong Kong films. Are the enemies a gang of
bandits? Are the protagonists joined together in an organization opposed to a
corrupt government? In either case, they have a social, a political and inevitably a religious identity. You cannot have one without the other two.

This distinctive trait is dramatically displayed in *Once Upon a Time in China
II [Wong Fei-hung ji yi: Naam yi dong ji keung]* (1992), another Jet Li vehicle,
with its portrayal of the White Lotus Sect, a group determined to expel all foreigners from China. White Lotus is a deity, but she is also an idea and an em-
powerment. Reminiscent of the Yellow Turbans and other revolutionary societies of a thousand or more years ago, the group is held together by a common
political goal and by the expectation of supernatural invulnerability. Their
commitment leads them to fight not only against their perceived foreign enemies but also against anyone whom they suspect of being sympathetic to them.
Anyone who does not agree with their ideology is *ipso facto* an enemy.

The fusion between politics and religion need not be nearly as overt as it is
in this film. When Bruce Lee confronts the murderers of his teacher in the
previously mentioned *The Chinese Connection,* the resultant struggle pits styles

of martial arts, kinds of spirituality and political allegiances against each other. Lee's opponents are the Japanese and their Chinese sympathizers during the occupation in 1937; Lee (portraying Chen Zhen, another character based on a historical person) defends the Chinese interest. There is a rather significant political quarrel, but the differences are cultural and spiritual as well. The utter chasm in paradigms is displayed when Chen declaims, "Now you listen to me. I'll only say this once. We are not sick men." The Japanese occupants were opprobrious of Chinese culture in all of its dimensions, and Chen's martial arts exploits were intended to defend them. His success, limited as it was, was a matter not only of achieving a small physical victory but of upholding a core set of values as well.[9]

Martial arts as integrated into spiritual orders. This is a really tricky point because it is all too easy to either overstate it or to understate it. Anyone familiar with the long-running *Kung Fu* television series knows that its protagonist, Kwai Chang Caine (addressed as "Grasshopper"), was brought up in a Shaolin monastery, where his master taught him Buddhist wisdom as well as fighting skills. But most Hong Kong martial arts films seem to be very thin on overt spiritual references. Martial arts films not made in Hong Kong, such as *The Glimmer Man* (1996) starring Steven Segal, often put a greater emphasis on a pseudo-Zen New Age spirituality.

When we look at productions in the Hong Kong genre, the filmmakers appear to make little effort to portray the spiritual background of martial arts. Nevertheless, this background is frequently assumed, and this assumption is incorporated into the plot. The protagonist may be a monk, but more often the protagonist has been taught his martial arts by a monk or even by someone associated with an order several generations removed. In real life, this was true of Wong Fei-hung, who, though not a monk, learned his fighting skills from a master whose spiritual genealogy went back to the original Shaolin temple.

Shaolin literally means "young (or new) forest," and the name refers simply to the location of the first temple of this order, which was originally Buddhist with few sectarian traits.[10] But the character of the temple changed drastically when, according to the legend, an Indian prince named Bodhidharma became a Buddhist monk and traveled to China, where he eventually became the leader of the Shaolin temple. The original reason for the temple's existence was as a place to translate the Buddhist scriptures into Chinese. When Bodhidharma (known as Tamo in China) took over, he also taught the monks under his care a new art of meditation, referred to as *dhyana* in Sanskrit, adapted as *chan (ch'an)* in Chinese, and eventually transformed into *Zen* when it came to Japan. The monks at the temple would spend virtually all of their time either sitting and writing or sitting and meditating, leaving them in very poor physical shape. To make matters worse, these overweight, under-energized monks were the targets of physical attacks by robbers and bullies. So to help his Shaolin monks lead a healthier life and to enable them to defend themselves against disruptive people, Bodhidharma also initiated a program of physical fitness and self-defense techniques. Since these monks had to be ready to defend themselves while going about their daily activities, the fighting skills could not rely on specific weapons but had to be carried out with bare hands. Thus kung fu was born.

Whatever truth there may be in the legend of Bodhidharma, it is clear that kung fu did not arise spontaneously and whole at any one point. Just as in India yoga was practiced in many different manners and contexts by this time, Chinese culture had also developed a number of physical techniques that were considered to be aids to meditation in Buddhism and in Daoism. The early followers of Daoism focused in particular on a breathing technique called *embryonic breathing*, and Buddhist schools developed a multifaceted program that involved breathing, physical exercises and meditation, called *Ch'i kung*.[11] Kung fu is a *wu-shu* (fighting skill or martial art) that emerged from Ch'i kung.[12] The original Shaolin temple was destroyed by the Qing dynasty in the 1700s, but its subsequent offspring rose to the forefront of the martial arts. Toward the end of the nineteenth century, when China found its existence as an independent nation threatened, the Shaolin fighters increasingly focused on their fighting skills at the expense of the Zen philosophy, eventually becoming leaders in the Boxer Rebellion in 1901. The "boxers" were the Shaolin-trained fighters. As we already saw, one of the original leaders in this effort was the lionized Wong Fei-hung.

Numerous Hong Kong films refer to Shaolin as a school of fighting in an off-hand way, but sometimes the setting is explicitly Shaolin. A rather crass example is *Shaolin Wooden Men [Shao Lin mu ren xiang]* (1976), an early Jackie Chan film. Chan plays a boy who witnesses the murder of his parents, the trauma of which leaves him unable to speak, thus earning him the name "the Mute." The Mute comes to live in a Shaolin monastery, where he masters all the various martial arts. He also learns that his teacher is responsible for his parents' death. To avenge his parents, the Mute must qualify for the highest level of Shaolin training, which culminates in a fight against thirty-six wooden-garbed Shaolin experts in a closed room. As trite and contrived as this film is, it is a clear example of the association between Shaolin and the martial arts, and it also shows how—in catering to the popular imagination—the Shaolin fighting culture can become elevated to fantastic levels.

Many Hong Kong films, however, do not belabor the association between martial arts and Buddhist groups, such as the Shaolin; they just assume it, as is the case with *Crouching Tiger, Hidden Dragon*. This film lives on the margin of true Hong Kong films. Filmed in Hong Kong and Taiwan, it is a deliberate attempt to fit in with the *wuxia* genre. However, reflecting the new trends associated with the absorption of Hong Kong into the People's Republic, the film's language is Mandarin, and it delivers a plot with greater ambiguity than is usually associated with Hong Kong films in general.[13] One important plot element is the motivation of a professional fighter named Li Mu Bai (the character played by Chow Yun-fat) who has learned his art in the context of Buddhist philosophy but now sees an inconsistency between his search for enlightenment and his profession of killing people. He wishes to give up violence altogether and devote himself to spirituality alone, but it turns out that the theft of his special sword, the Green Destiny, forces him to fight once again. We see here a paradox: the martial arts originate in the spiritual pursuit, but they can eventually become a hindrance to the spiritual pursuit.

The association between kung fu and Shaolin is also an element in *Iron Monkey*, a film that crosses over between *wuxia* and kung fu genres. As the evil governor continues to suppress the team of Iron Monkey, Wong Kei-ying and the youthful Wong Fai-hung, he enlists a group of kung fu fighters who turn out to be lapsed Shaolin monks, willing to sell their services for loathsome purposes. Despite their tainted characters, Kei-ying recognizes them as Shaolin by their fighting styles. Even though he is no longer attached to the order, he is a better fighter, not to mention a better person, than these professional killers.

Balance as the highest ideal. Virtually all of Chinese philosophy is predicated on the attempt to find the balance between the two opposing forces of the universe, the yin and the yang. When true harmony between the two is achieved, the entire world, from the minutest aspects of an individual's life to the largest matters of government and society, will be in compliance with the Dao (Tao), the ultimate "Way." Where Chinese schools of thought differ is in regard to the proper attainment of Dao. For example, according to Confucian teachings, when all people act according to their specific obligations, then the universe will return to a state of balance, whereas in Daoism (Taoism), once the universe is allowed to find its balance on its own, people will consequently act virtuously as well.

It is crucial to recognize that neither yin nor yang are either good or evil in and of themselves; rather, something is good when it properly balances yin and yang, and evil is a disruption of that balance. In their correct proportion, yin and yang are complementary, not oppositional. Yin is feminine, cold, dark, mysterious, passive, wet, expressive of the earth and represented by the dragon. Yang is masculine, hot, bright, clear, active, dry, expressive of heaven and represented by the tiger. Good and evil result from the appropriate balance or imbalance of yin and yang for each thing or event. Thus, for a well to be good, there must be more yin present than yang, or it will not have enough water. On the other hand, for a stove to be good, there must be more yang present than yin, or it will not be hot.

Now it would seem that most Hong Kong martial arts films are not much about balance. There are good people and evil people, and we hope that the good will triumph. Balance does not seem to be an option, let alone a goal. However, there are several places we may look to see the Chinese ideal of balance expressed. For example, in many films the subject matter includes traditional Chinese medicine, which seeks to provide the proper balance of yin and yang in the human body. We already mentioned above that the father of legendary kung fu hero Wong Fei-hung was portrayed as an herbalist doctor in both *Iron Monkey* and *The Legend of Drunken Master*. In fact, in *Iron Monkey* one of the points of tension between Fei-hung and his father Kei-ying is over the nutrition of the boy as he recovers from poisoning. In the *Legend of Drunken Master*, the young Fei-hung gets caught up in international intrigue when he and his servant, attempting to smuggle a healing root into his province for use by his father, accidentally pick up the highly valuable "seal of the Emperor." When he arrives at home without the root, Fei-hung's cunning stepmother tries to avert the father's wrath by substituting the root of a houseplant—which, unfortunately, turns out to be poisonous to Kei-ying's patient (a development that introduces the comic relief in this film).

In the series *Once Upon a Time in China*, we get to know Wong Fei-hung as an adult, now himself pursuing his father's vocation of herbalist doctor. The tension between the dehumanizing machine of the West and the diminishing strength of traditional Chinese culture that underlies the plots of these films also finds its way into the portrayal of medicine, particularly in *Once Upon a Time in China II.* When Wong Fei-hung travels to Hong Kong to deliver a lecture on the traditional practice of acupuncture, he gets caught between the White Lotus Sect, whose adherents claim that their spiritual power will give them magical healing, and the attempt by Dr. Sun Yat-sen (who will eventu- ally become the first president of China) to implement in China the most ben- eficial elements of Western medicine. Fei-hung needs to preserve the balance between an ignorant spiritualization of the healing arts, as demonstrated by the White Lotus Sect, and a Western physicalism that sees the human body as nothing more than a material object.

We can remain with the Wong Fei-hung of *Once Upon a Time* to see further and deeper application of this notion of balance. In addition to specific plot elements, such as traditional medicine, the quest for balance can also be a part of the fundamental motivation for the entire film. Even when there is a clear-cut protagonist who is in the right and an antagonist who is evil, the goodness of the protagonist may result from his maintaining proper balance. This is not about moral ambiguity, because the distinction between good and evil is evi- dent, but it is about the nature of the good, which can easily forget its own pre- carious nature and totter into the imbalance of evil. Thus, all of Fei-hung's life becomes a struggle to prevent the scales from tipping in the wrong direction. There are the reactionaries, such as the White Lotus, who do not face China's troubles realistically. There are the local leaders, whose self-interest has led them to sell out to foreign domination. A few isolated people, such as his Aunt Yee and Dr. Sun Yat-sen, have managed to reach a working compromise with Western values, but a working compromise is not the same thing as true, per- sonal balance.[14] This is something that Fei-hung struggles for and only com- pletely achieves inside of himself but not for his people.

The idea of cosmic balance between opposing elements also dictates Bruce Lee's eventual fate in *The Chinese Connection.* Chen Zhen, having avenged his master's death by killing the murderous gang and wreaking havoc among the collaborators with the Japanese occupiers, has fought violence with violence, yang with yang. And even though there is no question that in the film por- trayal Zhen is in the right, he has not achieved balance but has tilted the scales further into the direction of excessive yang. Consequently, he himself must die in order to bring things closer to equilibrium. Chen's death at the end is felt as highly unsatisfactory by many viewers (including myself), but understanding the need for a balance of yin and yang helps one understand this part of the story.

Portrayal of Western values as incompatible with Chinese ideals. Let's face it: in order to have a decent plot in a martial arts film, you have to have some antagonists, and antagonists are most likely going to be shown in an unfavorable light. Being shown in an unfavorable light will probably involve being described as different from the people you love and trust the most, and thus the antagonists are liable to be subjected to stereotypical depictions. So films with popular appeal are almost certain to have antagonists that embody stereotypes and misrepresentations.

In Hong Kong films, as in films produced in other locales, antagonists are frequently foreigners. This means that in films set in the last two hundred years, the people against whom the hero fights are often Europeans, Americans or those who sympathize with their imperialistic designs. In *The Legend of Drunken Master,* the villains try to defraud the Chinese people by smuggling valuable art objects out of China. It is important to recognize that in contrast to films set in other cultures, this is not a matter of Western materialism versus Eastern spiritual attitudes, because Chinese culture is not necessarily less materialistic than its Western counterpart. The issue is that Chinese materialism is considered more valuable than Western materialism, and the more powerful proponents of Western culture are obliterating the Chinese version. Thus the reason why this behavior by the Westerners is objectionable is that it will have a negative economic effect on China.

Once Upon a Time in China focuses on China's oppression by European powers. At the beginning of the story, Wong Fei-hung receives a large fan on which all of the treaties that are unfair to China are inscribed, and his instructions are to see to it that eventually the fan will be empty. But the odds against Fei-hung are overwhelming. No sooner has he taken charge than the soldiers aboard a European ship shoot the local greengrocer, who had inadvertently gone to the wrong dock. When Fei-hung seeks justice, he learns that local authorities would rather keep peace with the foreigners than redress the injustice. Furthermore, many men are duped into signing agreements to go to America, where they are promised untold riches but will in reality live as slaves. Some reprobate Chinese people of the province do not help matters any by mounting opposition to Fei-hung and even trying to earn some quick gold by selling women into slavery.

Now remember the point made earlier about the inseparability of the political, social and religious dimensions of life. From the perspective of Hong Kong films, Western exploitation and Christianity often go hand in hand. Westerners are depicted as shortsighted and greedy, and their religion does not seem to help them. Among the Westerners living in the area is an elderly Jesuit missionary, who proselytizes for the church while the labor recruiters attempt to enlist people in their deceptive scheme. The viewer may at first not be able to decide which is the more revolting. At the very beginning of the film, the Jesuit priest and two Western colleagues lead a procession of about two dozen Chinese acolytes through the street, hoisting a large crucifix and singing, "Hallelujah!" Entering the marketplace, a local musical ensemble starts to play as loudly as possible so as drown out this chant, adding to the embarrassment of the moment. The scene conveys the impression that here is an empty form of religion, irrelevant to China's problems at best, but more likely contributing to them.

In Stephen Teo's assessment of the role of Westerners in this film, "the Westerners are depicted as rapacious colonialists and slave traders who kidnap young men and women and ship them off to the 'Gold Mountain' (America). . . . The director goes as far as he can to depict arrogant uncouth and bellicose Westerners, stereotypical 'foreign devils' or *gweilos*. . . . Western powers have gained a foothold in China; their representatives are jingoists masquerading as missionaries, merchants and consular officials."[15] These comments are almost true. Nevertheless, they are belied by a crucial incident in the film, repeating an idea that does come up in other contexts as well.

A further murder places the local authorities into a serious predicament because they prefer to appease troublemakers rather than risk a confrontation with the foreign powers. Fortunately for them, they are able to save face because they all are too intimidated to risk their lives testifying against killers. But then the Jesuit priest, who has already shown himself to be visibly appalled at some of the abuses of the Chinese people, steps forward and declares that he witnessed the incident. Thus the prosecution against the evil powers can go forward, but at the next opportunity the priest is killed by Chinese collaborators.

Neither the priest nor the actor portraying him receive acknowledgment in the film's credits, and yet his contribution is very important to the message of the film. As Wong Fei-hung continues to find his way through the many cultural elements, the Western powers are a nemesis, and Christianity seems to be simply a prop for Western exploitation. But then the Jesuit priest—this individual who is personally devoted to Christ—demonstrates that he is a better person than most other people in the film, whether Western or Asian. He is willing to step forward, even though it costs him his life, when the Chinese will not. This incident does not mean that the film presents a positive view of Western religion in general, but it does say that an individual who is truly committed to Christ may provide an exception to the rule of corruption.

This last comment leads us to a concluding observation. We have taken a brief look at some of the elements of Chinese (spiritual) culture that come up in Hong Kong films. They are present, though rarely are they the intended message of Hong Kong films. Frequently, as we saw in the case of Wong Fei-hung's father in *The Legend of Drunken Master,* they are displayed in a negative light. Their presence in films of this genre shows that decent people, flawed though they may be, come out as winners in the end. The plots may be shallow, the acting superficial, the philosophy diluted. Still, right triumphs over wrong, and one leaves the film thinking that the world can become a better place after all.

Rattle and Film

U2, Nietzsche and Salvation in the Blues

DOUGLAS K. BLOUNT

• •

There is but one truly serious philosophical problem, and that is suicide.
Judging whether life is or is not worth living amounts to
answering the fundamental question of philosophy.

Albert Camus

In this essay I discuss two radically different answers to Albert Camus's fundamental question. Each of these answers, which find motivation in what I call "the blues of the human condition," maintains that life *is* worth living.[1] The first, put forward by the late-nineteenth-century German philosopher Friedrich Nietzsche, infers from our wretchedness that God has died; surprisingly, though, Nietzsche finds in God's death not an occasion for despair but rather an opportunity to make one's life a thing beautiful by one's own lights. Thus, in response to the blues, Nietzsche offers a requiem for God as a prelude to a reassessment of values. Such revaluing, he claims, makes possible a life worth living. The other answer to Camus's question, put forward by a band of Irish theologians known as U2, sees our present darkness in light of a kingdom yet to come, "a place that has to be believed to be seen."[2] On U2's view, the wretchedness of this life must be seen against the backdrop of God's grace and the hope of new life, which that grace provides. In response to the blues, then, U2 offers gospel.

God, some say, "is a most unwelcome guest in the world of rock 'n' roll."[3] Not so, however, for U2, known as much for its social conscience and spiritually evocative lyrics as for its distinctive music. Indeed, more than twenty-five years after emerging as one of the music industry's most creative forces, the band members' spiritual commitments—three of the four (Bono, The Edge and Larry Mullen Jr.) have been Christians since the band's earliest days, and the fourth (Adam Clayton) has recently come to faith as well—have taken an increasingly higher profile.[4] After they spent much of the 1990s dabbling in social commentary, mocking both Western consumerism and their own image as rock superstars, their Elevation Tour turned to such themes as "sin and redemption, heaven and hell, mercy and grace."[5] Brought to the fore in the CD *All That You Can't Leave Behind,* the release of which occasioned the Elevation Tour, these themes dominate the band's most recent album, *How to Dismantle an Atomic Bomb,* and the subsequent Vertigo Tour.[6] As a consequence, U2's concerts have come as much to resemble worship services as rock shows.[7]

Still, I suggest that one of the band's most explicit expressions of faith remains *Rattle and Hum,* a full-length motion picture chronicling the third leg of U2's Joshua Tree Tour.[8] In what follows, I develop this suggestion, interpreting *Rattle and Hum* as a presentation of Christian themes.[9] Most prominent among these are the twin themes of despair and hope—what one might call the blues of human wretchedness on the one hand and the gospel of promised redemption in Christ Jesus and his kingdom on the other.

No doubt the despair arising from human misery and the hope of promised redemption and the coming kingdom will seem to some an odd pairing. Bono, however, sees the two as naturally linked. "Gospel music," he says, "is the stuff of faith. It tells you about where you are going. The blues tells you where you are."[10] You cannot truly appreciate where you are going without knowing where you are. "I was never tormented," Bono says, "in the way those early rock and rollers [such as Little Richard, Jerry Lee Lewis and Marvin Gaye] were between gospel and the blues. I always saw them as parts of each other."[11] As grace has no meaning apart from law, so the hope of redemption has no meaning apart from wretchedness.

Indeed, while blues without gospel leads to endless despair, gospel without blues leads to self-deception. In a fallen world, the truth that brings salvation includes the fact of human wretchedness. However unpleasant that may be, the hope of redemption and the coming kingdom can be understood only in its light. Thus, there can be no gospel *without the blues.* "Rock 'n' roll, and the blues," Bono points out, "they're truthful. It says in the Scriptures, 'Know the truth, and the truth will set you free.' So, there is this feeling of liberation in the blues for me. There is salvation in the blues."[12] And, we might add, there is no salvation apart from the blues. As U2 sees it, then, one comes to hope only by way of despair; all roads to the gospel lead first through the blues. Grace offers hope only to those willing to look honestly at their world and themselves.

Of course, that one cannot arrive at gospel without blues does not mean that blues *must* lead to gospel. So, for instance, Nietzsche's response to the blues of the human condition goes in a radically different direction. On his view, the appropriate encore to such blues is not gospel but rather requiem.[13] God, Nietzsche tells us, is dead. He means not that God has literally died but rather that "belief in the Christian God has become unbelievable."[14] God has not *ceased* to exist but only for the simple reason that *he never existed in the first place.*[15]

God's death makes orphans of humankind. It also leaves us without purpose—meaningless cogs in the machine that is this world. For, of course, a dead deity cannot give purpose to our existence. And if God cannot give our lives purpose, neither can anyone else. For a thing's purpose involves the end for which it is *intended;* if no one exists to intend an end for humanity, then humanity lacks purpose. Purpose and divine providence are thus mere human inventions. Nietzsche states that "no one *gives* a human being his qualities: not God, not society, not his parents or ancestors, not *he himself*. . . . *We* invented the concept of 'purpose': in reality purpose is *lacking*."[16]

Without purpose, however, we are nothing but momentary blips on a cosmic screen that is viewed by no one. We enjoy neither a divine origin nor a divine destiny. Again Nietzsche writes, "Formerly one sought the feeling of the grandeur of man by pointing to his divine *origin:* this has now become a forbidden way, for at its portal stands the ape. . . . One therefore now tries the opposite direction: the way mankind is *going* shall serve as proof of his grandeur and kinship with God. . . . However high mankind may have evolved . . . it cannot pass over into a higher order, as little as the ant and the earwig can at the end of its 'earthly course' rise up to kinship with God and eternal life."[17] So, as momentary blips destined for oblivion, we have no hope of a world whose coming will give meaning to our present blues and make them worth bearing, no hope of a life whose dawning will redeem the wretchedness of this one. This present darkness is not merely the *first* act of our existence; rather, it *is* the play in *all* its fullness.

On Nietzsche's view, Christianity's most detrimental effect has been to obscure this fact by turning our attention from this world to another supposedly yet to come, to "an imaginary *teleology*."[18] As Robert Solomon and Kathleen Higgins put it, "What he disliked . . . about Christianity was its 'nihilism,' its disdain and contempt for the things of this world in favor of the 'next world.'"[19] For Nietzsche, then, to look toward a world still to come or a life yet to be lived is to reject one's only opportunity truly to live—which, of course, comes here and now. In proclaiming a coming kingdom in which all things are made new, Christianity repudiates *this* life. "Life," he writes, "is at an end where the 'kingdom of God' *begins*."[20]

So, while U2 responds to the blues of human wretchedness with the good news of redemption and the coming kingdom, Nietzsche responds to it with a requiem for God and a repudiation of any such kingdom. Salvation, on Nietzsche's view, comes not from God's willingness to become one of us, but rather from our power to transform ourselves into gods. If Nietzsche offers redemption, it comes not via the cross but rather power; if he offers absolution, it comes not via self-denial but rather self-assertion. Life in its fullness belongs only to those willing to exercise their own will to power. Nietzsche and U2 thus offer radically different responses to our miserable condition. In what follows, I discuss these responses in more detail.

Blues and Gospel: Human Wretchedness Redeemed

As *Rattle and Hum* opens, Bono introduces its first song, announcing, "This song Charles Manson stole from the Beatles; we're stealing it back." The song is "Helter Skelter," first released on the Beatles' so-called White Album and perhaps the most ill-fated song in the history of rock music.[21] For, as Bono acknowledges, it has become permanently linked to Charles Manson and the infamous Tate-LaBianca murders.[22] Over two nights in August 1969, Manson directed his followers to murder eight people, including Sharon Tate, actress and wife of film director Roman Polanski, and Leno and Rosemary LaBianca. Tate, who was eight months pregnant, was found dead along with four guests at her home in Beverly Hills; the LaBiancas were later found dead in their Los Angeles home. The connection with the Beatles' song stems from Manson's claim that the "White Album" was an encoded message to himself—a message prophesying a coming race war to be known as "Helter Skelter."

That U2 chose to open *Rattle and Hum* with a Beatles song underscores its appreciation of the Liverpudlian band. But the choice of "Helter Skelter" and the remark about Manson cannot fail to evoke memories of the brutality and savagery of the Tate-LaBianca murders. And this points us to the sad reality of the human condition. Most obviously, it points to the wickedness pervading our world. Manson and his disciples embody an all-too-common evil, one characterized by the exertion of one's will no matter what the consequences for others. Less obviously, the song also points to the vulnerability of innocence in an unjust world. For whatever else might be true about Manson's victims, they did not deserve what they got. And this points to yet another aspect of our wretched condition—the innocent suffer while the wicked prosper.[23]

On the heels of "Helter Skelter"—the performance of which comes in the stark black-and-white that dominates the film until its climax—The Edge performs his own "Van Diemen's Land," his solitary guitar contrasting dramatically with the frenetic, hard-driving energy of "Helter Skelter." "Van Diemen's Land" refers to the former penal colony now known as Tasmania.[24] Its speaker faces exile in Van Diemen's land, separated from those whom he loves, because he fought for justice rather than personal gain. So while "Helter Skelter" reminds us that the innocent suffer and the wicked prosper, "Van Diemen's Land" paints for us a portrait of one who sows justice for others only to reap injustice for himself. Significantly, however, it does not leave us in utter despair; the final verse anticipates a day when justice reigns, a day "when an honest man sees an honest wage." As we shall see, this theme of a day yet to come—when justice will reign—echoes throughout the film.

After "Van Diemen's Land," we see the members of U2 talking with the film's director, Phil Joanou. "What," Joanou asks, "has happened between the writing of the *Joshua Tree* album . . . and the tour and now the new songs?" The band hesitates and, with no response having been made, the film takes us to a performance of "Desire"—apparently leaving the question unanswered. Here one's attention is drawn to what is perhaps the most troubling aspect of the human condition—namely, one's *own* wretchedness. Thus far the wretchedness singled out in the film arises from external sources. "Desire," however, points to that which comes from within. This song functions, then, as a sort of confession by the band in response to Joanou's question. The song reflects a desire that increases in intensity like a slowly rising fever that cannot be assuaged: "And the fever / Getting higher / Desire, desire / Burning, burning."

The sense of losing one's self-control peaks as the camera spins rapidly in a circle, creating a blur of images.

As desire can drive one to self-loathing, so too despair can drive one to self-destruction. "Exit," which follows "Desire," "gets inside the head of a protagonist who's careening into psychosis."[25] The song, whose dark imagery and tone are expressed visually in Joanou's use of shadow, conveys "the state of mind of someone driven . . . to the very brink of desperation."[26] Whether the fruit of that desperation turns out to be murder or suicide the song leaves unclear, although its title makes the latter more likely.[27] In either case, the repeated references to "the hands of love"—hands that, we are told, can both build and pull down—bring to mind a biblical theme. Here God's words to Jeremiah are relevant: "Behold, I have put my words in your mouth. See, I have set you this day over nations and over kingdoms, to pluck up and to break down, to destroy and to overthrow, to build and to plant" (Jeremiah 1:9-10).[8]

The hands that build, as Bono sings, can also pull down. Niall Stokes sees this as reflecting "a new awareness [on U2's part] of the dangers of fanaticism implicit in faith."[28] The song's protagonist, however, is *not* a believer (e.g., "he wanted to believe in the hands of love" but apparently did not), so this is unlikely. Moreover, the point may be put the other way round; the hands that pull down also can build. In fact, this ordering reflects not only Jeremiah 1 but also a later text: "And it shall come to pass that as I have watched over them to pluck up and break down, to overthrow, destroy, and bring harm, so I will watch over them to build and to plant, declares the LORD" (Jeremiah 31:28). This text foreshadows the coming of Christ and his kingdom; for, as is indicated a few lines later, "Behold, the days are coming, declares the LORD, when I will make a new covenant with the house of Israel and the house of Judah. . . . But this is the covenant that I will make with the house of Israel after those days, declares the LORD: I will put my law within them, and I will write it on their hearts. And I will be their God, and they shall be my people" (Jeremiah 31:31, 33). I take the hands of love in "Exit" to refer to the hands of God.[29] If I am right, the song's protagonist wanted to believe in God but could not bring himself to do so. Unbelieving, he careens "into psychosis." Blues without gospel thus leads not simply to unending despair, but ultimately to self-destruction as well.

The finale of "Exit" incorporates the chorus of Van Morrison's "Gloria." So, as in "Van Diemen's Land," we are not left in utter despair. For, however briefly, we are reminded that God's promise to Jeremiah has been fulfilled in Christ Jesus. In the Latin Vulgate, the word *gloria* begins the angelic celebration of Christ's advent recorded in Luke 2:14.[30] As the song ends, the film shows Bono from behind striking the pose of one on a cross, underscoring the song's suggestion of hope and redemption—which, as the singer's pose indicates, come by way of sacrifice.

Thus far, then, the film concerns wretchedness arising both externally and internally. Injustice inevitably brings misery to both its victims and perpetrators. That which it brings on its perpetrators arises from within them and thus seems more troubling. Left unchecked, moreover, wretchedness arising from within leads ultimately to self-destruction. Still, the film affords a glimpse of that day when justice reigns and the hands of love build rather than pull down, when God writes his law on neither tablets of stone nor hearts of clay, but rather on hearts of flesh belonging to his people. In offering such a glimpse, "Gloria" is a prelude to what may well be U2's most misunderstood song.

Before the film moves to "I Still Haven't Found What I'm Looking For," The Edge describes the song as "a gospel song." "I mean, it doesn't sound much like a gospel song the way we do it," he admits, "but if you look at the lyric and the basic music, that's exactly what it is." As if to underscore these remarks, the film shows U2 performing the song with—as The Edge tells us— a gospel choir at a church in Harlem. Some see this song as repudiating the faith. If the members of U2 have yet to find what they seek, the thinking goes, they must have weighed Christianity and found it wanting; for how could a Christian say that he has *not* found what he seeks?[31] Significantly, however, The Edge characterizes the song as gospel rather than blues. Moreover, the song explicitly affirms the speaker's faith: "I believe," he insists, "in the kingdom come." Although the lines are left out of the filmed performance, the song also affirms that Christ has broken the bonds and loosed the chains that imprison us, taking the speaker's shame on himself. In light of this, I suggest that, far from repudiating the faith, "I Still Haven't Found What I'm Looking For" reaffirms it; what the speaker seeks is the kingdom of God. In other words, I take the song to be a plea for the coming of Christ's kingdom (cf. Philippians 3:20-21). Indeed, Bono has said that the kingdom "is taken by force," that "God doesn't mind if we bang on the door to heaven sometimes, asking him to listen to what we have to say."[32] Far from repudiating it, then, the song anticipates the fulfillment of promised redemption and thus presupposes an enduring faith.

That the kingdom has not yet come is obvious, given the wretchedness of our present condition. For the kingdom is marked by justice. When it comes, "all the colors will bleed into one." To the extent that injustice remains, then, we are assured that the kingdom has not yet come. The two songs that follow, "Freedom for My People" and "Silver and Gold," emphasize present injustice. "Freedom for My People"—which, along with Jimi Hendrix's instrumental version of "The Star-Spangled Banner," is one of two songs in the film not performed by U2—prefaces "Silver and Gold."[33]

"Silver and Gold" is a poignant plea for racial justice. To ensure that this point is not missed, Bono addresses the audience during the song: "It's a song written about a man in a shanty town outside of Johannesburg, a man who's sick of looking down the barrel of white South Africa." Sadly, such injustice includes oppression perpetrated by religious believers. Moreover, the speaker's plea to Jesus for help indicates that he also is a religious believer. The subject of religious believers victimizing one another—indeed, of Christians victimizing Christians—comes up again toward the end of the film, when U2 performs "Sunday Bloody Sunday." Like "Van Diemen's Land," however, "Silver and Gold" provides hope: neither chains nor shackles ultimately bind the speaker; freedom belongs to the oppressed, not to their oppressors. Yet again, the point is that those who commit injustice harm themselves more than those who suffer it (cf. Matthew 10:28). So, then, those who commit injustice become prisoners of their own wickedness; those who suffer injustice find hope in the coming of Christ's kingdom, when all things will be made new.

After "Silver and Gold," the setting shifts to Sun Studios in Memphis for "Angel of Harlem" and then to San Francisco for "All Along the Watchtower." The angel to whom the first song refers is Billie Holiday, the great jazz singer whose slow deterioration into drug and alcohol abuse led to an early death. Of her "luminous self-destruction," Elisabeth Hardwick writes, "The sheer enormity of her vices. The outrageousness of them. . . . Onto the heaviest addiction to heroin she piled up the rocks of her tomb with a prodigiousness of Scotch and brandy. She was never at any hour of the day or night free . . . except when she was asleep. And there did not seem to be any pleading need to quit, to modify."[34] A tribute to Holiday, "Angel of Harlem" laments her self-destruction. Interestingly, as the camera moves from one band member to another during the song, we see on the wall behind them pictures of Elvis Presley, who made many of his early recordings at Sun Studios and who also died from drug-related causes.

Bob Dylan's "All Along the Watchtower" presents us with a conversation between a joker and a thief. The joker desires to escape his situation, which apparently involves chaos and injustice. The thief counsels patience, for while some believe life is meaningless, he and the joker do not; moreover, some sort of end approaches. The song as Dylan wrote it ends with a reference to a growling wildcat and two riders approaching the tower. Given this reference, some see in the song an echo of Isaiah 21:8-9: "Then he who saw cried out: 'Upon a watchtower I stand, O Lord, continually by day, / and at my post I am stationed whole nights. / And behold, here come riders, / horsemen in pairs!' And he answered, / 'Fallen, fallen is Babylon; / and all the carved images of her gods / he has shattered to the ground.' " This passage obviously concerns judgment. So, as we listen to the song, we seem to overhear an exchange between two down-and-out individuals who find their present situations almost unbearable. What allows the thief to counsel patience, however, is his understanding that life has a purpose together with the lateness of the hour. Perhaps the lateness of the hour means that a new dawn approaches. In any case, two horsemen approach—an image that, in light of Isaiah's words, seems apocalyptic.

U2 replaces the lines mentioning the wildcat and two riders with these lyrics: "All I got is a red guitar / Three chords / And the truth / All I got is a red guitar / The rest is up to you."[35] The "three chords" allude to Curtis Mayfield's "People Get Ready"; The Edge had once told Bono that that song's three chords "could change the world."[36] U2 often performed this song, which concerns the coming of Christ's kingdom, during the Joshua Tree Tour. Apparently, then, the truth that Bono claims to have in "All Along the Watchtower" concerns the coming of the kingdom; and, given the song's apocalyptic imagery and the suggestion of a new day approaching when the down-and-out will find relief, this truth fits the song's motif.

The film's next three songs return our attention to the human condition. Two of them, "In God's Country" and "Heartland," illustrate U2's ambivalence toward the United States. "America both fascinates and frightens me," Bono has said. "I can't get it out of my system."[37] "In God's Country" portrays America as both savior and seductress. While she has much to offer, not all of it is good. Although "Heartland" presents a more favorable view of America, its performance accompanies film of the band visiting Graceland, Elvis's home in Memphis, Tennessee. Of course, Elvis—an unusually gifted singer whose success led ultimately to his destruction—exemplifies both the charm and corruption of American culture. With "Heartland" playing in the background, Mullen says of the visit, "I was a little bit disturbed by going to Graceland. When I got there, I enjoyed it and all that, but seeing the graves . . . it seemed very distant. I wish he hadn't been buried in there, in the back garden." While Elvis's success is evident in the house and on the grounds, so also is his excess.

Between "Heartland" and "In God's Country," we see U2 and B. B. King discussing and rehearsing "When Love Comes to Town," a song about regret and repentance. In it, the speaker laments wrongs done "before love came to town."[38] Here, as in "Exit," *love* clearly refers to God, specifically to Jesus Christ. A backstage conversation prepares us. "Right, with the B. B. King song," Bono says, "watch for the third verse. Not the first verse, the first chorus; not the second verse; but the third verse which comes after the chorus." We then see a conversation between Bono and King. "I hope," Bono says, "you liked the song." King responds, "I love the song. I think that the lyric is really—*real* heavy lyrics. You're mighty young to write such heavy lyrics." So before the song begins, the film draws our attention to its lyrics, especially its third verse. When the performance gets to that verse, the film cuts to a conversation in which Bono reviews the lyrics with King. Instead of hearing the third verse being sung, we hear Bono speak it. This draws our attention to the content of that verse, which tells us that the speaker "threw the dice" as Christ's side was pierced during the crucifixion. But he also saw "love conquer the great divide." "When Love Comes to Town" thus includes both an admission of wretchedness and a confession of hope, specifically Christian hope. It is both a lament and a celebration—a lament of wrongs done, a celebration of redemption in Christ.

As the film nears its climax, it moves to "Bad," a song about heroin addiction.[39] Significantly, it begins on the heels of Mullen's comments about Elvis and Graceland. As we hear the first strains of "Bad," we see him at Elvis's grave, looking at the eternal flame and tombstone. Elvis died from a drug overdose. So the film moves from this famous casualty of drug abuse to a song empathetic for one struggling with such abuse. The speaker anguishes over someone tormented by addiction but beyond his help. Were it possible, he says, he would free the addict from his bondage. When he begins singing, Bono is silhouetted; we see his outline, but he remains in shadow. As it did with "Exit," the film uses shadow to establish a dark, brooding mood. Although Bono comes into the light (as the speaker longs to see the addict do), the other band members remain obscured by shadow for much of the song. In the context of a film emphasizing the twin themes of despair and hope, drug addiction serves as a metaphor for the desperation we face more broadly, especially that arising from within. Toward the end of "Bad," U2 pays tribute to the Rolling Stones, incorporating lines from "Ruby Tuesday" and "Sympathy for the Devil." "Ruby Tuesday" concerns a groupie who longs for freedom but pays rather a high price for it. Written from its title character's point of view, "Sympathy for the Devil" portrays Lucifer—who has also paid a terrible price for personal autonomy—taking credit for various instances of injustice and oppression.

Although it has given us glimpses of gospel, *Rattle and Hum* has thus far stressed the blues. From "Helter Skelter" to "Bad," the film focuses our attention on wretchedness. Christ's kingdom receives mention, but only secondarily. And while references to the kingdom anticipate freedom from bondage—whether self-imposed or as the result of injustice—they are fleeting, passing quickly in the face of this present darkness. As the film climaxes, however, the emphasis shifts from blues to gospel, from despair to hope, from wretchedness to redemption.

As "Bad" ends, the screen fades to black for the first and only time in the film. When the picture returns, the visual impact is stunning. Red radiates from the screen like a sunrise, like the dawning of a new day. "Where the Streets Have No Name" begins gently, softly. As The Edge begins his familiar introduction on guitar, lights flash, illuminating the stage. An overhead shot shows the venue, Sun Devil Stadium in Tempe, Arizona. And then come the lyrics. The city of which they speak is, I suggest, the heavenly city of which Saint John writes, "Then the angel showed me the river of the water of life, bright as crystal, flowing from the throne of God and of the Lamb through the middle of the street of the city" (Revelation 22:1-2). In short, the song concerns the heavenly city, "a place high on a desert plain." In that place God's people will be afflicted no more—for there will be no more bondage, no more doubt, no more injustice, no more war. Thus, with the author of Hebrews, U2 seeks "the city that is to come" (Hebrews 13:14).

As mentioned above, the kingdom is marked by justice. So as the kingdom comes, those who long for justice see their dreams realized. "Where the Streets Have No Name" is followed by "MLK," a tribute to Martin Luther King Jr. Here we see Bono silhouetted against a bright light. Although the film has not reverted to the black-and-white that dominated it prior to "Where the Streets Have No Name," we cannot discern the color of the singer's skin. Of course, "I Still Haven't Found What I'm Looking For" anticipates the day of the kingdom's coming, when "all the colors will bleed into one"; and King himself dreamed of the day when his children would be judged not "by the color of their skin but by the content of their character."[40] The silhouetting of the singer thus contributes to a sense of expectation. Working with the motif made famous by King's "I have a dream" speech, Bono sings, "And may your dreams be realized." But those dreams envision a day when valleys are exalted and mountains debased, when rough places are made plain and crooked places straight—when, as Scripture says, "the glory of the LORD should be revealed, /and all flesh shall see it together" (Isaiah 40:4-5). And such a day will not come until Christ himself returns.

After "MLK," though gospel continues to be an important theme, the film's emphasis shifts back to the blues. "With or Without You" brings into view the fragility of human relationships. In apparent frustration, the speaker complains that, though he continually gives himself away for the sake of others, he can live neither with nor without them. As the song nears its conclusion, Bono inserts three lines that do not appear in its studio version: "We'll shine like stars in the summer night / We'll shine like stars in the winter light / One heart, one hope, one love." Of course, the last of these lines echoes the last verse of 1 Corinthians 13: "So now faith, hope, and love abide, these three; but the greatest of these is love."[41] So while the song reminds us of the blues, it nonetheless leaves us with hope.

Interestingly, from this point on, religion plays a prominent role in the wretchedness of which the film speaks. So, for instance, "Bullet the Blue Sky" rebukes "a preacher on the Old Time Gospel Hour stealing money from the sick and the old"; "Sunday Bloody Sunday" concerns the conflict between Catholics and Protestants in Northern Ireland—a conflict that has Christians killing Christians. U2 performs the song just after learning of a bombing in Enniskillen, Northern Ireland, which left eleven dead. As a consequence, the performance—filmed in the bleak black-and-white that dominates the movie through the performance of "Bad"—is unusually intense; in the film's most moving scene, Bono pauses during the song to deliver a stinging rebuke of those who support such terrorist acts.[42] The song itself both repudiates sectarian violence and pleads for unity.

Having focused our attention on the hatred out of which such violence arises, the film concludes with "Pride (In the Name of Love)," a tribute to those who sacrifice themselves in order to liberate others from bondage. Chief among those to whom the song pays tribute are Martin Luther King Jr. ("Free at last, they took your life / They could not take your pride") and Jesus Christ ("One man come, he to justify"; "One man betrayed by a kiss"). Here, as in "When Love Comes to Town," *love* refers to God. Thus, the song suggests that those who serve God do so not by seeking power for themselves but rather by sacrificing themselves for others (John 15:13).

As I understand it, then, *Rattle and Hum* turns our attention to the blues of the human condition. While "Helter Skelter" and "Van Diemen's Land" bring to mind blues arising from the wickedness of others, "Desire" draws attention to the blues arising from our own wretchedness. Ultimately, as "Exit" illustrates, such wretchedness leads to self-destruction. Even so, we find hope in the promised kingdom of God; "Gloria" celebrates the coming of Jesus of Nazareth, on whom that promise rests. So we live in the tension between blues and gospel, acknowledging faith in Christ and yet longing for his return. Of course, to long for his return is also to long for justice, which—as "Freedom for My People" and "Silver and Gold" remind us—we do not now enjoy. Like the speaker in "When Love Comes to Town," we enter into the kingdom by repentance. Sadly, as "Bad" points out, we cannot set others free from bondage, however much we desire to do so. Still, the invitation to repent remains open, and those who accept it will walk streets that have no name. Even so, they will struggle with their own wretchedness until Christ's kingdom comes in its fullness (Romans 7). Until then, we can do no better than humble ourselves for the sake of others (Philippians 2:3-4). So says U2.

Blues and Requiem: Human Wretchedness Embraced

As we have seen, Nietzsche responds to our miserable condition by proclaiming God's death—in which he delights. "Indeed, at hearing the news that 'the old god is dead,'" he writes, "we philosophers and 'free spirits' feel illuminated by a new dawn; our heart overflows with gratitude, amazement, forebodings, expectation."[43] The "new dawn" occasioned by God's death brings liberation, freedom from accountability. "The concept 'God,' " Nietzsche writes, "has hitherto been the greatest *objection* to existence. . . . We deny God; in denying God, we deny accountability: only by doing *that* do we redeem the world."[44] With God dead, then, we are free to be our own masters.

Prior to God's demise, Nietzsche suggests, we were like castaways stranded on an island, with few possibilities open to us. But denying God allows us to set sail with a clear and limitless horizon before us: "finally the horizon seems clear again, even if not bright; finally our ships may set out again, set out to face any danger; every daring of the lover of knowledge is allowed again; the sea, *our* sea, lies open again; maybe there has never been such an 'open sea.' "[45] So, before God died, we lived with a false view of the world—one according to which divine providence works all things "together for good" (Romans 8:28). Since such a view carried with it a divinely appointed morality, we thus found ourselves constrained, bound to live according to a morality based on error. But, having rejected that view, we are now free to pursue life in whatever way pleases us.

Moreover, on Nietzsche's account of things, what most pleases humankind is power. "Not necessity, not desire—no, the love of power is the demon of men," he writes. "Let them have everything . . . they are and remain unhappy and low-spirited: for the demon . . . *will* be satisfied. Take everything from them and satisfy this, and they are almost happy—as happy as men and de-mons can be."[46] This leads to a reassessment of values. "What is good?—All that heightens the feeling of power, the will to power, power itself in man. What is bad?—All that proceeds from weakness. What is happiness?—The feeling that power *increases*—that a resistance is overcome."[47] Belief in God, with its attendant morality, leads to the devaluing of strength in favor of weak-ness. In Christianity in particular, Nietzsche sees a decadent religion, one that elevates the lowly above the lordly. Having "taken the side of everything weak, base, ill-constituted, it has made an ideal out of *opposition* to the preservative instincts of strong life."[48] So, as he sees it, belief in God, especially *Christian* belief, leads to an inversion of values. Hence, the rejection of such belief opens the way for a reassessment of values; and such revaluing places strength in a position of honor and thus legitimizes humankind's love of power.

As Nietzsche sees it, God's death frees us to pursue whatever end pleases us. No deity holds us accountable, and without the artificial constraints of a false religion and its attendant morality and values, nothing stands between us and the unrestrained pursuit of what we naturally love above all else—to wit, power. No doubt some, concerned about its potential for exploitation, will balk at such a pursuit. But Nietzsche sees exploitation as essential to life. "It is just as absurd," he writes, "to ask strength *not* to express itself as strength, *not* to be a desire to overthrow, crush, become master, *[not]* to be a thirst for enemies, resistance and triumphs, as it is to ask weakness to express itself as strength."[49]

Gospel or Requiem?

Nietzsche and U2 thus offer radically different responses to the blues of the human condition. U2 proclaims the good news of God become human; Nietzsche, having proclaimed God's death, advocates that humans themselves become gods. One achieves salvation, according to Nietzsche, via one's own will to power. What he sees as salvific, however, U2 considers simply another manifestation of human wickedness. Indeed, as the band members see it, the mark of the kingdom *just is* justice for the oppressed; when Christ reigns, the weak will be liberated—not dominated, not exploited. On U2's view, salvation comes via divine grace, which has conquered "the great divide" between God and humankind. U2 thus finds redemption in the one who "broke the bonds" and "loosed the chains," taking our shame on himself. Nietzsche finds it in one's ability to make a life beautiful by one's own lights, in the opportunity to achieve whichever of infinitely many possibilities it pleases one to achieve. To be sure, this involves both a reassessment of values and a willingness to exploit others for one's own gain; still, the lives of those free spirits who abandon the old morality in order to pursue power will be worth living. In short, then, Nietzsche counsels us to pursue our own interests, which ultimately means accruing power for ourselves; in contrast, U2 counsels us to pursue the interests of others, to lose our lives in order that we might find them (Matthew 10:39; 16:25).

We are therefore presented with two different responses to the blues of the human condition, two different answers to the question of whether life is worth living. Although each of these answers affirms that life *is* worth living, each conceives of life's worth in radically different terms. U2 sees this present darkness in the light of a life yet to come; given the hope of the coming kingdom, our present suffering *is* worth enduring (Romans 8:18). Nietzsche believes the hope of such a kingdom to be nothing but self-delusion, "an imaginary *teleology.*" So rather than looking forward to an imaginary afterlife, we should, he counsels, focus on the present; rather than seeking the kingdom of an imaginary God, we ought to seek first our own kingdoms. We thus have a choice: on one hand are gospel, humility, self-sacrifice; on the other are requiem, will to power, self-assertion. Like Alice at the crossroads, we can choose either path. Which way should we go? Which response to the blues of our own wretchedness ought we favor?

At its most fundamental level, the disagreement between Nietzsche and U2 concerns whether God exists. Given life's blues, Nietzsche takes belief in God to be untenable; and, in a world without God, he sees no room for the old morality and its attendant values. In a world filled with injustice and pointless suffering, moreover, only the ruthless will thrive. U2, however, takes God's existence as a given and seeks to understand life's blues in light of it. So in choosing which of these ways to go, it seems that we need first to ascertain whether God exists.

Interestingly, however, neither Nietzsche nor U2 puts forward an argument on the question of God's existence. Nietzsche simply assumes that God does not exist; U2 assumes that he does. So we cannot determine which response to favor by examining the *reasons* put forward for the assumptions underlying them. It does not follow, however, that they provide us no basis for choosing between them. For, perhaps surprisingly, Nietzsche himself provides a criterion for making such a choice. In explaining his rejection of Christianity, Nietzsche writes, "What decides against Christianity now is our taste, not our reasons."[50] In the absence of God, he refuses to privilege reason over taste. After all, human reason has developed as it has in the midst of a struggle for survival; consequently, our reason has developed to help us survive, to secure our well-being. As Nietzsche points out, there "is no pre-established harmony between the furtherance of truth and the well-being of mankind."[51] Given this, taste seems as effective as reason at helping us choose between competing views. So if we choose between gospel and requiem, humility and power, abnegation and self-assertion on the grounds suggested by Nietzsche, we will choose on the basis of which we find most beautiful, most pleasing.

Now Nietzsche seems to me not to take seriously the words of the wood-god, Silenus, whose wisdom he extols. Asked by King Midas what is best for humanity, Silenus answers that nonexistence is best. Since, however, it is too late for us never to have been born, our best option is "to die soon."[52] But how can Nietzsche, having accepted the utter desperation of human existence, consistently advise against Silenus's way out? By his own lights, the truth is *unbearable. "Honesty,"* he writes, "would lead to nausea and suicide."[53] In short, the portrait of the world that Nietzsche paints makes life not merely a burden, but a burden *for which there is no point.* By successfully exerting one's will to power, one may for a time dominate one's world, thus temporarily winning the cosmic equivalent of king of the hill. But to what end?

If Nietzsche's assessment were correct, would death not be preferable— even to the divinity to which he invites us? Or to use a comparison taken from a passage quoted earlier, how do we essentially differ from ants and earwigs? And if these cannot "rise to kinship with God," how is it that we may aspire to divinity? I suggest that, by Nietzsche's own lights, we ought to prefer death to continued existence—even existence as gods. If so, then the choice between U2's response and Nietzsche's turns out to be nothing less than the choice between life and death. That we, like the ancient Israelites, face just such a choice Scripture makes clear. And, of course, it urges us to choose life—which, by all accounts, is the more beautiful of the two. "I call heaven and earth to witness against you today, that I have set before you life and death, blessing and curse. Therefore choose life, that you and your offspring may live, loving the LORD your God, obeying his voice and holding fast to him, for he is your life and length of days, that you may dwell in the land that the LORD swore to your fathers, to Abraham, to Isaac, and to Jacob, to give them" (Deuteronomy 30:19-20).

Appendix: Film Summaries

2001: A Space Odyssey

U.S., 1968

141 Minutes, Feature, Color

Rating: G

Director: Stanley Kubrick

Screenwriters: Stanley Kubrick and Arthur C. Clarke

DVD Features: English and French audio tracks; English, Spanish and French subtitles; interview with coscreenwriter

Cast: Keir Dullea, Gary Lockwood, William Sylvester, voice of Douglas Rain

Synopsis: Astronauts Dave and Frank (Keir Dullea and Gary Lockwood) plan to travel to Jupiter to do research. Their spaceship, *Discovery,* is largely operated and controlled by an intelligent, talking machine, Hal (the HAL 9000 computer). Hal, who is supposed to be much more intelligent than human beings, becomes bored with his human companions and attempts to seize control of the spaceship.

Adaptation

U.S., 2002

115 Minutes, Feature, Color

Rating: R (language, sexuality, drug use, violent images)

Director: Spike Jonze

Screenwriters: Charlie Kaufman and Donald Kaufman; based on the novel *The Orchid Thief: A True Story of Beauty and Obsession* by Susan Orlean

DVD Features: English and French audio tracks; English and French subtitles

Cast: Nicolas Cage, Meryl Streep, Chris Cooper, Cara Seymour

Synopsis: A highly fictionalized account of Charlie Kaufman's struggle to write a screenplay based on Susan Orlean's book *The Orchid Thief.* Orlean's book weaves accounts of the history of Florida and of the orchid trade with the story of John Laroche's arrest and trial for illegally harvesting orchids from a state preserve. Kaufman (Nicolas Cage) is anxious to preserve the original texture as he writes the screenplay. Kaufman's attempts unravel as he and his twin brother discover that the real story is exactly the kind of Hollywood story he did not want to write.

American Beauty

U.S., 1999

122 Minutes, Feature, Color

Rating: R (strong sexuality, language, violence, substance abuse)

Director: Sam Mendes

Screenwriter: Alan Ball

DVD Features: Audio commentary with director Sam Mendes and screenwriter Alan Ball; exclusive storyboards with commentary by director Mendes and director of photography Conrad Hall; *"American Beauty:* Look Closer," a featurette on the making of the film

Cast: Kevin Spacey, Annette Bening, Thora Birch, Wes Bentley, Mena Suvari, Chris Cooper

Synopsis: Lester Burnham (Kevin Spacey) is having a midlife crisis. He is alienated from his career-driven wife, Carolyn (Annette Bening), and his teenage daughter Jane (Thora Birch), who is falling for the drug-dealing boy next door, Ricky Fitts (Wes Bentley). Meanwhile, Lester has developed a crush of his own on Jane's friend Angela (Mena Suvari). Lester quits his job, begins weightlifting, buys a new car and begins smoking pot. Things come to a head when Lester discovers Carolyn is having an affair and Ricky's father (Chris Cooper) suspects that Ricky and Lester are having a homosexual affair.

Being John Malkovich

U.S., 1999

112 Minutes, Feature, Color

Rating: R (language and sexual content)

Director: Spike Jonze

Screenwriter: Charlie Kaufman

DVD Features: English, Spanish and French subtitles; documentaries; interviews; photo gallery

Cast: John Cusack, Cameron Diaz, Catherine Keener, Ned Bellamy, John Malkovich

Synopsis: Craig Schwartz (John Cusack) discovers a portal that allows him to enter the consciousness of John Malkovich for fifteen minutes. He forms a partnership with his friend Maxine (Catherine Keener) to charge people for a chance to "be John Malkovich." This is a life-transforming experience for many of those who do it. Schwartz's wife, Lotte (Cameron Diaz), becomes Malkovich and emerges with an unrestrained passion for Maxine. Schwartz has also fallen in love with Maxine and will do almost anything to have her.

Big Fish

U.S., 2003

125 Minutes, Feature, Color

Rating: PG-13 (violence, nudity)

Director: Tim Burton

Screenwriter: John August; based on the novel *Big Fish* by Daniel Wallace

DVD features: English and French audio tracks; English and French subtitles; featurettes on the making of *Big Fish;* Tim Burton featurette and audio commentary; three other filmmaker and cast featurettes

Cast: Ewan McGregor, Albert Finney, Billy Crudup, Jessica Lange, Helena Bonham Carter, Steve Buscemi

Synopsis: The fantastic story of a dying father, Edward Bloom (Albert Finney), and his estranged son, Will (Billy Crudup), who is trying to glean the truth about his father from his father's own exaggerated tales of his life. The son retells the story of his father's elusive life, a tale that assumes epic proportions as Edward rescues a town from a giant, becomes a war hero and has encounters with a mermaid, a werewolf and conjoined twins. Will learns to appreciate and forgive his absent and distant father, while Edward comes to realize his need for his son.

Bowling for Columbine

U.S., 2002

119 Minutes, Documentary, Color

Rating: R (language, violent images)

Director: Michael Moore

Screenwriter: Michael Moore

Special Edition DVD Features: Michael Moore interviews and Oscar-acceptance speech; commentary by receptionists and interns; "Return to Denver/Littleton" featurette; teacher's guide; segment from *Awful Truth II: Corporate Cops;* Michael Moore's "Action Guide"; film festival scrapbook: Moore in Cannes, Toronto and London; Moore on "The Charlie Rose Show"; photo gallery; original theatrical trailer; music video: Marilyn Manson's "Fight Song"

Cast: Michael Moore, Charlton Heston, Marilyn Manson, Dick Clark, Chris Rock, Matt Stone, George W. Bush, Bill Clinton

Synopsis: Prompted by the shooting massacre at Columbine High School in 1999, Michael Moore explores the causes of violence in America. Moore appraises several common explanations for violent behavior, including gun ownership, the breakdown of the family, the prevalence of violence in the media, the prevalence of violence at the political level and economic inequality. Moore's message is that the answers are not as clear as we might think.

The Bridges of Madison County

U.S., 1995

135 Minutes, Feature, Color

Rating: PG-13 (sexual content, adult situations, language)

Director: Clint Eastwood

Screenwriter: Richard LaGravenese; based on the novel *The Bridges of Madison County* by Robert James Walker

DVD Features: English and Arabic subtitles; production notes

Cast: Meryl Streep, Clint Eastwood, Annie Corley, Victor Slezak

Synopsis: Francesca Johnson (Meryl Streep) is lonely in a stale marriage of eighteen years. One day, while her husband and children are on a week-long trip to at the state fair, Robert Kincaid (Clint Eastwood), a photographer from National Geographic, drives down her driveway to ask for directions to the covered bridges of Madison County. She discovers in Robert someone who is loving, intriguing and adventurous. Francesca faces the most difficult decision of her life—to remain in her unfulfilling marriage or leave with Robert.

The Chinese Connection

Hong Kong, 1972

110 Minutes, Feature, Color

Original Title: *Jing wu men*

International English Title: *Fists of Fury*

Rating: R (violence)

Director: Wei Lo

Screenwriters: Wei Lo, Bruce Lee and Kuang Ni

DVD Features: English subtitles

Cast: Bruce Lee, Nora Miao, Maria Yi, James Tien, Robert Baker, Fu Ching Chen, San Chin, Yin-Chieh Han, Riki Hashimoto, Jun Arimura, Chung-Hsin Huang, Quin Lee, Feng Tien, Yin Chi Lee, Tony Liu

Synopsis: Chen Zhen (Bruce Lee) is a young martial arts expert who has been away from home for a while. When he returns, he finds his hometown under the control of the Japanese military, the Chinese people being treated as subhuman and his master murdered. Chen exacts revenge for his master's death by defeating the entire Japanese martial arts school and other oppressors. Still, in the end he is arrested and killed by an angry mob.

The Cider House Rules

U.S., 1999

126 minutes, Feature, Color

Rating: PG-13 (mature themes, sexual content, nudity, substance abuse, violence)

Director: Lasse Hallström

Screenwriter: John Irving; based on his novel *The Cider House Rules*

DVD Features: English and French audio tracks; audio commentary; deleted scenes; the making of *Cider House Rules*

Cast: Tobey Maguire, Charlize Theron, Delroy Lindo, Paul Rudd, Michael Caine, Jane Alexander, Erykah Badu

Synopsis: Dr. Walter Larch (Michael Caine) directs an orphanage in 1940s Maine. Homer Wells (Tobey Maguire) has grown up there. Larch trains him in medicine, but Homer refuses to perform abortions. Homer leaves the orphanage and works at a cider farm, run by Mr. Rose (Delroy Lindo). One day it comes to light that the daughter of Mr. Rose, Rose Rose (Erykah Badu), is pregnant by her own father. Homer is faced with a dilemma, and he must reevaluate his convictions regarding abortion.

Citizen Kane

U.S., 1941

119 Minutes, Feature, B&W

Rating: NR

Director: Orson Welles

Screenwriters: Orson Welles and Herman Mankiewicz

Special Edition DVD Features: English, Spanish, French and Portuguese subtitles; commentary by Orson Welles, biographer Peter Bogdanovich and film critic Roger Ebert; 1941 premiere newsreel; gallery of storyboards, rare photos and other studio memorabilia; documentary: *The Battle Over Citizen Kane*

Cast: Orson Welles, Joseph Cotten, Everett Sloane, Dorothy Comingore, Ruth Warrick, George Coulouris, Paul Stewart, Ray Collins, William Alland, Philip Van Zandt

Synopsis: The film opens with the death of Charles Foster Kane (Orson Welles) and the uttering of his cryptic last word, "Rosebud." The identity of Rosebud is the mystery that drives the movie. Ralston (Philip Van Zandt), a Hollywood newsreel producer, sends Thompson (William Alland) out in search of answers. Along the way Thompson answers many questions in the life of the famous but enigmatic Kane and raises many others. The plot develops through six separate narratives of Kane's life: an opening newsreel and then five stories told by his closest acquaintances.

Contact

U.S., 1997

153 Minutes, Feature, Color

Rating: PG (language, sexual content)

Director: Robert Zemeckis

Screenwriters: James V. Hart and Michael Goldenberg; based on the novel *Contact* by Carl Sagan

DVD Features: English and French audio tracks; English, Spanish and French subtitles; audio commentary by actress Jodie Foster, director Robert Zemeckis, producer Steve Starkey and others; computer animation concepts and tests; special effects designs

Cast: Jodie Foster, Matthew McConaughey, Tom Skerritt, James Woods, John Hurt, Angela Bassett, William Fichtner, David Morse

Synopsis: Ellie Arroway (Jody Foster) is an astronomer and atheist who believes science can explain all of reality. Her ideological foil is Palmer Joss (Matthew McConaughey), a religious scholar who warns against the dangers of deifying science and technology. Ellie is mainly interested in discovering whether intelligent life exists on other planets. Despite being shunned by her colleagues she persists and eventually receives a message from outer space containing information about how to build a space machine. After some political wrangling, the machine is built, with Ellie eventually slated to travel into the unknown.

Crouching Tiger, Hidden Dragon

Hong Kong and Taiwan, 2000

120 Minutes, Feature, Color

Original Title: *Wo hu cang long*

Rating: PG-13 (martial arts violence and sexuality)

Director: Ang Lee

Martial Arts Director: Yuen Woo-ping

Screenwriters: Du Lu Wang, Hui-ling Wang, James Schamus and Tsai Kuo Jung

DVD Features: English subtitles and English dubbing

Cast: Yun-Fat Chow, Michelle Yeoh, Ziyi Zhang, Chen Chang, Sihung Lung, Pei-pei Cheng, Fa Zeng Li, Xian Gao

Synopsis: When Li Mu Bai (Yun-Fat Chow) wishes to leave a life of martial arts in order to pursue enlightenment, he gives his special sword, the Green Destiny, to a friend. However, the sword gets stolen and so, together with Yu Shu Lien (Michelle Yeoh), he fights to recover it. The thief is the evil woman Jade Fox (Pei-pei Cheng), who has recruited the heiress Jen Yu (Ziyi Zhang) to be a part of her schemes. Jen, though, has her own entanglements. She is supposed to marry the wealthy man picked out by her family, but she is in love with the outlaw Lo "Dark Cloud" (Chen Chang), who shows up just before the wedding.

Eternal Sunshine of the Spotless Mind

U.S., 2004

108 Minutes, Feature; Color

Rating: R (language, drugs, sexual content)

Director: Michel Gondry

Screenwriters: Charlie Kaufman and Michel Gondry

Special Edition DVD Features: Commentary by director Michel Gondry and writer Charlie Kaufman; conversations with actor Jim Carrey, actress Kate Winslet and director Michael Gondry; "A Look Inside *Eternal Sunshine of the*

Spotless Mind"; deleted scenes

Cast: Jim Carrey, Kate Winslet, Elijah Wood, Kirsten Dunst, Tom Wilkinson

Synopsis: Because her relationship with Joel (Jim Carrey) has degenerated, Clementine (Kate Winslet) undergoes a procedure to have him erased from her memory. Joel arranges to have the same procedure himself. But in the process, Joel realizes that he wants to retain the memories. In his mind, he and Clementine search for a place to hide from the disintegrating power of the memory wipe. Everywhere they turn, the memories get erased. Finally, she whispers to him, "Meet me in Montauk." This one memory escapes detection. Joel wakes with no recollection of Clementine. He heads for work but jumps suddenly onto a different train, one heading for Montauk.

Hannibal

U.S., 2001

131 minutes, Feature, Color

Rating: R (extreme violence, sexual content, strong language)

Director: Ridley Scott

Screenwriters: David Mamet and Steven Zallian; based on the novel *Hannibal* by Thomas Harris

DVD Features: English, French and Spanish audio tracks; English, French and Spanish subtitles; commentary by director Ridley Scott; deleted scenes; photo gallery; *Breaking the Silence*—five featurettes on the making of the film

Cast: Anthony Hopkins, Julianne Moore, Gary Oldman, Ray Liotta, Giancarlo Giannini

Synopsis: Ten years after the events recounted in *Silence of the Lambs*, Hannibal Lecter, psychiatrist and culturally literate cannibal, is still on the lam, eluding capture by the FBI. But the bureau is not alone in seeking to bring Lecter to justice. Mason Verger, a wealthy evangelical child molester and Lecter's only surviving victim, is using every resource, licit and illicit, to capture Lecter and feed him to specially trained wild boars. The man-eating doctor outwits his pursuers; he has Verger himself fed to the boars and then dines with (and on) a corrupt FBI official.

Iron Monkey

Hong Kong, 1993

86 Minutes, Feature, Color

Original Title: *Siunin Wong Fei-hung tsi titmalau*

Rating: PG-13 (martial arts violence and brief sexuality)

Director: Yuen Woo-ping

Martial Arts Director: Yuen Woo-ping

Screenwriters: Lau Tai-Muk, Tan Cheung, Elsa Tang Pik-yin and Tsui Hark

DVD Features: Chinese and English audio tracks; English subtitles; interview with Quentin Tarantino; interview with Donnie Yen; score medley

Cast: Rongguang Yu, Donnie Yen, Jean Wang, Yee Kwan Yan, James Wong, Hou Hsiao, Sze-Man Tsang, Shun-Yee Yuen, Fai Li

Synopsis: The Iron Monkey (Rongguang Yu) is a local doctor who carries out a Robin Hood-style campaign against the corrupt local governor. The governor (James Wong) launches an all-out fight against the Iron Monkey just around the time that an herbalist doctor named Wong Kei-ying (Donnie Yen) and his son, a youthful Wong Fei-hung (Sze-Man Tsang), enter the town. Thinking that Wong Kei-ying is the Iron Monkey, the governor arrests Fei-hung. Together the Iron Monkey and Kei-ying free the son and defeat the governor as well as a band of renegade Shaolin monks.

It's a Wonderful Life

U.S., 1946

130 Minutes, Feature, B&W

Rating: NR

Director: Frank Capra

Screenwriters: Frank Capra, Frances Goodrich, Albert Hackett and Jo Swerling

DVD Features: English, French and Spanish audio tracks; French and Spanish subtitles; documentary on the making of *It's a Wonderful Life;* "A Personal Remembrance" narrated by Frank Capra Jr.

Cast: James Stewart, Donna Reed, Lionel Barrymore, Thomas Mitchell, Henry Travers, Beulah Bondi, Frank Faylen, Gloria Grahame, Ward Bond

Synopsis: George Bailey (James Stewart) runs his family's building and loan in the humble community of Bedford Falls. Things take a dire turn when George's bumbling Uncle Billy (Thomas Mitchell) misplaces $8,000, putting the loan office in jeopardy. When the avaricious town banker, Henry Potter (Lionel Barrymore), learns of this he has a warrant issued for George's arrest. In his despair George attempts suicide but is saved by his guardian angel, Clarence (Henry Travers), who proceeds to show George just what things would have been like had he never existed. George sees how the entire Bedford Falls community has benefited from his "wonderful life."

King of the Ants

U.S., 2003

102 minutes, Feature, Color

Rating: R (extreme violence, sexual content, strong language)

Director: Stuart Gordon

Screenwriter: Charles Higson; based on his novel *King of the Ants*

DVD features: Commentary (Stuart Gordon, Chris L. McKenna, George Wendt); featurette; trailer

Cast: Chris L. McKenna, Kari Wuhrer, George Wendt, Daniel Baldwin

Synopsis: Crooked contractor Ray Mathews (Daniel Baldwin) hires a feckless drifter, Sean Crawley (Chris L. McKenna), to kill someone. When Mathews refuses to pay for services rendered, Crawley threatens to spill the beans. Mathews then has Crawley kidnapped and tortured. The experience, far from breaking Crawley's spirit, reveals to him his true "vocation."

Legend of Drunken Master

Hong Kong, 1994

102 minutes, Feature, Color

Original Title: *Jui kuen II*

Rating: R (violence)

Director: Liu Chia-Liang

Screenwriters: Edward Tang, Tong Man-Ming and Yuen Kai-chi

DVD features: English audio track; interview with Jackie Chan; deleted scenes

Cast: Jackie Chan, Lung Ti, Anita Mui, Felix Wong, Chia-Liang Liu, Ken Lo, Kar Lok Chin, Ho Sung Pak, Chi-Kwong Cheung, Yee San Hon

Synopsis: Young Wong Fei-hung (Jackie Chan) and his servant attempt to smuggle a ginseng root for use by Fei-hung's father, but they accidentally pick up the highly valuable "seal of the Emperor." A gang, which is attempting to smuggle Chinese artworks into the West, tries to get back the seal. Fei-hung must defend himself by resorting to "drunken boxing," but his father has forbidden him to engage in any form of fighting. Thus he must decide whether to fight one more time in order to save his town and his culture.

Legends of the Fall

U.S., 1994

135 Minutes, Feature, Color

Rating: R (nudity, sexual content, adult situations, violence, language)

Director: Edward Zwick

Screenwriters: Susan Shilliday and William D. Wittliff; based on the novel *Legends of the Fall* by Jim Harrison

Special Edition DVD Features: English, French, Spanish and Portuguese audio tracks; English, Spanish, French, Portuguese, Georgian, Thai and Chinese subtitles; commentary by director Ed Zwick, actor Brad Pitt, cinematographer John Toll and production designer Lilly Kilvert; deleted scenes; production design featurette

Cast: Brad Pitt, Anthony Hopkins, Aidan Quinn, Julia Ormond, Henry Thomas, Karina Lombard

Synopsis: Spanning five decades, this epic details the turbulent lives of three brothers. When the fiancé, Susannah (Julia Ormond), of the youngest brother, Samuel (Henry Thomas), arrives by train in Helena, Montana, in 1913, the lives of everyone involved are forever changed. Susannah's heart is instantly captured by the middle son, Tristan (Brad Pitt), who is incapable of loving anyone. The entanglement of the crossed romances raises profound issues about the meaning of love, friendship and family.

Lemora: A Child's Tale of the Supernatural

U.S., 1975

85 minutes, Feature, Color

Rating: PG (sexual content, frightening images)

Director: Richard Blackburn

Screenwriters: Richard Blackburn and Robert Fern

DVD features: Commentary by director Richard Blackburn, coscreenwriter Robert Fern and actress Lesley Gilb; theatrical trailers; photo gallery

Cast: Lesley Gilb, Cheryl Smith, Richard Blackburn, William Whitton, Steve Johnson

Synopsis: After murdering his wife, Alvin Lee (William Whitton) takes off for parts unknown. He leaves behind his beautiful daughter Lila (Cheryl Smith), who becomes a ward of the local church. One day Lila, now thirteen, receives a letter stating that her father is near death and desperately seeks to be reconciled with his daughter. She immediately sets out on a journey of Christian love and forgiveness. She finds instead faith-shattering corruption and the waiting arms of a bloodthirsty monster named Lemora (Lesley Gilb).

The Matrix

U.S., 1999

136 Minutes, Feature, Color

Rating: R (violence and language)

Directors: Andy Wachowski and Larry Wachowski

Screenwriters: Andy Wachowski and Larry Wachowski

DVD Features: Commentaries by cast and production crew; documentary: "HBO First Look: Making *The Matrix*"; special effects documentaries: "What Is Bullet Time?" and "What Is the Concept?"; behind-the-scenes featurettes

Cast: Keanu Reeves, Laurence Fishburne, Carrie-Ann Moss, Hugo Weaving,

Gloria Foster, Joe Pantoliano

Synopsis: A computer hacker named Thomas Anderson, AKA Neo (Keanu Reeves), is shocked to discover that life as he knows it is really a computer-simulated illusion, the Matrix, designed to keep humans pacified while their bodies are used as a power source by a race of super-intelligent machines. Neo is contacted by a small team of rebels led by Morpheus (Laurence Fishburne), who believes that Neo is the prophesied "One" destined to lead the remnant of free humanity—now living in an underground city called Zion—to victory against the machines. Freed from the Matrix, Neo learns how the rebels are able to manipulate its rules and reenter it with enhanced powers.

The Matrix Reloaded

U.S., 2003

138 Minutes, Feature, Color

Rating: R (violence, sexuality)

Directors: Andy Wachowski and Larry Wachowski

Screenwriters: Andy Wachowski and Larry Wachowski

DVD Features: English and French audio tracks; English, Spanish and French subtitles; behind the scenes with cast and crew; documentaries: "The Freeway Chase," "Enter the Matrix," "What Is the Animatrix?" and "The Matrix Unfolds"

Cast: Keanu Reeves, Laurence Fishburne, Carrie-Ann Moss, Hugo Weaving, Jada Pinkett Smith

Synopsis: The first sequel to *The Matrix* picks up the action some months later as a machine army bores its way toward the underground city of Zion, threatening humanity with extinction. Zion's military command pursues a conventional defensive strategy, but Morpheus (Laurence Fishburne) puts his faith in Neo (Keanu Reeves), who continues to grow into his new powers as the One. Neo is harassed by Agent Smith (Hugo Weaving), who reappears as an independent operator with unlimited powers of self-replication.

The Matrix Revolutions

U.S., 2003

129 Minutes, Feature, Color

Rating: R (sci-fi violence, brief sexuality)

Directors: Andy Wachowski and Larry Wachowski

Screenwriters: Andy Wachowski and Larry Wachowski

DVD Features: English and French audio tracks; Spanish and French subtitles; documentaries: "Revolutions Recalibrated" on the making of the film and "CG Revolution" on special effects; "Super Burly Brawl," a featurette on the final Neo-Smith showdown; "Before the Revolution": a 3D Matrix timeline

Cast: Keanu Reeves, Laurence Fishburne, Carrie-Ann Moss, Hugo Weaving, Jada Pinkett Smith, Lambert Wilson, Collin Chou

Synopsis: Only a few hours remain before the machine army arrives in Zion, but Neo (Keanu Reeves) is marooned in the train station, a limbo between the Matrix and the real world controlled by a rogue program called the Merovingian (Lambert Wilson). Rescued by fellow rebels Morpheus (Laurence Fishburne), Trinity (Carrie-Ann Ross) and Seraph (Collin Chou), Neo confronts a new development: the Smith (Hugo Weaving) virus is now out of control, threatening to infect the entire Matrix. As the machine army breaks into Zion, its defenders fall back, fighting valiantly against overwhelming odds.

Mystic River

U.S., 2003

137 Minutes, Feature, Color

Rating: R (language and violence)

Director: Clint Eastwood

Screenwriter: Brian Helgeland; based on the novel *Mystic River* by Dennis Lehane

Special Edition DVD Features: English and French audio tracks; English, Spanish and French subtitles; commentary by actors Tim Robbins and Kevin Bacon; "Beneath the Surface," a featurette with cast and crew interviews; selections from "The Charlie Rose Show," including interviews with Clint Eastwood, Tim Robbins and Kevin Bacon; theatrical trailers

Cast: Sean Penn, Tim Robbins, Kevin Bacon, Laurence Fishburne Marcia Gay Harden, Laura Linney, Thomas Guiry, Emmy Rossum

Synopsis: Childhood friends Jimmy Markum (Sean Penn), Sean Devine (Kevin Bacon) and Dave Boyle (Tim Robbins) are playing together when child-abusers impersonating police abduct Dave. Years after Dave's escape from his abductors, the three friends are reunited following the death of Jimmy's oldest daughter, Katie (Emmy Rossum). Sean is a police detective on the case, gathering evidence that is ambiguous, pointing toward both Dave and Katie's boyfriend, Brendan Harris (Thomas Guiry), as suspects. As Sean pursues the case through official channels, Jimmy's rage and need for retribution fuel his own quest for Katie's killer.

Once Upon a Time in China

Hong Kong, 1991

134 Minutes, Feature, Color

Original Title: *Wong Fei-hung*

Rating: R (violence)

Director: Hark Tsui

Martial Arts Director: Yuen Woo-ping

Screenwriters: Leung Yiu-ming, Elsa Tang Pik-yin, Hark Tsui and Yuen Gai-chi

DVD Features: English, Spanish and French subtitles; commentary by Hong Kong film expert Ric Meyers

Cast: Jet Li, Biao Yuen, Rosamund Kwan, Jacky Cheung, Steve Tartalia, Kent Cheng, Jonathan Isgar, Shi-Kwan Yen, Mark King

Synopsis: Wong Fei-hung (Jet Li) is a doctor and a martial arts master who is attempting to fight for justice for his people in the face of the oppressive presence of Westerners and local authorities that support them. To make matters worse, a gang from a neighboring town captures local women in order to sell them into slavery. Wong Fei-hung and his friends eventually triumph in the immediate situation, but they have little hope of averting the eventual fate of China.

Once Upon a Time in China II

Hong Kong, 1992

113 Minutes, Feature, Color

Original Title: *Wong Fei-hung ji yi: Naam yi dong ji keung*

Rating: R (violence)

Director: Hark Tsui

Martial Arts Director: Yuen Woo-ping

Screenwriters: Chan Tin-suen, Tan Cheung, and Hark Tsui

DVD features: Cantonese, English and French audio tracks; English, Spanish and French subtitles

Cast: Jet Li, Rosamund Kwan, Donnie Yen Ji-dan, Max Mok Siu-chung, Xiong Xin-xin, Cheung Tit-lam, David Chiang, Shi-Kwan Yen

Synopsis: Wong Fei-hung (Jet Li) goes to Hong Kong to present a paper on acupuncture at a medical convention, where he meets Dr. Sun Yat-sen, the future president of China. Fei-hung's struggle against invidious foreign influences continues. But this time the White Lotus Sect, which has vowed to exterminate all foreigners and their sympathizers, adds to the fight.

Pleasantville

U.S., 1998

124 Minutes, Feature, B&W and Color

Rating: PG-13 (sexual themes, language)

Director: Gary Ross

Screenwriter: Gary Ross

DVD Features: Commentary by director Gary Ross and composer Randy Newman; "The Art of Pleasantville," a behind-the-scenes featurette; music video: "Across the Universe" by Fiona Apple; storyboard gallery

Cast: Tobey Maguire, Reese Witherspoon, Jeff Daniels, William H. Macy, J. T. Walsh, Joan Allen, Don Knotts

Synopsis: David (Tobey Maguire) and Jennifer (Reese Witherspoon) are transported into Pleasantville, the black-and-white world of a 1950s sitcom. They become a part of the story—as Bud and Mary Sue Parker. Life in Pleasantville is bland. The high school basketball team always wins. It never rains. The pages in all of the books are blank. Nothing ever changes. But Mary Sue breaks from the routine and has sex with her boyfriend. This sparks a community-wide liberation of sexuality and personal expression, symbolized by the appearance of color in Pleasantville.

Pretty Woman

U.S., 1990

119 Minutes, Feature, Color

Rating: R (sexual content, adult situations, language)

Director: Garry Marshall

Screenwriter: J. F. Lawton

DVD Features: commentary by director Garry Marshall; additional film footage; production featurette; music video: "Wild Women Do" by Natalie Cole

Cast: Richard Gere, Julia Roberts, Hector Elizondo, Ralph Bellamy

Synopsis: Edward Lewis (Richard Gere) is in Beverly Hills for a week, engaged in difficult business negotiations. He hires Hollywood prostitute Vivian Ward (Julia Roberts) to be his "employee" for the week since he doesn't want to be alone or burdened with "romantic hassles." Even though Edward and Vivian are from very different worlds, they are captivated by each other and are confronted with how empty each of their lives has become.

Rattle and Hum

U.S., 1988

99 Minutes, Feature, B&W and Color

Rating: PG-13 (language)

Director: Phil Joanou

DVD Features: English subtitles

Cast: Bono, The Edge, Adam Clayton, Larry Mullin Jr., B. B. King

Synopsis: This rock documentary chronicles the 1987 American tour of Irish rock band U2 as well as brief trips into the studio to record songs for the album, also titled *Rattle and Hum,* released the following year. Along the way, the band pays homage on stage and off to the pantheon of American rock legends, including Elvis Presley, Bob Dylan, Billie Holiday, B. B. King and Jimi Hendrix. African American gospel and the music of the Beatles are also featured.

Run Lola Run

Germany, 1998

81 Minutes, Feature, Color and B&W

Rating: R (violence and language)

Director: Tom Tykwer

Screenwriter: Tom Tykwer

DVD Features: English and German audio tracks; English and French subtitles; commentary by director Tom Tykwer and actress Franka Potente; music video: "Believe" by Franka Potente

Cast: Franka Potente, Moritz Bleibtreu, Herbert Knaup, Nina Petri, Armin Rohde

Synopsis: Lola (Franka Potente) receives a phone call from panicked boyfriend, Manni (Moritz Bleibtreu). As the delivery man in a major drug deal, he has lost 100,000 deutsche marks while riding the subway to deliver the money to his boss. They are to meet in just twenty minutes, and if Manni doesn't have the money, he's a dead man. She decides to seek help from her father, a bank executive. From here the film presents us with three different versions of what could be the future for Lola and Manni, depending on the choices they make and various random events. The consequences in the three scenarios range from tragic to happy.

Shaolin Wooden Men

Hong Kong, 1976

98 Minutes, Feature, Color

Original Title: *Shao Lin mu ren xiang*

Rating: NR

Director: Chi-Hwa Chen

Screenwriter: Wei Lo

DVD Features: English subtitles and English dubbing

Cast: Jackie Chan, Jang Lee Hwang, Kam Kong, Doris Lung Chun-erh, Yuen Biao, Simon Yuen Siu-tin, Chiang Kam, Cheung Bing-yuk, Miu Tak-san, Liu Ping

Synopsis: A boy witnesses his father's murder. Vowing revenge he enrolls in a Shaolin temple and masters the various styles of hung fu. Due to the trauma he suffered, he does not speak and is known as "the Mute" (Jackie Chan). Once he has demonstrated his fighting prowess by defeating thirty-six wood-clad Shaolin opponents, he sets out to find his father's killer. The Mute discovers that his master at the temple is the person he has been looking for all along. As he fights this man, he shows that he has not sacrificed his humanity in his quest for revenge.

The Truman Show

U.S., 1998

103 Minutes, Feature, Color

Rating: PG (adult themes, mild language)

Director: Peter Weir

Screenwriter: Andrew Niccol

Special Edition DVD Features: English and French audio tracks; English and Spanish subtitles; documentary: *The Making of The Truman Show;* deleted and extended scenes; photo gallery; theatrical trailers

Cast: Jim Carrey, Laura Linney, Ed Harris, Noah Emmerich, Natascha McElhone, Holland Taylor, Brian Delate

Synopsis: Truman Burbank (Jim Carrey), the first person to be adopted by a corporation, is the star of *The Truman Show*, a live television broadcast of his life twenty-four hours a day, seven days a week. Truman doesn't know that his life is a sham, that his town of Seahaven is a TV studio (the world's largest), that all the people in his life are merely actors, and that people worldwide have been watching him since the day of his birth. The film narrates the final days of the show, when Truman begins to connect the dots. His wife (Laura Linney) and his boyhood buddy (Noah Emmerich) do all they can to prevent Truman from discovering the truth.

Contributors

Douglas Blount is associate professor of philosophy at Southwestern Baptist Theological Seminary and managing editor of *Southwestern Journal of Theology*. He has published numerous articles in philosophical and theological journals and has contributed chapters to *Reason for the Hope Within* (Eerdmans, 1999), *God and Time* (Oxford University Press, 2002) and *The Lord of the Rings and Philosophy* (Open Court, 2003). He has articles in the *Holman Illustrated Bible Dictionary* (Holman, 2003) and the *New Dictionary of Christian Apologetics* (InterVarsity Press, 2006). Blount includes the study of film in his classes and gives special lectures on film and television.

Kelly James Clark is professor of philosophy at Calvin College. Clark has published many philosophical essays and authored *Return to Reason* (Eerdmans, 1990) and *When Faith Is Not Enough* (Eerdmans, 1997). He coauthored *101 Key Terms in Philosophy and Their Importance for Theology* (Westminster John Knox, 2004). He edited *Our Knowledge of God* (Kluwer, 1992), *Philosophers Who Believe* (InterVarsity Press, 1993) and *Readings in the Philosophy of Religion* (Broadview, 2000), and coedited *The Story of Ethics* (Prentice Hall, 2003). Clark gives public lectures on film and uses film in his courses.

Winfried Corduan is professor of philosophy and religion at Taylor University. Corduan is a leading Christian scholar on world religions. He has published in a variety of philosophical and theological journals and contributed articles to the *Evangelical Dictionary of Theology* (Baker, 2001) and the *Dictionary of Christianity in America* (InterVarsity Press, 1990). Corduan's books include *Neighboring Faiths* (InterVarsity Press, 1998), *A Tapestry of Faiths* (InterVarsity Press, 2002), *Pocket Guide to World Religions* (InterVarsity Press, 2006) and, as coauthor, *Philosophy of Religion* (Baker, 1988). Corduan includes films as illustrative material in his world religions courses.

Gregory E. Ganssle is lecturer in philosophy and Rivendell Institute Fellow at Yale University. Ganssle's publications have appeared in numerous philosophical journals. He has edited *God and Time: Four Views* (InterVarsity Press, 2001) and, with David Woodruff, *God and Time: Essays on the Divine Nature* (Oxford University Press, 2002). Ganssle is also the author of *Thinking About God: First Steps in Philosophy* (InterVarsity Press, 2004). His essay "God and Evil" appears in *The Rationality of Theism* (Routledge, 2003). Greg became interested in philosophy and film through many discussions with his children who are aspiring filmmakers.

R. Douglas Geivett is professor of philosophy at Biola University. Geivett's philosophical writings have appeared in many journals and edited volumes. He has contributed chapters to several volumes, including *The Rationality of Theism* (Routledge, 2003), *Does God Exist? The Craig-Flew Debate* (Ashgate, 2003), and *24 and Philosophy* (Blackwell, 2007). Geivett has authored *Evil and the Evidence for God* (Temple University Press, 1993) and coedited *Contemporary Perspectives on Religious Epistemology* (Oxford University Press, 1992) and *In Defense of Miracles* (InterVarsity Press, 1997). An acclaimed public speaker, Geivett frequently appears on radio programs and participates in debates around the country. He often discusses film in his public lectures and classes.

David P. Hunt is professor of philosophy at Whittier College. Hunt has published numerous philosophical articles and has contributed essays to several books, including *Divine Foreknowledge: Four Views* (InterVarsity Press, 2001), *Plato's Forms: Varieties of Interpretation* (Lexington, 2002), *Moral Responsibility and Alternative Possibilities* (Ashgate, 2003) and *Midwest Studies in Philosophy, Vol. 29: Free Will and Moral Responsibility* (Blackwell, 2005). Hunt's teaching regularly involves film. He has taught two film-related courses: "Philosophical Issues on Film" and "Philosophy in *The Matrix*."

Greg Jesson is a Ph.D. candidate in philosophy at the University of Iowa. Jesson's work has appeared in *Philosophia Christi, Intentionality Past and Future* (Rodopi, 2004), *War on Words: The Censorship Debate* (McMeel, 1993), *Reclaiming the Culture* (Word, 1996) and *Ontology and Analysis: Essays and Recollections About Gustav Bergmann* (Ontos Verlag, 2007), which he also edited. Jesson has lectured widely in the United States and Europe, and has participated in the Veritas Forum at Stanford and the University of California at

Santa Cruz. He has given a lecture series titled "Contemporary Cinema and the Christian Faith," and he is currently on the faculty of Augustana College.

James F. Sennett is associate professor of philosophy at Brenau University. Sennett has published numerous essays on a broad range of philosophical topics. He has written chapters for *God Matters* (Longman, 2003) and *Knowledge, Teaching, and Wisdom* (Kluwer, 1996), and his article "Alvin Plantinga" appears in the *Cambridge Dictionary of Philosophy* (1999). Sennett has also edited *The Analytic Theist: An Alvin Plantinga Reader* (Eerdmans, 1998) and coedited *In Defense of Natural Theology: A Post-Humean Reassessment* (InterVarsity Press, 2005). Sennett has lectured often on the place of cinema in contemporary American culture.

Sara L. H. Shady is associate professor of philosophy at Bethel University. Shady is a specialist in early- to mid-twentieth-century continental social and political philosophy. Her current research interests pertain to community and social relationships. Shady has published in *Religious Studies Review* and (forthcoming) *Christian Scholar's Review*, and presented papers at numerous professional conferences. Shady regularly includes film analyses in her classes and participates in film forums at her university.

Caroline J. Simon is Jacobson Professor of Philosophy at Hope College. Simon has published dozens of articles in scholarly journals and authored *The Disciplined Heart: Love, Destiny and Imagination* (Eerdmans, 1997) and coauthored *Mentoring for Mission: Nurturing New Faculty at Church-Related Colleges* (Eerdmans, 2003) and *Can Hope Endure? A Historical Case Study in Christian Higher Education* (Eerdmans, 2005). She has also contributed chapters to several edited volumes, including *Inquiring After God* (Blackwell, 2000) and *Philosophy, Feminism and Faith* (Indiana University Press, 2003). Simon regularly uses film in her philosophy courses and has also served on campus panels to discuss contemporary films.

James S. Spiegel is professor of philosophy and religion at Taylor University. Spiegel's essays have appeared in numerous philosophical and theological journals. His books include *Hypocrisy: Moral Fraud and Other Vices* (Baker, 1999), *How to Be Good in a World Gone Bad* (Kregel, 2004) and *The Benefits of Providence* (Crossway, 2005). He has contributed chapters to *Bob Dylan and Philosophy* (Open Court, 2005), *The Beatles and Philosophy* (Open Court,

2006) and *God Under Fire* (Zondervan 2002). Spiegel occasionally gives a public lecture titled "God and the Silver Screen" that explores philosophical and theological issues in contemporary film.

Brendan Sweetman is professor of philosophy at Rockhurst University. Sweetman's books include *Why Politics Needs Religion: The Place of Religious Arguments in the Public Square* (InterVarsity Press, 2006) and *Religion: Key Concepts in Philosophy* (Continuum, 2007). He has coauthored or coedited several other books, including *Truth and Religious Belief* (M.E. Sharpe, 1998) and *Contemporary Perspectives on Religious Epistemology* (Oxford University Press, 1992). He has published more than fifty articles and reviews in a variety of philosophical journals. Sweetman often moderates film discussions for an annual film series hosted by his department.

Ronald K. Tacelli, S.J., is associate professor of philosophy at Boston College. Tacelli has published in numerous philosophical journals and has contributed several articles to the *International Encyclopedia of Apologetics* (Ignatius, forthcoming). He coauthored the award-winning *Handbook of Christian Apologetics* (InterVarsity Press, 1994) and coedited *The Rationality of Theism* (Kluwer, 1999) and *The Resurrection Debate: Fact or Figment?* (InterVarsity Press, 2000). Tacelli uses film as a teaching tool in his great books course, "Perspectives on Western Culture," and has for many years organized Boston College's Friday Film Festival.

Dallas Willard is professor of philosophy at University of Southern California. An internationally renowned author and speaker, Willard has authored *Logic and the Objectivity of Knowledge* (Ohio University Press, 1984) and two volumes of translations from the early writings of Edmund Husserl. Willard has also published numerous bestselling books in spiritual formation, including *The Spirit of the Disciplines* (HarperSanFrancisco, 1988), *The Divine Conspiracy* (HarperSanFrancisco, 1998) and *Renovation of the Heart* (NavPress, 2002). He teaches in the field of aesthetics, and his public lectures often include critical analyses of contemporary film.

Notes

Chapter 1: The *Citizen Kane* Mutiny

I wish to thank my many "movie buds," with whom I spend delightful hours discussing and criticizing films of all kinds, for engaging me in critical examination of the ideas presented here. I had numerous and particularly helpful conversations on the topic with Brian "It's better if it's British" Johnson and Carolyn Kramlich, who is on a one-woman campaign to get Jack Nicholson cast for the lead in the remake of *Citizen Kane.*

[1]American Film Institute, "America's Greatest Movies" <http://www.afi.com/Docs/tvevents/pdf/movies100.pdf>. Accessed May 23, 2007. AFI issued a new "Top 100 Movies" list in the summer of 2007. While there were some interesting changes, *Citizen Kane* remained firmly ensconced at the top. Other lists in the "100 Years" series available at the AFI site include the one hundred greatest stars, one hundred funniest movies, one hundred top thrillers, one hundred top movie songs and one hundred top movie quotations. See <http://www.afi.com/tvevents/100years/100yearslist.aspx> for links to all the lists. The British Film Institute organ *Sight & Sound* has conducted an international poll of critics and directors every ten years since 1952 to determine the ten greatest films of all time. *Citizen Kane* has topped every poll but the first. See British Film Institute, "The History of the *Sight & Sound* Top Ten Poll" <http://www.bfi.org.uk/sightandsound/topten/history>. Accessed May 23, 2007. A poll of American film critics reported in *The Village Voice* on January 4, 2000, ranked *Citizen Kane* the greatest film of the twentieth century, as did a *Time Out* critics poll published in 1995. While similar polls of movie fans (rather than professionals) invariably list *The Godfather* as the most popular film of all time, *Citizen Kane* routinely makes it into the top five of such polls as well.

[2]Louis Giannetti, *Understanding Movies*, 10th ed. (Upper Saddle River, N.Y.: Pearson Prentice Hall, 2005), pp. 511-47. According to the Wikipedia article on *mise en scène* from April 2007, "When applied to the cinema, mise en scène refers to everything that appears before the camera and its arrangement—sets, props, actors, costumes, and lighting. Mise en scène also includes the positioning and movement of actors on

the set, which is called blocking." The article begins by noting that *mise en scène* "has been called film criticism's 'grand undefined term,' but that is not because of a lack of definitions. Rather, it's because the term has so many different meanings that there is little consensus about its definition." "Mise en scène [April 10, 2007]," *Wikipedia: The Free Encyclopedia* <http://en.wikipedia.org/wiki/Mise_en_scène>. Accessed May 23, 2007.

[3]In a script where almost every line is significant, artistic and full of content, this is one of my two favorites. The other comes from the lips of Bernstein, responding to Thompson's observation that Thatcher had made a lot of money in his life: "Well, it's no trick to make a lot of money, if all you want is to make a lot of money."

[4]For my personal musings on this subject, see James F. Sennett, "The *Cogito* Meets the *Imago:* The Image of God and the Concept of a Person," in *Taking Every Thought Captive: Essays in Honor of James D. Strauss*, ed. John Castelein and Richard A. Knopp (Joplin, Mo.: College Press, 1997), pp. 327-54.

[5]Dorothy Sayers, *The Mind of the Maker* (New York: Harper and Row, 1970), pp. 21-29, esp. p. 22.

[6]All Scripture quotations in this essay are taken from the New International Version.

[7]See <www.comicbookmovie.com>.

[8]Although Batman is often cited for his lack of supernatural powers, such lack has, from the very beginning, been more than compensated for by his access to state-of-the-art technological equipment and weaponry—a situation made possible, of course, by Bruce Wayne's limitless wealth, another of Kane's tools. The wild capabilities of his specialized toys provide Batman with the scientific-age equivalent to super powers. One is reminded of Arthur C. Clarke's famous dictum, "Any sufficiently advanced technology is indistinguishable from magic."

Chapter 2: Story-Shaped Lives in *Big Fish*

[1]Stanley Hauerwas, "The Moral Authority of Scripture," in *From Christ to the World: Introductory Readings in Christian Ethics*, ed. Wayne Boulton, Thomas Kennedy and Allen Verhey (Grand Rapids: Eerdmans, 1994), p. 46.

[2]At the circus, which Edward will travel to shortly, the ringmaster, Amos tells Edward, "You were hot s*** back in Hickville, but here in the real world, you got squat. You don't have a plan. You don't have a job. You don't have anything but the clothes on your back. . . . Kid, you were a big fish in a small pond. This here is the ocean, and you're drowning. Take my advice and go back to Puddleville. You'll be happy there."

[3]In the novel *Big Fish*, this point is made explicitly. The kind of people who come to Spectre are described as "normal people and their plans. This rain, this dampness—it's a kind of residue. The residue of a dream. Of a lot of dreams, actually. Mine and yours." Soon after, the narrator comments, "There seemed to be no real life here,

none of the anxious expectancy of a hunger about to be sated." Daniel Wallace, *Big Fish* (New York: Penguin, 1998), pp. 42, 45.

[4]An excellent example of this approach is Joel B. Green, ed., *In Search of the Soul: Four Views of the Mind-Body Problem* (Downers Grove, Ill.: InterVarsity Press, 2005).

[5]Alasdair MacIntyre, *After Virtue* (Notre Dame, Ind.: University of Notre Dame Press, 1981), p. 216.

[6]Michael Novak, *Ascent of the Mountain, Flight of the Dove* (San Francisco: Harper and Row, 1978), pp. 49, 62.

[7]This is the attitude that we should have toward our narratives that provide genuine self-understanding. We believe that we are discovering, not creating, patterns. As Hannah Arendt puts it, narration "reveals meaning without committing the error of defining it." Hannah Arendt, foreword to *Daguerreotypes and Other Essays* by Isak Dinesen (Chicago: University of Chicago Press, 1979), p. xx. However, we are often more pattern creators than pattern discoverers (especially as we tell stories that competitively "make" us better than others).

[8]MacIntyre, *After Virtue*, p. 205.

[9]Adriana Cavarero, *Relating Narratives* (Oxford: Routledge, 2000), p. 2.

[10]Ibid., p. 3.

[11]C. S. Lewis, "On Stories," in *Of This and Other Worlds*, ed. Walter Hooper (London: Collins, 1982).

[12]Frank Kermode, *The Sense of an Ending* (New York: Oxford University Press, 1967), p. 4.

[13]"Coming home he felt like a stranger. Everything had changed. His wife had rearranged the living room, bought a new dress, made new friends, read strange books, which she brazenly placed on her bedside table. And I grew so quickly. His wife couldn't see it as clearly, but he could. Coming back he saw this incredible growth, and seeing it realized how much smaller this made him, relatively speaking. So in a way it was true: as I grew, he shrank. And by this logic one day I would become a giant, and Edward would become nothing, invisible in the world." Wallace, *Big Fish*, p. 123.

[14]Ibid., p. 15.

[15]The novel (ibid., pp. 21-22) makes this point clearly:

> *"I wanted to be a great man,"* he whispers.
>
> "Can you believe it? I thought it was my destiny. A big fish in a big pond— that's what I wanted. That's what I wanted from day one. I started small. For a long time I worked for other people. Then I started my own business. I got these molds and I made candles in the basement. That business failed. I sold baby's breath to floral shops. That failed. Finally, though, I got into import/ export and everything took off. I had dinner with a prime minister once, Wil-

liam. A prime minister! Can you imagine, this boy from Ashland having dinner in the same room with a—. There's not a continent I haven't set foot on. Not one. There are seven of them right? I'm starting to forget which ones I . . . never mind. Now all that seems so unimportant, you know? I mean, I don't even know what a great man *is* anymore—the, uh, prerequisites. Do you, William?"

"Do I what?"

"Know," he says. "Know what makes a man great."

"I think," I say after a while, waiting for the right words to come, "that if a man could be said to be loved by his son, then I think that man could be considered great."

For this is the only power I have, to bestow upon my father the mantle of greatness, a thing he sought in the wider world, but one that, in a surprise turn of events, was here at home all along.

[16]It was suggested by several readers that I should omit references to the book because the film is a different medium from the book and the film has a life of its own. I ignored this advice. Acknowledging the limitations of any humanly constructed narrative, one should approach any subject matter with as much information, garnered from a wide variety of sources, as possible. I take it that this is precisely what Christians should do with the Bible: it provides information, independent of any particular event in our lives, that helps us interpret the events in our lives.

Chapter 3: Defining Love Through the Eye of the Lens

[1]Bruce Barton, quoted in Virginia Ely, *I Quote* (New York: George W. Stewart, 1947), p. 205.

[2]C. S. Lewis, *The Four Loves* (New York: Harcourt Brace Jovanovich, 1960) esp. pp. 87-127.

[3]Michel Quoist, *Prayers*, trans. Agnes Forsyth and Anne de Commaille (New York: Sheed and Ward, 1963), p. 53.

[4]Bertrand Russell, *The Autobiography of Bertrand Russell*, vol. 1 (London: George Allen and Unwin, 1969), pp. 126, 147.

[5]I want to avoid both the self-righteousness of the scribes and Pharisees and any view that minimizes the seriousness of immoral actions and their heartbreaking consequences. The danger is that people are looking for a way to do what they want to do with no negative consequences. Certainly, treating one's spouse with less than real love is always serious and, if it persists, potentially disastrous, but using that to justify one's own immoral actions is always wrong and accelerates the destruction of the relationship.

[6]Martin Buber, *I and Thou* (Edinburgh: T & T Clark, 1953), p. 87.

[7]William Ernest Hocking, *Human Nature and Its Remaking* (New Haven: Yale University Press), p. 398; cf. John 3:16.

Chapter 4: Escaping into Reality

[1]See Peter Weir's introduction to Andrew Niccol, *The Truman Show: The Shooting Script* (New York: Newmarket Press, 1998), p. xiii. The epigraph at the opening of this chapter also comes from this script.

[2]This is reflected in a scene in ibid., pp. 8-9.

[3]For a very fine exploration of issues related to truth, see Michael P. Lynch, *True to Life: Why Truth Matters* (Cambridge, Mass.: MIT Press, 2005).

[4]An actress named Sylvia (who is played by real-life actress Natascha McElhone) plays the role of Lauren on the set of Seahaven. In the rest of this chapter, I'll refer to her as Sylvia.

[5]In the shooting script, Truman peers into the sky, apparently thinking the item may have become dislodged from an airplane. But he sees nothing. See Niccol, *Truman Show*, p. 3.

[6]This exchange does not occur in the film, but it's there in the shooting script. See ibid., pp. 19-20.

[7]The original screenplay has a very different ending. See <http://www.imsdb.com/scripts/Truman-Show,-The.html>. Accessed May 23, 2007.

[8]This reminds me of the crucial moment in another film with similar themes: *36 Hours* (1964). Major Jefferson Pike (James Garner) is fooled by an elaborate Nazi ruse, until a guard at what is supposed to be an American military hospital clicks his heels while saluting him. (This film pairs Garner with Eva Marie Saint. I give it two thumbs up.)

[9]I'm thinking of some expressions of the emerging church movement. For example, Eddie Gibbs and Ryan Bolger define the emerging church in this way: "Emerging churches are communities that practice the way of Jesus within postmodern cultures." They then state the nine practices encompassed by this definition: "Emerging churches (1) identify with the life of Jesus, (2) transform the secular realm, and (3) live highly communal lives. Because of these three activities, they (4) welcome the stranger, (5) serve with generosity, (6) participate as producers, (7) create as created beings, (8) lead as a body and (9) take part in spiritual activities." See Eddie Gibbs and Ryan K. Bolger, *Emerging Churches: Creating Christian Community in Postmodern Cultures* (Grand Rapids: Brazos, 2005), pp. 44-45. Depending on their specific meaning, these are admirable practices. But there is no mention here of the role of the church in preserving and commending a knowledge tradition. For the emerging church, practicing the way of Jesus "within postmodern cultures" entails a discomfort with "standing up for the truth" (see ibid., p. 124). Emerging churches "do not hope for a belief change for their conversation partners as much as a life change" (ibid., p. 134). This is a needless dichotomy. For more on the complexities involved here, see my chapters "Is God a Story? Postmodernity and the Task of Theology" and "Post-

modernity and the Quest for Theological Knowledge," in *Christianity and the Post-modern Turn: Six Views*, ed. Myron B. Penner (Grand Rapids: Brazos, 2005).

[10]Truman's situation is extreme (and unrealistic); we're not in the dire position that he is. Sustaining the level of conspiracy of deceit depicted in *The Truman Show* would be incalculably difficult. We have little to worry about ourselves, if we live in a wide enough community. Also, while Truman's world is a deceit, he has grown up with much *reliable* testimony about a great many things. The irony is that his society's deception depends on educating and reinforcing him in beliefs that are not only justified, but also true. He has much useful information that enables him to understand his own parochial world and much of the world beyond. I concur with Jonathan Adler, who argues that our vulnerability to error when we believe on the basis of testimony is exaggerated. See Jonathan Adler, *Belief's Own Evidence* (Cambridge, Mass.: MIT Press, 2002), chap. 5.

[11]Attempts to discredit our cognitive capabilities are currently popular, and film is often exploited for this purpose. But a film need not promote a skeptical agenda to be epistemologically interesting. Our film *The Truman Show* has, understandably, been mined for skeptical themes. See, e.g., Kimberly A. Blessing, "Deceit and Doubt: The Search for Truth in *The Truman Show* and Descartes's *Meditations*," in *Movies and the Meaning of Life: Philosophers Take on Hollywood*, ed. Kimberly A. Blessing and Paul J. Tudico (Chicago: Open Court, 2005), pp. 3-15. But this emphasis misses the deeper epistemological import of the film.

[12]Alvin Plantinga, "Against Materialism," *Faith and Philosophy* 23, no. 1 (January 2006): 4.

[13]For an accessible introduction to evidentialism, see Richard Feldman, *Epistemology* (Upper Saddle River, N.J.: Prentice Hall, 2003), one of the best introductions to general epistemology.

[14]For further reflections on these and other lessons, please visit the website <www.faith-film-philosophy.com>.

[15]Kaitlyn Geivett read an early draft of this chapter and made valuable suggestions, helping me to see, as always, things in *The Truman Show* that I had not seen before.

Chapter 5: The Sleeper Awakes

[1]The filmmakers, Andy and Larry Wachowski, have acknowledged the Gnosticism connection in interviews, and a number of scholarly articles (not to mention a host of websites) have commented on Gnostic themes in the films. A good analysis of the first film in Gnostic (and, in this case, Buddhist) terms may be found in Frances Flannery-Dailey and Rachel Wagner, "Wake up! Gnosticism and Buddhism in *The Matrix*," *Journal of Religion and Film* 5 (October 2001). The best survey of Gnosticism is still Hans Jonas, *The Gnostic Religion*, 3rd ed. (Boston: Beacon Press, 2001).

[2]Clement of Alexandria *Excerpta ex Theodoto* 78.2, quoted in Jonas, *Gnostic Religion*, p. 45.

[3]For the "noise of the world" theme, see Jonas, *Gnostic Religion*, pp. 73-74.

[4]Others include *Blade Runner, Total Recall, The Thirteenth Floor* and *Vanilla Sky*, just to name a few.

[5]Robert Nozick, *Anarchy, State, and Utopia* (New York: Basic Books, 1974), p. 43.

[6]The theological parallel to this problem is obviously the one posed by the doctrine of divine foreknowledge. Some Christian responses to the latter problem may be found in James K. Beilby and Paul R. Eddy, eds., *Divine Foreknowledge: Four Views* (Downers Grove, Ill.: InterVarsity Press, 2001).

[7]I would say the same thing about the Christian doctrine of *divine* providence. Its virtues are many, but they do not include providing, by itself, a solution to the problem of divine foreknowledge and human free will. That solution must be found elsewhere.

[8]Aristotle *Nicomachean Ethics* 1.7, trans. Terence Irwin (Indianapolis: Hackett, 1985).

[9]Augustine *Confessions* 8.5, trans. F. J. Sheed (Indianapolis: Hackett, 1993).

[10]René Descartes *Meditations* 1.

Chapter 6: Consciousness, Memory and Identity

[1]Walker Percy, *Lost in the Cosmos: The Last Self-Help Book* (New York: Farrar, Straus & Giroux, 1983), pp. 17-19.

[2]Friedrich Nietzsche, *Beyond Good and Evil*, sec. 217, as quoted by Mary (Kirsten Dunst) in *Eternal Sunshine of the Spotless Mind*. Walter Kaufmann's translation reads, "Blessed are the forgetful: for they get over their stupidities too." Friedrich Nietzsche, *Beyond Good and Evil*, trans. Walter Kaufmann (New York: Random House, 1966), p. 146.

[3]Summaries of these films are given in the appendix.

[4]René Descartes, *Discourse on the Method*, in *Descartes' Philosophical Writings*, trans. J. Cottingham, R. Stoothoff and D. Murdoch (Cambridge: Cambridge University Press, 1985), 1:127. See also René Descartes, *Meditations on First Philosophy*, in ibid., 2:16-17.

[5]Behaviorism in philosophy is not the same thing as behaviorism in psychology (such as that of B. F. Skinner). Philosophical behaviorism is a thesis about the meaning of mental terms. Sometimes it is known as *analytic behaviorism*.

[6]Gilbert Ryle, *The Concept of Mind* (London: Hutchinson, 1948).

[7]Classic sources for identity theory include J. J. C. Smart, "Sensations and Brain Processes," *Philosophical Review* 68, no. 2 (1959): 141-56, and D. M. Armstrong, *A Materialist Theory of the Mind* (London: Routledge and Kegan Paul, 1968).

[8]There are many nuances to functionalism. A couple of influential pieces include Hilary Putnam, "Minds and Machines," in *Dimensions of Mind*, ed. Sydney Hook (New

York: Collier Books, 1960), and Sydney Shoemaker, "Some Varieties of Functionalism," in *Identity, Cause and Mind* (Cambridge: Cambridge University Press, 1984).

[9]It ought to be mentioned that there are many different kinds of dualistic theory. Descartes's theory is the one most discussed. Other dualists hold theories closer to that of Thomas Aquinas. Still others hold other kinds.

[10]Susan Orlean, *The Orchid Thief: A True Story of Beauty and Obsession* (New York: Random House, 1998).

[11]Jean Paul Sartre, *Existentialism and Humanism*, trans. Philip Mairet (London: Methuen, 1948), pp. 33, 34.

[12]Walker Percy, "A Semiotic Primer of the Self," in *Lost in the Cosmos: The Last Self-Help Book* (New York: Farrar, Straus & Giroux, 1983), pp. 85-126. Percy's analysis owes a great deal to Søren Kierkegaard.

[13]Percy, *Lost in the Cosmos*, pp. 147-48.

[14]John Locke, *An Essay Concerning Human Understanding*, ed. Peter Nidditch (Oxford: Oxford University Press, 1975), p. 335 (2.27.9).

[15]I wish to thank the editors for detailed comments and David Ganssle for help with Internet research. I also want to thank David, Nick, Elizabeth and Jeanie for encouraging me to take up this project.

Chapter 7: What Would Have Been and What Could Be

[1]Two recent books feature scholarly discussions of historical counterfactuals: Robert Cowley, ed., *What If? The World's Foremost Military Historians Imagine What Might Have Been* (New York: G. P. Putnam's Sons, 1999), and Robert Cowley, ed., *What If? 2: Eminent Historians Imagine What Might Have Been* (New York: G. P. Putnam's Sons, 2001).

[2]As Aristotle puts it, "To say of what is that it is not, or of what is not that it is, is false, while to say of what is that it is, and of what is not that it is not, is true." Aristotle, *Metaphysics*, in *The Basic Works of Aristotle*, trans. W. D. Ross (New York: Random House, 1941), p. 749. This correspondence theory of truth, of which Aristotle is the progenitor, remains the standard view.

[3]My analysis here draws from that of Nelson Goodman, *Fact, Fiction and Forecast*, 4th ed. (Cambridge, Mass.: Harvard University Press, 1983), chap. 1.

[4]This is a variation of the principle of sufficient reason, famously articulated by G. W. Leibniz in such works as "Primary Truths" (1686) and "Principles of Nature and of Grace" (1714).

[5]This longstanding principle comes from the ancient philosopher Parmenides, by way of Aristotle. See Aristotle *Physics* 1.8.

[6]Another term for this law is the *principle of sufficient reason*. Definitive statements of this principle were given by Leibniz, such as his assertion that "nothing happens for

which a reason cannot be given why it should happen as it does rather than otherwise." G. W. Leibniz, "The Nature of Truth," in *Philosophical Writings*, trans. Mary Morris and G. H. Parkinson (London: J. M. Dent and Sons, 1973), p. 94.

[7]For good examples of this view, see B. F. Skinner, *Beyond Freedom and Dignity* (New York: Knopf, 1971), and John Hospers, "Meaning and Free Will," *Philosophy and Phenomenological Research* 10, no. 3 (1950): 316-30.

[8]Compatibilism comes in a variety of forms. It has been endorsed by such philosophers as Baruch Spinoza, John Locke, David Hume, John Stuart Mill and W. T. Stace.

[9]Tykwer's view, in fact, might be quite the opposite, given his remarks in an interview about *Run Lola Run*. In a discussion about Lola, Tykwer says, "The bad things she's doing, she's forced to do and I think the way she acts makes clear to us that this could happen to us in exactly the same way." Tom Mes and Joep Vermaat, "Tykwer's Run," *Projecta* <http://www.projecta.net/tykwer3.htm>. Accessed May 23, 2007.

[10]Libertarianism, too, comes in many varieties and has been endorsed by such philosophers as William James, C. A. Campbell and Peter Van Inwagen.

[11]Tykwer himself intimates this idea, as he notes that "the animation is also very strictly related to the moment in the staircase where she runs down, which is always where she meets this boy with the dog and so is the first moment when fate turns into a new direction. Of course, because that's the idea that now anything can happen and anything new can happen, and this is very much related to the ideology of animation and of cartoons, because cartoons give you the impression of 'anything goes.'" Mes and Vermaat, "Tykwer's Run."

[12]That Capra makes theistic assumptions in this film is evident in the fact that Clarence is an angel. And a theology of angels is most typical of theistic religions.

[13]The view is named after Luis de Molina, the sixteenth-century Jesuit theologian who formulated the doctrine. See Luis de Molina, *On Divine Foreknowledge*, trans. Alfred Freddoso (Ithaca, N.Y.: Cornell University Press, 1988).

[14]William Lane Craig, *The Only Wise God: The Compatibility of Divine Foreknowledge and Human Freedom* (Eugene, Ore.: Wipf and Stock, 2000), p. 135 (emphasis in original). For another recent exposition of Molinism, see Thomas P. Flint, *Divine Providence: The Molinist Account* (Ithaca, N.Y.: Cornell University Press, 1998).

[15]For a fuller discussion of this criticism, see Robert M. Adams, "Middle Knowledge and the Problem of Evil," *American Philosophical Quarterly* 14, no. 2 (1977): 109-17.

[16]For good discussions of this "grounding objection" to Molinism, see Adams's "Middle Knowledge and the Problem of Evil" and Steven B. Cowan, "The Grounding Objection to Middle Knowledge Revisited," *Religious Studies* 39, no. 1 (2003): 93-102.

[17]William Hasker, *God, Time, and Knowledge* (Ithaca, N.Y.: Cornell University Press, 1989), p. 186.

[18]Richard Swinburne, *The Coherence of Theism* (Oxford: Oxford University Press, 1993), p. 181.

[19]Free-will theists also face the theological problem of explaining hundreds of fulfilled predictive prophecies in Scripture. Many different events are foretold long before they come to pass, from the division of the Roman Empire to the circumstances of the Messiah's birth and death (cf. Daniel 7; Micah 5:2; Zechariah 9:9; Isaiah 52:13—53:12).

[20]For compatibilist treatments of this issue, see D. A. Carson, *Divine Sovereignty and Human Responsibility* (Eugene, Ore.: Wipf and Stock, 2002), and James S. Spiegel, *The Benefits of Providence: A New Look at Divine Sovereignty* (Wheaton, Ill.: Crossway, 2005).

Chapter 9: From a Society of Fear to a Community of Trust

[1]Michael Moore, introduction to *Bowling for Columbine*, special ed. DVD, directed by Michael Moore (Century City: MGM, 2003).

[2]Michael Moore, speech given at Toronto Film Festival, *Bowling for Columbine*, special ed. DVD, directed by Michael Moore (Century City: MGM, 2003).

[3]According to Moore's website, the sources for these figures are as follows: Germany, Bundeskriminalamt; France, *International Journal of Epidemiology;* Canada, Statistics Canada; the U.K., the Centre for Crime and Justice Studies in Britain; Australia, the Australian Institute of Criminology; Japan, the National Police Agency of Japan; the U.S., the Center for Disease Control. See <www.michaelmoore.com/words/wacko-attacko>. Accessed May 23, 2007.

[4]Although the origin of the cartoon has been questioned, Moore claims that he wrote the script and that the animation was done by the studio of Harold Moss. See <www.michaelmoore.com/words/wackoattacko>. Accessed May 23, 2007.

[5]Michael Moore, lecture at the University of Denver, March 24, 2003, *Bowling for Columbine,* special ed. DVD, directed by Michael Moore (Century City: MGM, 2003). A transcript of the lecture is also available online at <www.michaelmoore.com/books-films/bowlingforcolumbine/about/dvd-denver.php>.

[6]Ibid.

[7]Ibid.

[8]The examples cited in the film include U.S. actions in Guatemala (1953), Southeast Asia (1963-75), Chile (1973), El Salvador (1954), Afghanistan (1980-present), Nicaragua (1981), Iraq (1982-present), Iran (1983), Panama (1989), Kuwait (1991) and Sudan (1998). Moore's antiwar comments during his Oscar acceptance speech in 2003 suggest that he sees the current U.S.-led war with Iraq to be another example of a foreign policy that promotes violence as a means of conflict resolution.

[9]A similar argument is made by Martin Buber. See Martin Buber, *Between Man and Man* (New York: Routledge, 1947).

[10]Other major personalist philosophers include Nikolai Berdiaev, Peter Anthony Bertocci, Borden Parker Bowne, Edgar S. Brightman and Gabriel Marcel.

[11]John Macmurray, *Reason and Emotion* (Atlantic Highlands, N.J.: Humanities Press, 1978), p. 101.

[12]This modern characterization of the self can be traced to René Descartes's claim, *cogito ergo sum* ("I think, therefore I am").

[13]John Macmurray, *The Self as Agent* (Atlantic Highlands, N.J.: Humanities Press, 1999), pp. 66-67.

[14]Ibid., p. 17.

[15]John Macmurray, *Persons in Relation* (Atlantic Highlands, N.J.: Humanities Press, 1999), p. 159.

[16]Macmurray, *Self as Agent*, p. 15.

[17]Macmurray, *Persons in Relation*, pp. 66-79. The opposition of love and fear is also a biblical theme. See, e.g., 1 John 4:18.

[18]Ibid., pp. 15-43.

[19]Ibid., p. 40. The degree to which people would trust a "generalized other," however, is a strong indicator of the health of the social bonds in a society. For a recent discussion of this issue, see Robert Putnam, *Bowling Alone* (New York: Simon and Schuster, 2001), pp. 134-47.

[20]Macmurray, *Persons in Relation*, pp. 40-43.

[21]Ibid., p. 176.

[22]Ibid., p. 146.

[23]John Macmurray, *Freedom in the Modern World* (London: Faber and Faber, 1968), p. 59.

[24]This is a common theme in most of Moore's films, including *The Big One* and *Fahrenheit 9/11*, and in his television series *TV Nation* and *The Awful Truth*. Moore addresses the abuses of pharmaceutical companies in his film *Sicko*, released in 2007.

[25]For a thorough study of the relationship between the economic health of a community and the decline of that community, see Putnam, *Bowling Alone*.

[26]Moore, speech given at Toronto Film Festival, *Bowling for Columbine*, special ed. DVD.

[27]John Macmurray, *Constructive Democracy* (London: Faber and Faber, 1942), pp. 21-22.

[28]For an extended version of this argument, see Macmurray, *Persons in Relation*, chaps. 5 and 6.

[29]Macmurray, *Freedom in the Modern World*, pp. 214-15.

[30]Macmurray, *Persons in Relation*, p. 188.

[31]John Macmurray, *Through Chaos to Community?* (London: National Peace Council, 1944), p. 13.

[32]Macmurray, *Persons in Relation*, p. 217.

[33]Moore, lecture, University of Denver. Some argue that Moore unfairly targets the Bush administration here, and his controversial film *Fahrenheit 9/11* seems to make the Bush administration a scapegoat for social ills. On the other hand, it might be more accurate to say that Moore identifies the abuse of power itself as the source of social ills. This can be seen in his criticisms of several political administrations, corporations and the media.

[34]The passages to which Moore is referring are Matthew 19:21-24; 25:31-46.

[35]John Macmurray, *Search for Reality in Religion* (London: George Allen and Unwin, 1965), p. 57.

[36]See, e.g., Matthew 19:16-30; Mark 10:17-23; Luke 12:13-21; 18:18-29; 1 Timothy 6:17-19.

[37]The version of the song "Take the Skinheads Bowling" used in the film is Teenage Fanclub's cover of Camper Van Beethoven's original.

Chapter 10: Vengeance, Forgiveness and Redemption in *Mystic River*

[1]Sissela Bok, *Secrets: On the Ethics of Concealment and Revelation* (New York: Vintage, 1984), p. 103.

[2]Dennis Lehane, *Mystic River* (New York: HarperTorch, 2001).

[3]Ed Gonzales, "Mystic River," *Slant Magazine* <http://www.slantmagazine.com/film/film_review .asp?ID=837>. Accessed May 23, 2007.

[4]Peter A. French, *The Virtues of Vengeance* (Lawrence: University Press of Kansas, 2001). Given that *Mystic River*'s director, Clint Eastwood, began his acting career in "spaghetti Westerns," it is interesting that French sees classic Western films as a natural narrative laboratory for exploring the justifiability of some occasions of vengeance. As we will see, Eastwood's Boston neighborhood has a social structure with relevant similarities to a frontier town.

[5]Aeschylus's three-play series, *Orestea*, is the oldest extant complete dramatic trilogy.

[6]French, *Virtues of Vengeance*, p. 69.

[7]French's conception of moral anger seems to be like righteous indignation in being morally permissible anger experienced on the right occasions, for the right people, for the right reasons. It may be stronger than some conceptions of righteous indignation in being not only morally commendable but, under some circumstances, morally required.

[8]Solomon Schimmel, *Wounds Not Healed by Time: The Power of Repentance and Forgiveness* (New York: Oxford University Press, 2002), p. 22.

[9]French, *Virtues of Vengeance*, p. 111.

[10]Ibid., p. 33. See also pp. 110-12.

[11]Ibid., p. 64.

[12]Viewers watching *Mystic River* through French's lens may wonder whether there are

factors that contaminate Jimmy's enactment of due diligence. Jimmy's own past crimes mean that he comes with soiled hands to the role of avenger. The crucial philosophical issue to be adjudicated by a careful reading of French and attention to the film is whether Jimmy is a flawed embodiment of French's conception of virtuous vengeance or whether French's account is flawed.

[13]This context is more clearly and fully established in the novel on which the movie is based, but it is there in the film: "Is he with you?" asks Sean.

[14]Joram Graf Haber, *Forgiveness* (New York: Rowman & Littlefield, 1991), p. 90.

[15]Miroslav Volf, "Forgiveness, Reconciliation and Justice," in *Forgiveness and Reconciliation: Religion, Public Policy and Conflict Transformation,* ed. Raymond G. Helmick, S.J., and Rodney L. Petersen (Philadelphia: Templeton Foundation Press, 2001), p. 40.

[16]Ibid., p. 41.

[17]Ibid., p. 44. It is conceivable that the light shed by embrace, love and forgiveness will reveal that justice was all on the side of the forgiver and that the offender was completely in the wrong. Volf seems to be on solid theological ground in his assumption that the only wholly innocent victim was Christ. Tellingly, Christ prays from the cross, "Father, forgive them, for they know not what they do" (Luke 23:34).

[18]Hannah Arendt, *The Human Condition* (Garden City, N.Y.: Doubleday Anchor Books, 1959), p. 216.

[19]Marilyn McCord Adams, "Forgiveness: A Christian Model," *Faith and Philosophy* 8 (July 1991): 295.

[20]Ibid., p. 294.

[21]Ibid., p. 296.

[22]Ibid.

[23]Ibid., p. 299.

[24]See Geraldine Smyth, O.P., "Brokenness, Forgiveness and Healing," in *Forgiveness and Reconciliation: Religion, Public Policy and Conflict Transformation,* ed. Raymond G. Helmick, S.J., and Rodney L. Petersen (Philadelphia: Templeton Foundation Press, 2001), p. 330.

[25]Adams, "Forgiveness," p. 296.

[26]Perhaps it is the lack of any theological resources provided within the film to explain Sean's forgiveness that makes it seem to come out of the blue.

[27]The novel on which the film is based, published in 2001, also ends with a parade. Author Dennis Lehane could not have had 9/11 in mind, although Eastwood and his scriptwriter certainly could have in retaining the parade scene. The script's spare elegance is strong evidence that anything retained must have been deemed central to the film's central themes of vengeance and forgiveness.

[28]Nigel Biggar, *Burying the Past: Making Peace and Doing Justice After Civil Conflict*

(Washington, D.C.: Georgetown University Press, 2001), p. 272.

[29]Jeffrie G. Murphy, *Getting Even: Forgiveness and Its Limits* (New York: Oxford University Press, 2003), p. 34.

[30]Jean Bethke Elshtain, *Just War Against Terror: The Burden of American Power in a Violent World* (New York: Basic Books, 2003), pp. 56, 112.

[31]Ibid., p. 57. Elshtain's quotation from Capizzi is found in Joseph E. Capizzi, "On Behalf of the Neighbor," *Studies in Christian Ethics* 14, no. 2 (2002): 81-108.

[32]Elshtain, *Just War Against Terror,* pp. 59, 25. Perhaps it is not a coincidence that Elshtain, like French, looks to Western movies for narratives that model morally appropriate responses to violence. What she calls justice and contrasts with revenge bares striking similarities to French's "virtuous vengeance." See ibid., p. 24.

[33]Miroslav Volf, *Exclusion and Embrace* (Nashville: Abingdon Press, 1996), p. 306.

Chapter 11: Moral Monsters

I would like to thank Andrew Peach for his comments on an earlier draft of this chapter, and Doug Geivett and Jim Spiegel for their help, encouragement and patience.

[1]Reuters, "Horror Films Boom Amid War, Anxiety," May 1, 2005.

[2]By *scholasticism* I mean the philosophical discourse that dominated medieval Christian Europe—a discourse that reached its pinnacle in the writings of Thomas Aquinas. See Thomas Aquinas *Summa Theologiae* 1-2, 19.

[3]For an entertaining, if somewhat overenthusiastic, chronicling of horror's abiding attraction, from ancient times to the (then) present, see H. P. Lovecraft, *The Annotated Supernatural Horror in Literature*, ed. S. T. Joshi (New York: Hippocampus, 2000) <http://gaslight.mtroyal.ab.ca/superhor.htm>. Accessed May 23, 2007.

[4]Consider a handful of acknowledged horror classics: Terence Fisher's *Horror of Dracula* (1958), George A. Romero's *Night of the Living Dead* (1968), William Friedkin's *The Exorcist* (1973), Tobe Hooper's *The Texas Chain Saw Massacre* (1974), Narciso Ibáñez Serrador's *¿Quién puede matar a un niño? [Who Can Kill a Child?]* (1976), John Carpenter's *Halloween* (1978) and Scott Derrickson's *Hellraiser: Inferno* (2000). Each of these films witnesses (in Romero's case, somewhat reluctantly) to horror's essential need for moral grounding.

[5]Charles Higson, *The King of the Ants* (London: Abacus Books, 1998), pp. 218-19.

[6]Ibid., p. 282.

[7]Ibid., p. 41.

Chapter 12: Religion and Science in *Contact* and *2001: A Space Odyssey*

[1]See Richard Dawkins, *The Blind Watchmaker* (New York: Norton, 1987); Francis Crick, *The Astonishing Hypothesis* (New York: Touchstone, 1995); Steven Weinberg,

Dreams of a Final Theory (New York: Pantheon, 1992); and Carl Sagan, *Cosmos* (New York: Random House, 2002). See also Carl Sagan, *Contact* (New York: Simon and Schuster, 1985). The film *2001* was based on a short story, "The Sentinel," by Arthur C. Clarke, who, along with director Stanley Kubrick, wrote the screenplay for the film. Clarke later published a novel, *2001: A Space Odyssey.*

[2]This is the opening claim of Sagan's 1980 TV series, *Cosmos.*

[3]Ellie notes that the reason the message from outer space is expressed in mathematics is because mathematics (and physics) is a universal language. Or as Galileo put it, "The book of nature is written in mathematics."

[4]This is only the merest sketch of these arguments, of course, which is all that can be attempted here. For readers interested in pursuing them further, see Brendan Sweetman, *Religion: Key Concepts in Philosophy* (London: Continuum Books, 2007); also William Lane Craig, *The Kalam Cosmological Argument* (Eugene, Ore.: Wipf and Stock, 2000); Richard Swinburne, *The Existence of God*, 2nd ed. (Oxford: Oxford University Press, 1991); R. Douglas Geivett and Brendan Sweetman, eds., *Contemporary Perspectives on Religious Epistemology* (Oxford: Oxford University Press, 1992); and R. Douglas Geivett, *Evil and the Evidence for God* (Philadelphia: Temple University Press, 1993), chaps. 6 and 7.

[5]Crick, *Astonishing Hypothesis*, p. 3.

Chapter 13: Bottled Water from the Fragrant Harbor

I will follow the romanization that goes with particular films and use the pinyin transliteration—with the Wade-Giles version in parenthesis, if necessary—for general Chinese cultural terms.

[1]A brief bibliography for this genre would include Chris Berry, ed., *Chinese Films in Focus: 25 New Takes* (London: British Film Institute, 2003); David Bordwell, *Planet Hong Kong: Popular Cinema and the Art of Entertainment* (Cambridge, Mass.: Harvard University Press, 2000); Poshek Fu and David Desser, eds., *The Cinema of Hong Kong: History, Arts, Identity* (New York: Cambridge University Press, 2000); Verina Glaessner, *Kung Fu: Cinema of Vengeance* (London: Lorimer, 1974); Sheldon Hsia-peng Lu, ed., *Transnational Chinese Cinema: Identity, Nationhood, Gender* (Honolulu: University of Hawaii Press, 1997); Law Kar and Frank Bren, *Hong Kong Cinema: A Cross-Cultural View* (Lanham, Md.: Scarecrow Press, 2004); Harry H. Kuoshu, *Celluloid China: Cinematic Encounters with Culture and Society* (Carbondale: Southern Illinois University Press, 2002); George S. Semsel, Xia Hong and Hou Jianping, eds., *Chinese Film Theory: A Guide to the New Era* (New York: Praeger, 1990); George Stephen Semsel, *Chinese Film: The State of the Art in the People's Republic* (New York: Praeger, 1987); Stephen Teo, *Hong Kong Cinema: The Extra Dimension* (London:

British Film Institute, 1999); Jeff Yang, *Once Upon a Time in China: A Guide to Hong Kong, Taiwanese, and Mainland Chinese Cinema* (New York: Atria Books, 2003); and Esther C. M. Yau, ed., *At Full Speed: Hong Kong Cinema in a Borderless World* (Minneapolis: University of Minnesota Press, 2001).

[2]This is in contrast to films made in Shanghai. See Kar and Bren, *Hong Kong Cinema*, p. xvi.

[3]Teo, *Hong Kong Cinema*, p. 98.

[4]The international English title of *Jing wu men* is *Fists of Fury*. This same title had been used in America for Lee's first film, *Tang shan da xiong* (1971), which carried the international title *The Big Boss*.

[5]Chinapages, "Introduction of [*sic*] Peking (Beijing) Opera" <http://www.chinapages.com/culture/jje.htm>. Accessed May 23, 2007.

[6]The English dubbed version leaves out the name of Madam White Snake, but it uses it in the English subtitles of the Cantonese.

[7]In the 1950s and 1960s, an actor named Kwan Tak-hing portrayed Wong Fei-hung in eighty films. Teo, *Hong Kong Cinema*, p. 51.

[8]Incidentally, the comical butcher in *Once Upon a Time*, referred to as Lang in the English dubbed version, was in real life Lam Sai-wing, a butcher who became one of the real Wong Fei-hung's outstanding disciples and a great kung fu master in his own right. Ibid, p. 104.

[9]Lee insisted that his character should not be exempt from the consequences of violence <http://www.imdb.com/title/tt0068767/trivia>. Accessed May 23, 2007.

[10]Shaolin Gung Fu Institute, "History of the Shaolin Temples" <http://www.shaolin.com/shaolin_history.aspx>. Accessed May 23, 2007.

[11]On embryonic breathing, see David S. Noss and John B. Noss, *A History of the World's Religions*, 9th ed. (New York: Macmillan, 1994), p. 301.

[12]Michael S. Diener et. al., *Lexikon der Östlichen Weisheitslehren* (Munich: Scherz, 1985), p. 76.

[13]The language was an obstacle in the production of this film. Malaysian actor Michelle Yeoh had to memorize her lines purely through sound reproduction; Chow Yun-fat, at home in Cantonese, displays an accent in his Mandarin; and other actors showed regional inflections. The producers wound up dubbing in Mandarin for regions where Mandarin is the primary language. This makes *Crouching Tiger* a film that virtually everyone watches with dubbing or subtitles <http://www.imdb.com/title/tt0190332/trivia>.

[14]The term *aunt* is used frequently for any woman whom one holds in great esteem or affection. Called "Auntie Yee" in the English dubbing, her Cantonese generation name is "Yellow Flies the Great Wild Goose" and "Thirteen Maternal Aunt" as her personal designation within the generation, so that she is called "Aunt 13" in the sub-

titles. (Thanks to Nicholas Corduan for helping me to make sense of some of the complexities of Chinese vocabulary here and in other places.)

[15]Teo, *Hong Kong Cinema*, pp. 170-71.

Chapter 14: Rattle and Film

[1]Blues has its origin in jazz and features depressing themes, a sluggish tempo and flatted third and seventh notes. See Marc McCutcheon, *Descriptionary: A Thematic Dictionary*, 2nd ed. (New York: Checkmark, 2000), p. 278. It is therefore both a fitting metaphor and an apt medium for reflecting on themes of human wretchedness.

[2]The quotation is from U2's "Walk On," the fourth song on *All That You Can't Leave Behind* (Interscope, 2000).

[3]Jason White, "The Spiritual Journey of U2," in *The U2 Reader: A Quarter Century of Commentary, Criticism, and Reviews*, ed. Hank Bordowitz (Milwaukee: Hal Leonard, 2003), p. 173.

[4]See Steve Stockman, *Walk On: The Spiritual Journey of U2* (Lake Mary, Fla.: Relevant, 2005). On Adam Clayton, see Michka Assayas, *Bono in Conversation with Michka Assayas* (New York: Riverhead, 2005), pp. 44-79, esp. pp. 64-68.

[5]Terry Mattingly, "The Scripture According to Bono," in *The U2 Reader: A Quarter Century of Commentary, Criticism, and Reviews*, ed. Hank Bordowitz (Milwaukee: Hal Leonard, 2003), p. 172.

[6]U2, *All That You Can't Leave Behind* (Interscope, 2000); *How to Dismantle an Atomic Bomb* (Interscope, 2004).

[7]See Mattingly, "Scripture According to Bono," pp. 171-72; and Steve Braden, "U2's Hi-Tech Tent Revival," in *The U2 Reader: A Quarter Century of Commentary, Criticism, and Reviews*, ed. Hank Bordowitz (Milwaukee: Hal Leonard, 2003), pp. 175-78.

[8]*Rattle and Hum*, directed by Phil Joanou (Hollywood: Paramount Pictures, 1988). See Mark Chatterton, "Rattle & Hum (Feature Film/Video)," in *U2: The Ultimate Encyclopedia*, 2nd ed. (London: Firefly, 2004). In the wake of the film, U2 also released an album titled *Rattle and Hum* (Island, 1988).

[9]While the interpretation offered gets at what seems to me the message U2 intends *Rattle and Hum* to have, what I say below remains largely—perhaps entirely—unaffected even if it is not. For those who find this a startling claim, I note that it fits quite well with U2's own understanding, according to which human authors do not so much impart meaning to their works as discover it in them. So, for instance, "[Bono] says he is still shattered from the show two nights earlier. . . . 'Stepping back inside these songs—you know *the way these songs change meaning as they go*—they took me on a real ride.'" Chris Heath, "U2 Band of the Year," *Rolling Stone*, January 18, 2001, p. 41 (emphasis added). "And Bono often does not know exactly what he is writing

until after he sings it. . . . [The Edge] cites *Atomic Bomb*'s 'Miracle Drug,' inspired by the real-life story of Christopher Nolan. . . . 'What's interesting about "Miracle Drug," ' the Edge continues, 'is that later on, Bono realized . . . "I've been doing all this work to get retro-viral drugs for Africa. I was so sure this song was just about Christy Nolan." ' " David Fricke, "U2 Drops Bomb," *Rolling Stone,* December 30, 2004-January 13, 2005, p. 62. "I find that it's only after six months of touring it and talking to different people that you get to the inner truths of the song," says Clayton, *"which is not always something Bono intended.* Gradually the sand and debris is swept away and the core is revealed." Niall Stokes, *U2 into the Heart: The Stories Behind Every Song* (New York: Thunder's Mouth, 2001), p. 58 (emphasis added).

[10]Robert Hilburn, "Where Craft Ends and Spirit Begins," *Los Angeles Times,* August 8, 2004 <http://www.calendarlive.com/music/hilburn/cl-ca-hilburn8aug08,0,7106726 .htmlstory>. Accessed May 23, 2007.

[11]Anthony DeCurtis, "Bono: The Beliefnet Interview," February 20, 2001 <http://www.macphisto.net/article147.html>. Accessed May 23, 2007.

[12]Adam Block, "Bono Bites Back," *Mother Jones,* May 1, 1989 <http://www.mother jones.com/arts/qa/1989/05/bono.html>. Accessed May 23, 2007.

[13]Hence, the madman who announces God's death finishes his work with a requiem: "It is still recounted how on the same day the madman forced his way into several churches and there started singing his *requiem aeternam deo.*" Friedrich Nietzsche, *The Gay Science,* ed. Bernard Williams, trans. Josefine Nauckhoff and Adrian Del Caro, Cambridge Texts in the History of Philosophy (New York: Cambridge University Press, 2001), sec. 125, p. 120.

[14]Ibid., sec. 343, p. 199.

[15]See Friedrich Nietzsche, *Twilight of the Idols,* in *Twilight of the Idols and the Anti-Christ,* trans. R. J. Hollingdale (New York: Penguin, 1968), sec. 1:7, p. 23.

[16]Ibid., sec. 6:8, p. 54 (emphasis in original).

[17]Friedrich Nietzsche, *Daybreak: Thoughts on the Prejudices of Morality,* ed. Maude-marie Clark and Brian Leiter, trans. R. J. Hollingdale, Cambridge Texts in the History of Philosophy (New York: Cambridge University Press, 1997), sec. 1:49, p. 32 (emphasis in original).

[18]Friedrich Nietzsche, *The Anti-Christ,* in *Twilight of the Idols and the Anti-Christ,* trans. R. J. Hollingdale (New York: Penguin, 1968), sec. 15, p. 125 (emphasis in original).

[19]Robert C. Solomon and Kathleen M. Higgins, *What Nietzsche Really Said* (New York: Schocken, 2000), pp. 25-26. On the alleged nihilism of Christianity, see Alan Smithee, *Nihilism and the Purpose-Driven Life: What Does It Matter Anyway?* (Hollywood: Requiem, 2001).

[20]Nietzsche, *Twilight of the Idols,* sec. 5:4, p. 45 (emphasis in original).

[21]The album's actual title is *The Beatles* (Apple, 1968).

[22]For an account of the murders, see Vincent Bugliosi and Curt Gentry, *Helter Skelter: The True Story of the Manson Murders* (New York: Norton, 2001).

[23]See Job 9:23-24; 21:7-26; Psalm 73:2-14; 94:3-7; Ecclesiastes 8:14; Habakkuk 1:2-4, 13.

[24]Stokes, *U2 into the Heart*, p. 80. Stokes is a leading advocate of contemporary Irish music and the founder of the Dublin-based *Hot Press,* which has been characterized as "the first serious Irish journal" to concentrate on such music. *Hot Press* was also the first journal to give serious attention to U2 and accounted for much of the band's early publicity. See Chatterton, "Hot Press" and "Stokes, Niall," in *U2: The Ultimate Encyclopedia,* 2nd ed. (London: Firefly, 2004). pp. 106, 217.

[25]Stokes, *U2 into the Heart*, p. 76.

[26]Ibid.

[27]Even the author of the song's lyrics claims not to know himself. According to Stokes, Bono says, " 'Exit'—I don't even know what the act is in that song. Some see it as a murder, others suicide—and I don't mind. But the rhythm of the words is nearly as important in conveying the state of mind." Ibid.

[28]Ibid.

[29]The album *Rattle and Hum* contains numerous references to "love" that also seem to be thinly veiled references to God. So, for instance, in "Love Rescue Me" (which sounds like an angst-ridden version of "Love Lifted Me"), "When Love Comes to Town" and "God Part II" (in which the speaker repeatedly affirms his belief in love), *love* almost certainly refers to God.

[30]The incorporation of Van Morrison's song into "Exit" brings to mind U2's own "Gloria," which also includes phrases borrowed from the Latin Vulgate. U2's "Gloria" is the first song on *October* (Island, 1981).

[31]On such misunderstanding, John Smith writes, "Shallow souls on Christian and secular fronts totally missed the point of 'I Still Haven't Found What I'm Looking For.' For the shallow opponents of Christianity it served as a departure from sermonizing faith. For fundamentalists, who neither understood nor empathized with the Lord's Prayer (Thy Kingdom Come, Thy will be done on earth as it is in Heaven!), they had betrayed the simplistic slogan of 'Jesus is the answer.' . . . That the song reaffirmed Christ's vicarious embracing of our guilt and sin and reasserted the declaration of faith ('You know I believe it') was overlooked in a frenzy of Sunday school responses." John Smith, "The New U2," in *The U2 Reader: A Quarter Century of Commentary, Criticism, and Reviews,* ed. Hank Bordowitz (Milwaukee: Hal Leonard, 2003), p. 180.

[32]Mattingly, "Scripture According to Bono," p. 173.

[33]"Freedom for My People" (written by Macie Mabins, Sterling Magee and Bobby

Robinson) is performed in the film by Adam Gussow and Sterling Magee; Jimi Hendrix's performance of "The Star-Spangled Banner" is from the Woodstock Festival of 1969.

[34]Elisabeth Hardwick, "Billie Holiday," *The New York Review*, March 4, 1976 <http://www.ladyday.net>. Accessed May 23, 2007.

[35]To prevent the horsemen from dropping out of the song altogether, however, Bono also modifies another line: "While all the women came and went / Barefoot servants, too" becomes "While horsemen came and went / Barefoot servants, too."

[36]Dianne Ebertt Beeaff, *A Grand Madness: Ten Years on the Road with U2* (Tucson, Ariz.: Hawkmoon, 2000), p. 19.

[37]Stokes, *U2 into the Heart*, p. 90.

[38]Perhaps the song's most poignant regret involves promises, made to a lover, that the speaker "was soon to forget," leaving her standing alone at the altar.

[39]See Laura Jackson, *Bono: His Life, Music, and Passions* (New York: Citadel, 2001), p. 56.

[40]Both audio and transcription of the "I have a dream" speech (delivered by King in Washington, D.C., on August 28, 1963) can be found at the website of History and Politics Out Loud <http://www.hpol.org/record.php?id=72>. Accessed May 23, 2007.

[41]The other two lines echo Philippians 2:15.

[42]See Chatterton, "'Sunday Bloody Sunday' (Live) (*Rattle & Hum* Film/Video Track)," in *U2: The Ultimate Encyclopedia*, 2nd ed. (London: Firefly, 2004).

[43]Nietzsche, *Gay Science*, sec. 343, p. 199.

[44]Nietzsche, *Twilight of the Gods*, sec. 6:8, p. 54 (emphasis in original).

[45]Nietzsche, *Gay Science*, sec. 343, p. 199 (emphasis in original).

[46]Nietzsche, *Daybreak*, sec. 4:262, p. 146 (emphasis added).

[47]Nietzsche, *Anti-Christ*, sec. 2, p. 115 (emphasis in original).

[48]Ibid., sec. 5, p. 117 (emphasis in original).

[49]Friedrich Nietzsche, *On the Genealogy of Morality*, ed. Keith Ansell-Pearson, trans. Carol Diethe, Cambridge Texts in the History of Political Thought (New York: Cambridge University Press, 1994), sec. 13, p. 28 (emphasis in original).

[50]Nietzsche, *Gay Science*, sec. 132, p. 123.

[51]Friedrich Nietzsche, *Human, All Too Human: A Book for Free Spirits*, trans. R. J. Hollingdale, Cambridge Texts in the History of Philosophy (New York: Cambridge University Press, 1996), sec. 517, p. 182.

[52]Friedrich Nietzsche, *The Birth of Tragedy*, in *The Birth of Tragedy and Other Writings*, ed. Raymond Geuss and Ronald Speirs, trans. Ronald Speirs, Cambridge Texts in the History of Philosophy (New York: Cambridge University Press, 1999), sec. 3, pp. 22-23. See also sec. 7, p. 40.

[53]Nietzsche, *Gay Science*, sec. 107, p. 104 (emphasis in original).

Index